School Sector and Student Outcomes

Notre Dame Advances in Education

Michael Pressley
General Editor

SCHOOL SECTOR AND STUDENT OUTCOMES

Edited by

MAUREEN T. HALLINAN

University of Notre Dame Press
Notre Dame, Indiana

Copyright© 2006 University of Notre Dame
Notre Dame, Indiana 46556
All Rights Reserved
www.undpress.nd.edu

Published in the United States of America

Library of Congress Cataloging-in-Publication Data

School sector and student outcomes / edited by Maureen T. Hallinan.
   p.   cm. (Notre Dame Advances in Education)
Includes bibliographical references and index.
ISBN-13: 978-0-268-03101-5 (pbk. : alk. paper)
ISBN-10: 0-268-03101-0 (pbk. : alk. paper)
1. Educational sociology. 2. School management and organization.
3. Academic achievement. I. Hallinan, Maureen T.

LC191.S262   2006
306.43'2—dc22

                                       2006001501

∞ *The paper in this book meets the guidelines for permanence and durability of the Committee on Production Guidelines for Book Longevity of the Council on Library Resources.*

Contents

	Acknowledgments	vii
	Introduction	1
1	Public and Private Education: Conceptualizing the Distinction Charles E. Bidwell and Robert Dreeben	9
2	Innovation in Educational Markets: An Organizational Analysis of Third Sector Private Schools in Toronto Scott Davies and Linda Quirke	39
3	Public and Private School Differences: The Relationship of Adolescent Religious Involvement to Psychological Well-Being and Altruistic Behavior Barbara Schneider, Lisa Hoogstra, Fengbin Chang, and Holly Rice Sexton	73
4	Religious Participation as Cultural Capital Development: Sector Differences in Chicago's Jewish Schools Adam Gamoran and Matthew Boxer	101
5	The Practice of Ability Grouping: Sector Differences in Implementation Maureen T. Hallinan and Brandy J. Ellison	125
6	Student Learning: Sector Differences in Achievement Gains across School Years and during the Summer William Carbonaro	153

7	Sector Differences in Opportunities for Parental Involvement in the School Context	181
	Gail M. Mulligan	
8	Children's Cultural Capital and Teachers' Assessments of Effort and Ability: The Influence of School Sector	201
	Susan A. Dumais	
	Contributors	223
	General Index	225
	Author Index	229

Acknowledgments

Most of the papers published in this volume were originally presented at a conference entitled "Effects of School Sector on Educational Outcomes" held at the University of Notre Dame in November 2002. Support for this conference was provided by the Institute for Educational Initiatives at the University of Notre Dame. Subsequent to the conference, additional papers were invited for the edited volume, based on their relevance to the issue of school sector effects.

The editor is grateful to the chapter authors for their serious analyses of the role of school sector in the education of youth. Their theoretical and empirical chapters provide a scholarly, in-depth analysis of a topic that is often treated superficially. I also am grateful for their cooperation with the many facets of the publication process, including revisions and deadlines.

Special thanks go to members of the Center for Research on Educational Opportunity at the University of Notre Dame for their assistance in organizing the conference and preparing the volume for publication. Warren Kubitschek's role in reviewing the chapters before publication and his sage advice regarding revisions made a significant contribution to the high quality of the final volume. Sylvia Phillips organized the conference with her typical graciousness, while Cheryl Pauley's contributions to the editing process were indispensable. The generous assistance of CREO graduate students is appreciated. In addition, I would like to thank St. Mary's College for allowing us to use their conference facilities.

This volume is part of the Notre Dame Advances in Education series, edited by the Rev. Ronald J. Nuzzi, Ph.D., Director, Alliance for Catholic Education Leadership Program, and John L. Watzke, Ph.D., Coordinator of Supervision, Alliance for Catholic Education. The series explores various themes in private, Catholic, and public education that contribute to our understanding of schools and challenge educational leaders, policymakers, and concerned stakeholders. The Institute for Educational Initiatives, under the directorship of the Rev. Timothy Scully, CSC, generously provided support for the series, which we acknowledge with gratitude.

Versions of chapters 1–3 and 5–7 in this volume have been published in *Catholic Education: A Journal of Inquiry and Practice,* as follows:

1. Bidwell, C. E., & Dreeben, R. (2003). "Public and private education: Conceptualizing the distinction." *Catholic Education: A Journal of Inquiry and Practice, 7*(1), 8–33.
2. Davies, S., & Quirke, L. (2005). "Innovation in educational markets: An organizational analysis of private schools in Toronto." *Catholic Education: A Journal of Inquiry and Practice, 8*(3), 274–304.
3. Schneider, B., Sexton, H., & Hoogstra, L. (2004). "The importance of religion in adolescents' lives." *Catholic Education: A Journal of Inquiry and Practice, 7*(3), 366–388.
5. Ellison, B. J., & Hallinan, M. T. (2004). "Ability grouping in Catholic and public schools." *Catholic Education: A Journal of Inquiry and Practice, 8*(1), 107–129.
6. Carbonaro, W. (2003). "Sector differences in student learning: Differences in achievement gains across school years and during the summer." *Catholic Education: A Journal of Inquiry and Practice, 7*(2), 219–245.
7. Mulligan, G. (2003). "Sector differences in opportunities for parental involvement in the school context." *Catholic Education: A Journal of Inquiry and Practice, 7*(2), 246–265.

Introduction

The current controversy regarding school choice draws attention to several important questions about school sector differences and their consequences for student outcomes. Advocates of school choice see such a policy as a way for parents to provide better schooling for their children. They argue that school choice creates an educational marketplace in which competition for students within and across sectors improves the quality of all schools. More fundamentally, many advocates of school choice see it as a parental right and a justice issue.

Critics of school choice contend that the policy unfairly benefits those students who are already advantaged. The families of these students are more likely to have the social and financial capital to identify successful schools and to provide transportation for their children to attend those schools. Opponents also argue that school choice removes the more advantaged students from low-quality public schools, further weakening these schools. When academically strong students exit the public school system to attend private schools, public education in general suffers. Many critics assert that extending school choice to private schools violates the constitutional principle of separation of church and state by providing public support for religious schools.

The impetus to allow school choice across sectors in the selection of schools is based on the assumption that student outcomes differ across sectors. While there is empirical evidence of sector differences in school effects, the nature of these differences is not well researched. Whether public and private schools differ fundamentally in terms of organization and governance, curriculum and pedagogy, characteristics of administration, faculty and students, and school climate and context has not been systematically studied. Further, on the conceptual level, the way that schools might be expected to differ by sector and the mechanisms that may account for sector differences have not been well specified. With the exception of early work by Coleman, Hoffer, and Kilgore (1982) and later research by Bryk, Lee, and Holland (1993), few researchers have compared student achievement across school sectors, and virtually no research systematically examines sector effects on nonacademic student outcomes.

This volume aims to provide a set of carefully reasoned conceptual analyses and methodologically rigorous empirical studies that examine sector differences in U.S. elementary and secondary schools. Most of the chapters were presented at a conference entitled "Effects of School Sector on Educational Outcomes," held at the University of Notre Dame on November 9–10, 2002. The remaining chapters were invited to supplement the conference papers and to expand our understanding of sector differences and their effects. Taken as a whole, the volume provides an extensive examination of the nature of school sector differences. The conceptual analyses identify the sources of these differences, trace their history, and describe the mechanisms that link school sector to school processes and outcomes. The empirical analyses document how sector differences operate and the resulting consequences for student learning and social behavior.

In chapter 1, Charles Bidwell and Robert Dreeben present a sociological and historical analysis of the institution of schooling and the emergence of public and private schools in the United States. They argue that school sectors developed as a result of differences in the social organization of schools. U.S. schools vary in the extent to which their control mechanisms are centralized or decentralized and in the degree to which they occupy broad or narrow niches for the provision of educational services to society. Bidwell and Dreeben suggest that the public-private school template does not provide a perfect fit with the underlying differences between schools. They maintain that the defining characteristics of schools are better described in terms of social organizational dimensions than in terms of school sector.

Scott Davies and Linda Quirke investigate the impact of markets on Canadian schools in chapter 2. They examine three issues: First, do markets increase innovation as schools develop client niches? Second, do markets allow schools to weaken their formal structures? And third, do markets force schools to more closely monitor their effectiveness? Unlike most U.S. jurisdictions, Ontario has no charter schools or voucher programs, and thus parental choice is being expressed in new private markets. Davies and Quirke analyze data from twenty-two private, nonreligious, and nonelite schools in Ontario. They find that markets encourage some forms of innovation, such as smaller classes and a more tailored curriculum, but that parental input, which tends to be conservative, limits innovation. Their results also show that competition does not preclude a loosely coupled organization. Most private schools in the study avoided the test culture and regulated forms of accountability that characterize most contemporary Canadian public schools. Finally, the study shows that private schools do not monitor their effectiveness closely, but rather provide accountability through their relationships with parents and the community.

In chapter 3, Barbara Schneider, Lisa Hoogstra, Fengbin Chang, and Holly Rice Sexton elucidate the role of religion in the lives of public and private school adolescents. Addressing a widespread belief that being religious improves an adolescent's psychological well-being and altruistic behavior, they examine the effect of religious affiliation on student self-esteem, self-efficacy, and altruistic participation. Using data from the National Education Longitudinal Study of 1988–2000, they compare the social and religious behaviors of students in private and public schools. Their analyses show that regardless of school sector, the greater a student's religiosity, the higher his or her self-esteem, sense of self-efficacy, and involvement in community service. School sector acts as an added influence on psychological well-being and social participation. Schneider et al.'s results indicate that Catholic schools have the strongest effects on student altruistic behavior compared to private nonreligious or other religious schools. Public schools have the weakest effects on adolescent psychological well-being. While school effect studies typically focus on academic achievement, these findings underscore the importance of examining the effects of sector on nonacademic outcomes and, in particular, of studying school influences on a student's moral and social development.

Adam Gamoran and Matthew Boxer address the question of how Jewish schools and families reproduce cultural outcomes, including religious practices and attitudes. In chapter 4, they conceptualize students' cultural capital as a commitment to and engagement with the traditions and practices of the Jewish people. This cultural capital is created at home through family affiliation and practices and at school through the curriculum. Relying on data from nine Jewish schools, Gamoran and Boxer examine the relationship between family and school in the formation of cultural capital, and they find that schools provide an independent source of Jewish cultural capital. Moreover, Jewish schools supplement the religious activities that families provide at home and compensate for them when such activities are lacking. Families, however, appear to have a stronger influence on students' religious expression than schools. This finding is consistent with the large body of sociological research on school effects.

Ability grouping is a widely practiced method of differentiating students for instruction in public and private schools. The practice is highly controversial, with proponents stressing its efficiency and effectiveness and critics charging that it favors some students over others. In chapter 5, Maureen Hallinan and Brandy Ellison discuss the evolution of ability grouping in public and Catholic schools and the way that this organizational technique is currently practiced in both sectors. Their empirical analyses of ability grouping in six public and one Catholic high school reveal significant differences in how public and Catholic school students are assigned to ability groups. The data also show sector differences in student characteristics at similar ability group levels and in the flexibility of ability group assignments. The results indicate that the Catholic school curriculum is more demanding than the public school curriculum at every ability group level. The relationship between school sector and the organizational differentiation of the curriculum helps to account for achievement differences between the two school sectors.

The recent availability of the Early Childhood Longitudinal Study (ECLS) enables researchers to address new questions about student learning at the beginning of their school careers. The authors of chapters 6, 7, and 8 take advantage of this new survey to examine sector effects on kindergarten and first grade students. In chapter 6, William Carbonaro addresses two important questions about sector effects: Do sector differences in achievement vary across grade level, and does school sector affect summer learning rates? Analyzing kindergarten, summer, and first grade data from the ECLS survey, Carbonaro finds distinct differences in the way that sector affects learning in a student's early school career compared to the high school years. Further, he reveals the danger of ignoring summer learning when studying sector effects. His analyses suggest that the organization and culture of elementary schools may differ from that of high schools, in either public or private sector, or both, accounting for differential effects of sector by grade level.

Gail Mulligan investigates another way that differences in school sector affect student outcomes in chapter 7. Research shows that parents of children in private schools are more involved in their children's schooling than parents of public school students. While this finding has been attributed mostly to differences in family characteristics and educational orientation, Mulligan argues that school factors also play an important role. Schools influence parental involvement through their practices, policies, culture, and communication networks. Analyzing the kindergarten data of the ECLS survey, Mulligan finds that public schools offer significantly more opportunities for parental involvement than private schools. This finding is surprising, since research is fairly consistent in showing that private school parents are more involved in school activities than public school parents. If the latter have more opportunities for school involvement than private school parents but fail to take advantage of these opportunities, then motivational or other factors may be at play. Mulligan offers a number of explanations for greater parental involvement in private schools. Given the relationship between parental involvement and student achievement noted in educational research, these results identify a previously unexamined way that school sector may influence student learning.

In the final chapter, Susan Dumais builds on Pierre Bourdieu's theory of social reproduction to examine whether cultural capital affects the school outcomes of young children. She argues that public and Catholic schools differ in the impact of cultural climate on student outcomes. Her analyses of the ECLS-K data show that Catholic school kindergartners are more likely to participate in arts activities than public school students. Moreover, the parents of kindergarten students in Catholic schools are more likely to be involved in school activities and more comfortable with school involvement than the parents of public school students. Interestingly, the data show that a student's cultural capital does not affect teachers' evaluations of the student's effort or ability. These results highlight previously unexamined social processes associated with school sector that may affect student outcomes.

In theoretical and empirical research presented in these chapters, and in research on school sector in general, sector is typically treated as a dichotomous variable. However, the term actually covers a wide variety of school characteristics. Many of these characteristics, such as religious orientation or source of funding, exist in only one sector. Other characteristics, such as opportunities for parental involvement in school, may be found in both sectors, though in varying degrees. Still others, such as curricular differentiation, exist to the same degree in both sectors but may be linked to student outcomes by different mechanisms. Current research on sector differences fails to take this complexity into account, nor does contemporary research specify the many ways that school sector influences school outcomes.

Most of the chapters in this volume, while providing rigorous empirical analyses of school sector effects on student outcomes, maintain the tradition of treating sector as a dichotomous variable. An exception is the Bidwell-Dreeben chapter in which the authors reconceptualize school sectors and identify critical characteristics of schools that may be more useful than sector in explaining various school outcomes. At the same time, there are features of public and private schools that are unique to each sector and that are best studied as such. A promising direction for sociologists of education to take would be to identify the commonalities and differences among public, private, and religious schools to determine which factors have the strongest effects on various student outcomes.

One theme that runs through nearly all the chapters in this volume is that families play an important role in shaping student outcomes in both public and private schools. This finding is well established in the literature. Beginning with the first Coleman Report (Coleman et al., 1966), sociologists of education have accumulated a large body of research demonstrating that the effects of family background and resources are stronger than those of school on student achievement. One contribution that the chapters in this book make to this literature is the insight that families influence a wider number of student characteristics than are typically considered. Families provide human, social, and cultural capital to students that increases the likelihood that they will succeed in school. These resources have direct effects on student achievement as well as indirect effects, mediated by religion, parental involvement, political participation, and other school-parent-community factors. The chapters show that public and private schools utilize these resources differently, which may account, in part, for sector differences in various student outcomes.

No serious study of school sector effects can ignore the possibility that findings distinguishing between public and private schools may be attributable to selection factors. Public schools accept all students who apply, while private schools may screen admissions on the basis of ability, achievement, behavior, and any other characteristic they view as relevant. Further, private schools typically charge tuition, thus making them inaccessible to many middle- or low-income families. Parents who do invest in private education are likely to insist that their children work hard to attain academic goals. Unless selection factors are controlled, they remain a possible explanation of any sector differences observed in public and private school comparisons. While it is not possible to control experimentally for selection factors, statistical models allow researchers to take these factors into account when analyzing survey data. The sector effect is often reduced in these models but rarely disappears.

Most of the arguments in this volume are not based on multivariate analyses of survey data and hence cannot control for selection effects. Carbonaro's study is an exception. He estimates a multivariate model that controls for selection bias and finds that it reduces but does not eliminate selection effects. The remaining chapters are either theoretical or rely on descriptive analyses of data. In these cases, it is possible that observed sector differences may be attributable to family background and related factors rather than to sector. However, in these chapters the authors attempt to determine what characteristics of public and private schools might explain the observed effects. In so doing they identify cognitive and social processes that link school sector characteristics to students' academic and social behavior.

In a volume dedicated to understanding how school sector influences students' cognitive and social development, it would be remiss not to note the current fiscal crisis facing Catholic schools, which comprise the largest private school system in America. Catholic schools currently educate about 6 percent of American youth. In the past, these schools were staffed primarily by the unpaid labor of priests, brothers, and sisters. However, the number of religious educators is declining rapidly, due to resignations, retirements, and the lack of new recruits. The loss of this primarily volunteer workforce has necessitated hiring lay faculty and administrators. Their salaries, as well as other expenses, have forced Catholic schools to raise tuition to a level that is prohibitive to many families. As a result, student enrollment in Catholic schools is declining annually and dioceses are closing schools every year.

The statistics for several urban school systems are illustrative. For the archdioceses of Chicago, Boston, Detroit, and St. Louis, and the diocese of Brooklyn, the numbers of school closings in 2003–2004 are 10 (4%), 9 (5%), 12 (8%), 7 (4%), and 2 (1%), respectively. In 2004–2005 the numbers of closings for these same school systems are 19 (7%), 2 (1%), 16 (12%), 10 (6%), and 21 (14%). If this rate of shrinkage continues, the Catholic school system will educate far fewer students in the future. On the other hand, Catholic enrollment may stabilize or even increase after significant changes are made in the organization and management of these schools. Either way, the Catholic school system is likely to remain the largest component of the private school sector, and changes in its size will have consequences for public school education.

Regardless of the eventual size of the Catholic school system, its current fiscal crisis has focused attention on the importance of maintaining religious and nonreligious private schools in a pluralistic society. Understanding how school sector affects student outcomes is essential for a commitment to private education in a country with an overwhelmingly large public school system. Appreciation for the unique contributions of both school sectors motivates educators to learn from each sector how best to improve student learning.

The chapters in this volume trace the emergence and evolution of the dual school system in the United States and describe several dimensions of schools that vary by sector. By presenting theoretical analyses of social and cognitive processes that differ in public and private schools, the chapters have heuristic value and should generate a number of conceptually grounded studies of sector effects. The authors analyze sector effects on new data sets and find support for sector differences in student learning and related outcomes. In providing a better understanding of how schools differ by sector and how these sector differences affect student outcomes, the contributors to this volume hope that the research presented here will stimulate new investigation in this area and help educators improve both public and private schools.

References

Bryk, A. S., Lee, V. E., & Holland, P. B. (1993). *Catholic schools and the common good.* Cambridge, MA: Harvard University Press.

Coleman, J. S., Campbell, E. Q., Hobson, C. J., McPartland, J., Mood, A. M., Weinfield, F. D., & York, R. L. (1966). *Equality of educational opportunity.* Washington, DC: U.S. Government Printing Office.

Coleman, J. S., Hoffer, T., & Kilgore, S. (1982). *High school achievement: Public, Catholic, and private schools compared.* New York: Basic Books.

1 | Public and Private Education

Conceptualizing the Distinction

Charles E. Bidwell and Robert Dreeben

In this chapter, we have two tasks. First, we will conceptualize the widely used distinction between the public and private sectors of national systems of education by searching for prime environmental and social organizational dimensions along which the two kinds of schools may differ. Second, within the terms of this conceptualization, we will evaluate the usefulness of this distinction between school sectors for understanding school production, that is, the degree to which a school produces achievement gains among its students. We will conclude that the same environmental and social organizational dimensions apply to both public and private schools. Consequently, observed differences between them are matters of degree, rather than kind, reflecting tendencies for the two sets of schools to occupy different locations in the property space formed by these dimensions. These trends reflect differences of institutional history. They are analytically important, but significant trends toward the convergence of the two school types also are apparent.

The conceptualization that we present is couched at the organizational level. It specifies mechanisms that should account for observed differences in organizational form, instructional activity, and pedagogical outcomes between public and private schools. We intend this organization-level analysis to complement individual-level analysis of the effects of public and private schools on students' cognitive achievement. This individual-level analysis was the subject of the research of Coleman and his collaborators (Coleman & Hoffer, 1987; Coleman, Hoffer, & Kilgore, 1982) that gave momentum to research on sectoral differences and that remains the chief topic of subsequent popular and scholarly discussion of the public-private distinction.

The public school-private school distinction has been taken for granted by scholars and laypersons alike for much of the twentieth century, receiving sporadic attention from sociologists. In the 1950s, Alice and Peter Rossi (A. S. Rossi, 1954; P. H. Rossi, 1954) focused on students attending the public and private schools of Bay City, Massachusetts. The 1960s saw the publication of *The Education of Catholic Americans* (Greeley & Rossi, 1966). Little of significance followed these studies until the publication of *High School Achievement* (Coleman et al., 1982) and *Public and Private High Schools* (Coleman & Hoffer, 1987). Following upon their appearance, the comparison of American public and private schools has become a perennial topic for public policy discourse and sociological research.

Although the public-private distinction has occupied a privileged place in current policy debates, its pride of place has not been justified on conceptual grounds, which gives our enterprise particular importance. For this reason, we should ask what properties of schools and school systems are conceptually important for understanding why they take the organizational forms they do, operate the way they do, and produce what they do. In other words, we should ask whether the distinction has any bearing on schooling (Bidwell & Kasarda, 1980), its nature and quality, and the curriculum, instruction, learning, and character of schools.

We have no definitive explanation for the currently sustained popular and scholarly interest in comparing public and private education. Public policy concerns no doubt have been sharpened by widespread criticism of the public schools in a period of conservative political ascendancy and by a growing fascination with the uses of social science research to design and assess the impact of policy.

As for the scholars, research in the sociology of education, like the whole sociological enterprise, is acutely responsive to movements in the policy domain. Moreover, the stress in recent studies on community as a key to understanding differences in public and private schools has gained force as it resonates with a broader literature on the social capital represented in community-like networks of face-to-face interaction. These networks are regarded as a key to the adaptiveness and productivity of organizations (Brown & Duguid, 2000; Cohen & Prusak, 2001; Lave & Wenger, 1991). No doubt there is further resonance with the communitarian movement in social science (Etzioni, 1996).

For sociologists, the public-private comparison gains added significance from efforts to conceptualize organizational environments and to understand how organizational forms and processes interact with the environment (e.g., Baker, 1992, on the political environment in which American Catholic education developed). Among the most productive of these efforts has been the attempt to situate organizations in their institutional environments. This effort began with the old institutionalism associated with the work of Philip Selznick (1957) and his students (Gusfield, 1955; Perrow, 1961; Stinchcombe, 1965; Zald, 1970). Recently it has inspired the neoinstitutional literature on organizations, given its impetus by Meyer and Rowan (Meyer, 1977; Meyer & Rowan, 1977) and DiMaggio and Powell (1983).

INSTITUTIONAL SECTORS AND SUBSECTORS

For most sociologists of education, the term "sector" has been applied specifically to the distinction between public schools and the varieties of private education. However, for students of organizations, it has a broader denotation that directly addresses relationships between organizations and their institutional environments. We begin our discussion with these relationships.

Consider the differentiation of modern societies into institutional sectors. Meyer and Scott (1994) treat institutional sectors in a way that is reminiscent of Parsons (1951) on the differentiation of modern societies into functionally distinct domains of socially organized activity. They define these sectors as sets of organizations that are devoted to the same array of productive activities, emerging, persisting, and dying in socially ordered environments. Each sector has its own institutional history and its own organizational forms. Each also has a distinct environment, with respect to both formal control and regulation and market conditions. Sectors can be divided into finer and finer subsectors until one reaches a limit of analytical usefulness. Our concern is with education as an institutional sector of American society, that is, as the set of organizations that either provide educational services or that interact with these providing organizations. Specifically, we are concerned with two of its principal subsectors: the public and private systems of elementary and secondary education.

We first consider matters of institutional history, with particular attention to the circumstances under which the institutionalized differentiation of the two subsectors developed. Next, we discuss how the institutional environments of these subsectors have affected their organizational forms, with particular stress on the regulatory and market-ordered characteristics of these environments. Subsequently, we turn from the level of subsectors to the local schools that are situated in these environments, that is, the places where the work of teaching is done. We ask how the market locations and organizational forms of these schools affect the capacity of their faculties and administrators for organizational learning and, consequently, how they affect the degree to which the students whom they enroll are taught well. We go on to consider how these relationships may be affected by the selectivity of a school's inputs of students, personnel, and materials and the degree to which a school is chartered, in the sense of having a distinctive mission or of offering a distinctive brand of education.

History

We begin with colonial New England. In the colonies, educational responsibilities were vested in parents, following English practice (Cremin, 1970). Renaissance traditions identified the household "as the primary agency of human association and education" (p. 124), and teaching, accordingly, made up a portion of a woman's child-care responsibilities in the home (Perlmann & Margo, 2001). In 1642, for example, the colonial government passed a law "requiring masters of families to teach their children and apprentices to read" (Morgan, 1944, p. 87). It also required them to oversee how satisfactorily parents carried out their didactic functions "concerning their calling and employment of their children, especially of their ability to read and understand the principles of religion and the capital laws of this country" (Cremin, 1970, p. 124). When some towns appointed a woman to be a dame school teacher, a hitherto solely domestic activity took on a public coloration through acts of legislation and their enforcement by an authority located outside the household.

The distinction between the family and government authority had its origin in the provisions of the Elizabethan Statute of Artificers, which regarded the household as the most fundamental educational unit, and the Poor Law of 1601, which recognized the need for agencies outside the household (e.g., workhouses). Carl Kaestle (1973), for example, refers to English usages dating from the Renaissance that distinguished lessons offered in a classroom from individual (tutorial) lessons, and education designed for the public good as distinct from personal gain. Using modern language, we would apply *private* to the realm of the family and *public* to the society outside it. But the modern distinction made little sense at that time because all social functions were subsumed under the religious authority of the colony, and the household itself was the site of economic, religious, domestic, recreational, and educational activities that had not yet become differentiated into separate spheres.

Schools as entities outside the household had barely emerged. Reading instruction took place in the home, with mothers teaching their own children, and in dame schools, with mothers teaching neighbors' children as well. Parents also were enjoined to train their children for a trade. Should they fail to do so, the state could order children apprenticed to another family, who would provide appropriate instruction. According to church doctrine, the famous Old Deluder Satan

Law of 1647 stipulated that when townships increased to a size of fifty households, they "shall then forthwith appoint one within their town to teach all such children as shall resort to him to write and read" (Cremin, 1970, p. 181), with sanctions for noncompliance duly noted. The rationale for the law was straightforward: "It being one chief project of that old deluder, Satan, to keep men from the knowledge of the scriptures, as in former times keeping them in an unknown tongue" and to cloud the original scripture "with false glosses of saint-scheming deceivers" (quoted in Fischer, 1989, p. 132).

Teaching children to read the Bible in English in order to understand and observe the religious principles of the colony was a matter of the highest priority. Note that this law mandated a teacher, not a school. In smaller places, the law implied that education need not transpire inside the venue of a school building. In larger places, with one hundred or more households, the law required the establishment of a grammar school for the preparation of ministers; although the historical record shows that very few were built over the next century; and in both smaller and larger places, compliance was poor.

John Demos (1970), for example, indicates that Plymouth showed little interest in founding or running schools in the first forty years of the colony's existence. At the same time that teaching and schooling were legally mandated, there were "numerous arrangements whereby ministers, schoolmasters, and school dames set up shop independently, attracted such pupils as they could, and collected tuition from parents" (Cremin, 1970, p. 184). Cremin further notes that "schooling went on anywhere and everywhere, not only in schoolrooms, but in kitchens, manses, churches, meetinghouses, sheds erected in fields, and shops erected in towns; that pupils were taught by anyone and everyone, not only by schoolmasters, but by parents, tutors, clergymen, lay readers, precentors, physicians, lawyers, artisans, and shopkeepers" (1970, pp. 192–193), adding "that education became increasingly a matter of 'public concernment' in the colonies" (p. 193).

But education was not to be confused with schooling. Education was an indivisible element in a broader process of cultural transmission across generations that did not depend simply on schools (Bailyn, 1960). A variety of incipient forms of educational arrangements existed at this time that modern (but not contemporaneous) usage would identify as public and private: private in the senses of family based and entrepreneurial, and public in the senses of nonfamilial and state directed. Because public referred to what was nonfamilial, the public realm contained private entities, such as venture schools, not just governmental ones (the latter consistent with twentieth-century usage). By the mideighteenth century, reading instruction offered by women in town-supported schools increased in prevalence; this development was accompanied by the formation of higher level schools that taught writing and other useful subjects, such as ciphering and bookkeeping (Perlmann & Margo, 2001).

Lest we confuse modern and colonial usages of public and private (Bailyn, 1960), however, we should emphasize how little meaning the distinction had several centuries ago because the two were so intermingled. We can readily identify a household responsibility for educating children, both for their salvation and for preparing them to find a vocation and earn a living, the latter representing a moral as well as a practical responsibility. Nevertheless, we must also recognize the explicit influence of Bible, church, and state on the conduct of parents (Morgan, 1944). Warning against presentist interpretations of the past, particularly rampant in Progressive-era accounts of American educational history, Bailyn (1960) indicates that the boundary between the family and its surrounding community was hazy at best, blurring the distinction between public and private.

By the second half of the seventeenth century, youth dealt with the hardships of colonial life differently from their parents by showing greater independence (Bailyn, 1960). Concern developed about the decline in community control and in the ability of parents to restrain their children within the bounds of traditional family life. Starting with the 1647 legislation, reliance on schools increased gradually, transferring "the maimed functions of the family to formal instructional institutions" (Bailyn, 1960, p. 27). In effect, the colonists relied on legislative action to cope with what were considered to be failures by families to raise their children in conformity to religious and social standards. During the same period, the decline of indentured service for employing labor meant that masters became more reliant on young apprentices to get out the product and accordingly spent less time on moral instruction and more on practical demands. As the familistic quality of traditional apprenticeship declined, its more utilitarian aspects came to the fore. Bailyn states that: "In all, there took place a reduction in the personal, non-vocational obligations that bound master and servant and a transfer of general educational functions to external agencies. With increasing frequency masters assigned their apprentices to teachers for instruction in rudimentary literacy and in whatever non-vocational matters they had contracted to teach" (1960, p. 32).

The advent of evening schools for apprentices in the late seventeenth and early eighteenth centuries was a response to the decline in practical and especially moral instruction taking place in such family-like settings as homes and tradesmen's shops. One effect of this development was efforts by sectarian groups to further their religious interests by establishing schools, the financing of which became an issue of high priority. The efforts at finance were numerous: benefactions, rents, land sales, payments in kind, gifts of community property, and so forth, all tending to be insufficient. These efforts were public in a modern sense in that funds were raised through market transactions (e.g., sales and rents). They were also private in another modern sense: They entailed individually owned property. The instability of funding stimulated the gradual introduction of local taxation in some communities to supplement but not replace the various forms of unstable financing already in existence. While taxation did not guarantee adequate support, it nevertheless added another element of the public (as well as increased stability) into the financing of education in a sense consistent with our modern understanding of governmental support being public. In due course, schooling supported by taxes would become the key criterion for judging whether or not schooling was public.

During the late eighteenth and early nineteenth centuries, different kinds of schools began to populate the landscape. Kim Tolley (2001, p. 227) indicates that they gained financial support in several ways: for example, by tuition payments, by funds raised by sponsoring groups, and by town subsidies. Among these were the academies (also called seminaries) "incorporated to ensure financial support beyond that available through tuition alone." Support through tuition alone was the hallmark of venture (entrepreneurial) schools (Seybolt, 1935). Academies operated in a market, as did dame schools for young children and specialized schools serving older populations that provided training in practical and commercial subjects. They advertised in newspapers and differed from the more familistic forms of education available in the colonial period.

Although disputes among scholars have simmered over the similarities and differences among venture schools, Latin schools, and academies, the fact remains that they differed within and among themselves in curriculum, financing, and denominational affiliation. They were alike in that they responded to consumer demand and were part of a public economic domain not controlled by the state, though there were examples of academies established by state legislation (Tolley, 2001). Kaestle (1973, p. 41) describes a similar phenomenon in late-eighteenth-century New York City: tuition-based pay schools, available to the poor as well as to the well-to-do, even though the latter often availed themselves of private (tutored) instruction at home. In the usage of the time, these schools were considered public because instruction was classroom based, not private because they were tuition based. Tuition-supported financing, of course, is now regarded as a defining property of private schooling.

According to William Reese (1995, p. 7), Samuel Adams in 1789 promoted a "System of Public Education" in Boston. A committee of "distinguished citizens" supported a law for the election of what would become "the first formal school board in an American city," which "would administer and supervise public education, inspect the schools, hire teachers, and set the school curriculum and schedule." The committee comprised members from the commercial elite who designed schools that served their interests (e.g., by stressing English and practical and commercial subjects over the classics) and restricted entry to children who already had been tutored, or attended dame schools, and could read and write. Despite the selectivity of these schools, the education of the poor also grew in salience: poverty, pauperism, and vagrancy frightened the merchant elite of Boston. Similar apprehensions were experienced in New York and other cities.

Kaestle (1973, p. 18) reports that well-to-do New Yorkers believed that "[p]ublic education meant an experience that would impress on young men their public responsibilities and give them the abilities to act as public figures," that is, according to the collective good rather than personal gain. Remedies for the problems of the poor were also sought in philanthropically supported charity (or free) schools and in Sunday schools founded by evangelical churches. "After the War of 1812 . . . the elites who made up the School Committee, like town notables across the eastern seaboard, debated whether taxpayers should educate the poor by creating primary schools. Should the children of all social classes attend Boston's system of schools?" (Reese, 1995, p. 10).

In the late eighteenth and early nineteenth centuries, the idea of schools controlled by secular political authority began to take root. It was expressed in debates over who should be educated with taxpayers' money, what kinds of schools (e.g., free, charity, common, pay) should benefit from government support, and what kinds of expenses (e.g., salaries, buildings) should be the government's responsibility (Kaestle, 1973). This notion of public has a meaning we clearly understand today. And to the extent that issues of equality began to infuse the discussion, there is still another meaning of public that pertains to the idea of citizenship and rights to social, political, and economic participation.

With so many ways to define public and private in the eighteenth and nineteenth centuries, distinguishing sharply between public and private schools at that time appears less than useful. In New York, for example, both the state and the city supported denominational schools, and in the bitter controversies between Bishop John Joseph Hughes and the Protestant Free and Public School Societies, Hughes fought hard for financial support for Catholic schools from the government (Kaestle, 1973; Ravitch, 1974). While in the vocabulary of the 1840s, public and Catholic schools were clearly contrasted (Kaestle, 1973), it was not clear whether Catholic was equated with private. But in light of the religious and ethnic conflicts at the time, for Bishop Hughes and his supporters, given their hostility to the nascent system of common schooling, public meant Protestant (Ravitch, 1974).

Characteristic of this age is the multiplicity of meanings residing in the idea of public. The emerging tax-supported schools clearly fit our modern definition. But schools supported by tuition payments, philanthropic contributions, subscriptions, and religious sponsorship also met the criteria of what public encompasses; for example, exercising choices in a market of competing providers of schooling, or nation-building by maintaining and expanding citizenship. In the nineteenth century, the idea of the public in education came to signify a movement of schools into the domain of the state, into that of the market, and into the civil society. It was marked not only by a concern with public welfare in a sense of the whole, but also with the welfare of more parochial groups, such as schools devoted to the interests of religious denominations transcending the household.

The midnineteenth century witnessed the establishment of a variety of schools with mixed public and private characteristics (in the twentieth-century sense), the academies of the period being cases in point. These were incorporated schools (Tolley, 2001) to which tuition was also paid. Most were under religious auspices, both Catholic and Protestant, but also offered secular curricula. Their student bodies were diverse, both in socioeconomic terms and in drawing children from multiple locales, and in that sense cosmopolitan (Beadie, 2001). As to funding, Bruce Leslie (2001, p. 265) comments that "in some cities Catholic challenges for public funds prompted clearer private/public distinctions, [while in places] outside cities mingling private and public funds remained second nature."

The impetus for tax-supported secondary schools, however, developed in the latter part of the nineteenth century from urban origins, not as an outgrowth of the rural and small-town academy movement, even though the academies sought funding from the state. Macroeconomic forces that spurred the growth of an urban, white-collar middle class were probably the main reason for the expansion of urban high schools at this period and later for their spread to the countryside. Leslie (2001, p. 267) observes: "The public/private and religious/secular distinctions solidified after the Civil War. The Fourteenth Amendment provided a constitutional tool to separate church and the states (no longer only church and 'the state') while growing Catholic power fueled the issue emotionally and politically. Labeling high schools 'public' and academies 'private' began to have meaning." With the later decline of academies, the public-private distinction extended to the differences between other kinds of schools that we now familiarly and without confusion label as private (both religious and secular) and public.

In sum, the term "private" is less than helpful in tracking historically the twentieth-century distinction between public and private. In the American colonial context, the description of education as a household (both parental and apprenticeship) function captures the phenomenon. A break from the household provision of education came with the development of tuition-based venture schools, existing in a market and dependent on consumer demand. This invention created a social reality to which the terms "public" and "private" gained relevance. The meaning of these terms expanded as new contingencies arose in the realm of education, among them the multiplicity of types of school sponsorship and the search for devices to create financial stability (Tolley, 2002). Apposite examples were the decision by some schools to solicit state, community, and philanthropic support, and by states to undertake the provision of education.

As the public-private distinction became sharper and more widely acknowledged, its bases narrowed because the social realities that had given rise to the varied criteria of the public and private in education disappeared. Education left the household. Most of the small entrepreneurial schools vanished. The academies and seminaries, with their multiple modes of financing, gave way as the high school came onto the scene. Schools as collections of classrooms became the dominant organizational form, regardless of how they were owned or financed. By the beginning of the twentieth century, the public-private distinction was firmly institutionalized, with a meaning that now was taken for granted. In essence, the distinction denoted, and continues to denote, a difference of formal control and regulation, namely, ownership by governmental or nongovernmental entities.

Acknowledgment of the legitimacy of the public-private distinction, so understood, has been accompanied by the belief that the public schools provide schooling that is at once an entitlement and a duty of citizenship and, for both reasons, must be universally accessible. Within the broader frame of state oversight, in the private subsector the citizenship duty can be fulfilled in schools devoted to the particular interests of persons, families, and groups. Consequently, the public and private subsectors differ in the scope of governmental control and regulation to which they are subordinate and in the degree to which their missions, curricula, and instruction are responsive to many or few particular interests. In the public subsector, governmental control is more pervasive and the particular interests often are more numerous. However, they often are also individually less binding.

An important organizational element in the scope of governmental control and regulation, particularly in light of the idea of the citizenship entitlement to schooling, is the ability of schools to select their student populations. In the twentieth century, it has come to be generally the case that schools in the private sector are free to select who attends them; in the public sector, tax-supported and government-controlled schools are customarily not free to select. There are, however, notable exceptions to this generalization, with the New York City public schools providing numerous cases. Here we find places such as the Bronx High School of Science, Stuyvesant, and earlier Townsend Harris; Music and Art, Needle Trades, and Culinary Arts High Schools. These examples represent schools that vary according to student interest, artistic talent, and academic ability, some of them requiring competitive examinations for entrance. (Note here that religious persuasion is not a criterion for public school selection, while American society continues to struggle with race.)

Aside from these exceptions, which exist in other locations as well, the requirement for admission to schools in the public sector is residence in a specified catchment area. The fact that schools can select their student populations means that they are in a position to adapt their curricular and instructional programs to the characteristics of the student body. They can reduce potential disjunctures between curricular or other program interests and the interests of students and their families. These advantages accrue because wherever schools can choose students, students can choose the school. Public schools, by contrast, and with the exceptions noted, must take all comers. The selection process then is shifted to diverse local real estate markets and away from the school.

Environments of Control

Having completed our historical overview, we turn to the consequences of these differences for the external environments of control in which American elementary and secondary schools are found. Our analysis centers on individual schools. As we have noted, certain private schools, as well as public ones, are parts of larger systems, as is true of diocesan Catholic schools, or are under some sort of supervision by an external body, as is true of many Lutheran schools. Because of our central interest in how control affects the workings of classrooms, we will treat these larger systems as parts of the environment of the schools that they contain, and their structures of control as part of the external control of these schools.

The control of an organization's activities may be exerted through formal internal regulation (in the case of individual schools, regulated by the principal), market discipline, and external laws and administrative regulation. All three are important components of the environments of control of both public and private schools. We propose that these environments exert greater pressures for the standardization of organizational forms and procedures in the public than in the private subsector. These pressures have three sources: bureaucratic formalization and consequent standardization of procedures; organization of markets for personnel, students, and textbooks; and exposure to mandated innovation.

As our historical review shows, by the middle of the nineteenth century, diverse arrangements for schooling had converged on a state-run system, marked by what Meyer has called "fragmented centralization" (Meyer, 1983). With time, the centralizing tendencies extended into the private subsector, though less pervasively and with less force. Although the effective formal control and funding of the state-run schools, like that of the private schools, was in local hands, by the early years of the twentieth century the entire educational sector displayed what Rowan (2002b, p. 5) calls an "industry standard." That is, appearing throughout both public and private elementary and secondary education, instruction was conducted in English in the same secular subjects, and in graded classrooms of similar layout.

Similar teaching and other occupational specialties also emerged in the two subsectors, accompanied by shared conventional understandings about training and entry, forming a common occupational structure for K-12 education. This structure provided the basis for a common set of practices for recruiting, hiring, and retaining staff. Organizational and substantive diversity in the supply of education now was concentrated in the small private subsector, which, however, remained substantially constrained by the industry standard.

In the past two decades, the public subsector's control environment has become less fragmented and more centralized. Control over funding has moved away from local bodies toward state and federal agencies. More important, public schools and systems are exposed to increasing pressures to account for student learning. These pressures arise in part from statewide testing programs that carry performance sanctions of some force, including state-administered incentives for improved instructional performance as measured by achievement test scores. They arise also from an increasingly central role of private agencies such as the Educational Testing Service and ACT in evaluating schools' instructional performance.

Consequently, public schools and school districts have become more bureaucratic and hence more standardized in at least three senses. First, they have experienced increasing formalization that extends into the technical core of the school to affect, for example, staff recruitment and evaluation, curricula, and student management. Second, the formal rules of procedure in these areas are universalistic, so that exceptions and deviations, whether or not they are adaptive, are hard to make. Third, this formalization and universalism now extend into the evaluation of instructional performance. This trend makes key performance indicators, such as achievement test scores and rates of college attendance, visible and significant in the eyes of school and system administrators and relevant public actors. These changes have converged to place substantial limits on the autonomy and discretion of both administrators and teachers. With respect to the public subsector, it is no longer possible to characterize the schools as engaged in a world of institutionalized myth, as they once were by Meyer and Rowan (1977). In any event, Meyer and Rowan meant this characterization to apply only to the American case, and Rowan (2002a) has recanted with respect to American public schools as well.

Recently, and to an increasing degree in the public's perception as well as in that of professional educators, the universalistic character of public schools has become associated with the bureaucratic elements of school organization, while the particularistic character of private education has become associated with the familistic attributes of community. However, there is a good measure of truth in the proposition that most schools (except the small, independent ones) possess significant bureaucratic elements. That is, as education has become a citizenship entitlement and obligation, the work of virtually all schools has become subject to formal, universalistic regulation by state agencies and by nonstate (private) bureaucracies, for example, dioceses and such commercial ventures as the Edison Project. This development precisely follows Max Weber's (1978) depiction of bureaucratization as inevitable.

Nevertheless, the trends toward bureaucratic standardization are less consistently and pervasively apparent in the private subsector. There, specific market niches and a local control that is based on nongovernmental ownership combine to buffer the schools from bureaucratic pressures. Among these schools, hiring and firing of staff can be somewhat more particularistic, and curricula may be less extensively specified. Moreover, the discipline of achievement testing is slack. For the greater number of these schools, however, the discipline imposed by accountability for their graduates' later educational attainments may be more severe.

Each of these aspects of school operation can be focused on the particular interests of a relatively homogeneous clientele. The degree of exposure to diverse interests is itself an important dimension of subsector variation. We will consider it when we turn to questions of organizational form and control.

Schools and Markets

Both public and private schools exist in environments that are organized in significant ways as markets. Perhaps the most powerful force that moves public more than private schools toward standardization is the organization of the markets in which they find personnel, students, and textbooks. Their broader market niches and greater exposure to governmental control and regulation allow them substantially less selectivity in recruiting and retaining staff and students, so that neither is likely to align well with the interests of clienteles and these schools' governing bodies.

Textbooks constitute a high proportion of the content that is taught in elementary and secondary classrooms, and they are supplied in a concentrated market. Because the textbook market is dominated by a handful of publishers, the industry is marked by a slow rate of product innovation and supplies texts that are sufficiently general and superficial in content so that they can be used in a diversity of school settings. Consequently, textbooks constitute a powerful barrier to local instructional innovation, thereby creating strong pressures for curricular and instructional standardization.

Schools in the private subsector should be buffered to a significant degree from the constraints of this market. The narrow market niches that private schools occupy, combined with a less formalized technical instructional core, should make it possible for private school teachers, more often than their public school counterparts, to use teaching materials that they have prepared themselves. They also should go more often outside the textbook market for the books that they have their students read, draw more often selectively and with supplementation on commercially published textbooks, and use materials sold in commercial markets that cater to religious and other narrow niche schools (e.g., creationist science textbooks).

Finally, the narrow market niches that private schools occupy buffer them from mandated innovation. It has become a truism that American public education is now a field littered with the remains of instructional innovations that have failed (Cuban, 1993; Tyack & Cuban, 1995). In contrast to the textbook market, the market in which instructional training, information, and program development are supplied to schools is extremely heterogeneous, including numerous independent private organizations and governmental agencies. In this market, products appear and disappear at a rapid rate. Consequently, the school or district that enters the instructional innovation and development market finds an abundance of short-lived possibilities—the curricular and instructional fads that seem to dominate instructional reform in the United States.

Schools that serve a specific, delimited clientele, that is, private more often than public schools, are in a position to be highly selective in entering this market, if they enter it at all. A diverse clientele restricts such choices, as do popular and governmental pressures for accountability. Hence, public schools are more likely than privates ones to enter the innovation market unselectively and often.

Difference and Convergence

We must not push the matter of difference too far. The development of the public and private subsectors displays a trend toward similarity as well as difference of environmental and organizational attributes. With education defined as an entitlement and obligation of every citizen, private schools have become public in significant ways.

While some private schools are freestanding (e.g., elite college preparatory schools, secular as well as religious), others are parts of overarching administrative structures, Roman Catholic schools being the prime example. Although private schools do not get their funds from the government, they nonetheless get them by participating in financial markets of one kind or another: for example, by seeking bank loans, accepting philanthropies, and investing endowments. They hire employees increasingly from secular labor markets for teachers and administrators (in the case of Catholic and other religious schools, less and less from the pool of religious whose work is based more on faith than market position).

For all schools, public and private, the academic curriculum has become standardized around state mandates, following worldwide patterns of convergence for teaching basic elementary school skills and a core of high school subjects, including: English (or a mother tongue), science, mathematics, social studies, and foreign language (Meyer, Kamens, & Benavot, 1992). To the same end, the constraints of college entrance requirements are felt equally keenly by both public and private high schools that offer college preparation.

Some current reform movements in public education constitute a new pressure toward the convergence of the public and private in education. They can be seen as attempts to infuse the public schools with communal patterns of organization and conduct while maintaining universalistic regulation through such devices as grading, yearly promotion, a standard academic curriculum, and rules of decorum. It remains to be seen whether these attempts will move the organizational form of at least some public schools in a communal direction. It also remains to be seen whether schools in the private sector, subject to continuing pressure toward equality in educational life chances, will become increasingly subject to formal, universalistic regulation.

Market Niches, Organizational Form, and Organizational Learning

Now we consider how a local school's capacity to instruct well may be affected by its organizational form and location in the educational services market. Given the uncodified nature of instructional practice (Dreeben, 1996; Herbst, 1989), in most schools this capacity must be a matter of local knowledge about how to deal with the kinds of students whom a school enrolls, within limits set by the availability of material resources for teaching. For this reason, capacity for instructional effectiveness depends substantially on opportunities for organizational learning about instruction by a faculty and a school's administrators. These opportunities, in turn, are effects of market location and organizational form. Capacity for organizational learning is a prime condition, but not a sufficient one, for viable local pedagogical knowledge, a caveat that must be kept in mind throughout the following discussion.

Behavior in social settings is governed, with greater or lesser effect, by rules; that is, by regulations, routines, norms, and expectations (March, Schulz, & Zhou, 2000). Organizational learning denotes the processes through which the members of an organization diagnose and solve problems of work and gain compliance with these solutions, thereby adapting to changing circumstances that affect the work that they do. The sensed problems and solutions have to do with the rules that govern the conduct of work.

Organizational learning involves a group's learning from experience and its capacity for social control. It depends in particular on the informal processes through which a group within an organization alters or invents rules and gains compliance with the newly formulated rules. It includes the processes through which the need for rule change is sensed, multiple interests in the ways the work is done are aggregated and, if in conflict, negotiated, new understandings about the work are framed and disseminated, and new rules and action become tightly coupled.

In schools, the rules that bear most directly on instruction include those that govern (1) the content and organization of the curriculum; (2) the distribution of instructional and related resources among classrooms, teachers, and students; (3) standards of instructional or academic performance; (4) the conduct of instruction (including efficiency; rates of gain adjusted for pertinent traits of a student body); and (5) the school schedule and thereby the definition of time allotments to different subjects and activities, and the assignment (and hence matching) of teachers with students in classrooms. Organizational learning in the instructional workplace centers primarily on conventions, norms, and expectations concerning how instruction is conducted and what constitutes satisfactory and unsatisfactory results.

Studies of organizations in several institutional sectors, including commerce, manufacturing, and research and development, suggest that the effectiveness of organizational learning is a function of lateral, collegial networks, including their density and centrality. These network attributes affect the ease and accuracy of communication in a group, its capacity for informal social control, and the degree to which its members can act autonomously (i.e., the degree to which the network is buffered from intrusion) (Brown & Duguid, 2000; Cohen & Prusak, 2001; Lave

& Wenger, 1991). Recent work on high school faculties (Bidwell & Yasumoto, 1999; McLaughlin & Talbert, 2001; Siskin, 1994) suggests that such collegial networks have significant effects on a faculty's collective capacity to make and implement adaptive changes in local rules of instruction. There is some evidence that the effects of this capacity extend to rates of gain in students' cognitive achievement (Yasumoto, Uekawa, & Bidwell, 2001).

Because the members of such networks tend to develop common understandings about the nature of their work and how to go about it, we can think of them as small adaptive communities. The research on the formation of these communities, limited as it is to high school faculties, shows that such communities are more likely to form within teaching fields, constrained by the division of instructional labor, than they are to embrace entire faculties, let alone faculties and administrators. These findings leave open the question of conditions that might favor the emergence of schoolwide adaptive communities, including the conditions under which they incorporate local school administrators. Intuitively, it seems reasonable to think of school size and of the intensity of faculty specialization as probable fostering or inhibiting conditions.

Niches and Hierarchies

We consider the autonomy of faculties and faculty groups and of local school administrators (either separately or in conjunction with teachers) to be a function of the diversity of interests in the external environment and of the degree to which they are buffered from intrusion by the interested actors. Note that we consider the interests of the central administrators of a school system to be a part of the external environment of the schools in the system.

When the staff of a school is exposed to diverse interests, its situation permits negotiation over both the ends and means of the instruction that it provides, a political process that potentially gives it leeway to frame its own local pedagogical rules. When it is exposed to an environment that is homogeneous in the interests that it contains, it loses autonomy with respect to the ends of the schooling that it offers. In effect, it is in a condition of substantive domination by the external actor, while autonomy with respect to means (i.e., procedural rules) is a question of the degree to which the dominant external actor trusts the technical competence of the staff. We will propose that this trust is a function of the chartering and selectivity of the school.

A useful way to analyze the bearing of external actors and their interests on the autonomy of teachers and local administrators is to consider the degree to which their market niches and organizational form buffer them from the interests of these actors. By definition, the width of market niches determines the diversity of external interests to which schools are exposed, while organizational form affects the degree to which faculty members and administrators individually or collectively become active agents in the determination of instructional rules and in securing the implementation of these rules. The narrower the niche, the more homogeneous are the interests of the actors in the external environment. The weaker such buffering, the greater a school's vulnerability to the interests of the persons and groups that are active in its environment, including persons and groups in the administrative echelons of school systems. Therefore, the more vulnerable it should be to bureaucratic standardization and mandated innovation, affecting the location of rule setting, changing, and suspending.

Buffering as a consequence of organizational form requires a more extended discussion. We propose that this buffering is a function of formal hierarchies of authority. The more centralized such a hierarchy, the stronger the buffering effect. Internally, organizations, including schools, gain autonomy to set, change, or suspend rules as power becomes dispersed among numerous actors. They also gain autonomy over rules as interest diversity increases, allowing room for maneuver as one interest is played off against another, that is, as a consequence of negotiation between actors in the environment and in the organization. In either of these situations, rule setting, changing, and suspending become functions of internal hierarchy, negotiation among interested actors within the school, and experiential learning by the school's administrators or teachers. An organization such as a school loses this autonomy as the number of actors decreases either because of coalition-forming negotiation among external actors in a market-ordered environment or because of centralization in a hierarchically ordered environment.

Our reasoning points to a trade-off of control between the faculty workplace as hierarchically subordinate or as vulnerable to the play of diverse interests. While a hierarchy, whether internal or external to a school, buffers from diverse external interests by aggregating and expressing them, it also places the school in a structure of formal domination. The more decentralized the hierarchy, the less effective the buffering, so that the force of external control then depends on the diversity and number of actors and interests. This is the situation of many public schools in the United States, where school boards and district administrators comprise only a part of the array of interested actors who potentially can influence a school's regulations and routines.

External Hierarchies

With respect to external authority, in a formal sense a school that is operated by the state is buffered because the state in principle acts to represent the full range of interests of the citizens for whom education is an entitlement. The resolution of any difference of interests takes place before policies are made and resources are allocated. In a formal sense, Roman Catholic diocesan schools should be more effectively buffered from particular interests than parochial ones, with diocesan authorities performing the same functions of interest aggregation and expression that are performed by governmental authorities in the public sphere.

Despite the centralizing trends that we have noted in the United States, effective authority over public schools remains primarily local, so that the state hierarchy is substantially decentralized. As we have suggested, most American public schools are located in broad market niches. Therefore, these schools are vulnerable to direct intervention by such local, interested actors as aggrieved or ambitious parents, interest groups, employers, and business organizations. An extreme example is provided by the current wave of charter school establishment in Arizona. There, state law allows virtually any plausible group to begin a charter school, with minimal governmental supervision. As a result, the numerous charter schools being opened are highly responsive to the particular interests of the founding groups, on which they are entirely dependent for resources and students (Clemens, 2002).

In fact, despite the centralizing effects of the accountability movement, public schools may be more effectively buffered from the state agencies to which they are formally responsible than from the local actors who stand outside the formal structure of control. This difference in the effectiveness of buffering can be attributed to the concentration at the local level of actors who supply two major resources to schools, namely, funds and political support. It brings us to the second type of buffering, which is a consequence of degrees of resource dependence between external actors and organizations. As classic resource dependence theory suggests, the greater the dependence of an organization on any single actor (individual or collective) or coalition of actors in its environment, the greater the control of that actor or coalition over the organization's effective goals, modes of operation, and output (Aldrich & Pfeffer, 1976; Pfeffer & Salancik, 1978). At the same time, the more these actors or coalitions value an organization's output of goods or services, the greater its autonomy in relation to them and the greater its potential control of their activities.

As external hierarchies become steeper, so that the centralization of authority increases, a school becomes dependent on the central authority and is in a situation similar analytically to the resource dependent school in a narrow niche. In addition, public schools in communities where active stakeholders are few are likely to be in this situation either because district administrators can dominate the school's environment or because they can easily form coalitions or be co-opted into coalitions with the community actors. Schools that serve sectarian communities (in which family, community, and school boundaries are blurred and overlapping) and those that serve elite clienteles are similarly situated, whether this clientele is private (as in the case of elite secular private schools) or public (as in the case of schools in affluent communities).

Internal Hierarchies

Internal hierarchy is of particular importance when external interests are diverse because it affects the distribution of power to act on instructional rules. To the extent that authority becomes concentrated in the hands of the principal, the school's faculty should become effectively buffered from local external interests. However, in most public school systems, principals are notably weak actors in the chain of command, lacking the power resources required to make their formal authority effective (Bidwell, 2001). Here, private schools are likely to have the advantage, perhaps apart from those in diocesan systems large and complex enough to approximate public school districts. This advantage should derive from their substantial autonomy in their external environments, providing space, other things being equal, for the emergence of strong leadership by the principal.

Organizational Learning and Students' Learning

When a school is heteronomously controlled, that is, when it is subject to strong external domination, a prime condition is present for both inhibited experiential learning and for tight coupling of rules and action. Its curriculum and modes of instruction should be highly stable, uniformly realized, and unresponsive to pedagogical movements and changing local circumstance. These effects of heteronomy should be stronger the greater the legitimacy and consequent authoritative quality of the external control and the sparser the opportunities available to the staff for employment elsewhere. Authoritative control should produce a strong tendency toward habitual compliance, weakening individual teachers' and administrators' sensitivity to either pedagogical innovation or local change, while centralization generally implies centralization of means of enforcement as well as means of decision making. This tendency should be stronger the smaller the school (and, therefore, the faculty) and the less specialized the faculty. That is, as the number of teachers and the number of specialties increase, so should the number of points in the hierarchy for breaks in communication from the center and the number of opportunities for faculty contact with colleagues and professional groups outside the school.

When a school is autonomous, without effective external control, the incidence of experiential learning among its administrators and faculty and the coupling of rules and action are a function in part of the centralization of its internal administrative hierarchy, working similarly to the centralization of external control. However, as central internal authority weakens, control should disperse within a faculty, the more so the larger its size and the more specialized its roles. This dispersion should endow multiple pedagogical interests in the faculty with some freedom of play. Hence, it should provide focal points in the faculty workplace for local experiential learning, the formation of external ties (potentially allowing more cosmopolitan forms of pedagogical learning), and the coupling of locally differentiated rules and instructional action. Under these conditions, although the incidence of experiential learning is high, it also is likely to be differentiated and divergent, rather than coordinated and convergent. Moreover, although rules and acts may be tightly coupled, the substance of these tightly coupled, localized loci of control is also likely to be divergent, giving the aggregate appearance that rules and action are imperfectly linked.

This argument implies that a faculty and its administrators cannot easily form an adaptive community. That is, they cannot easily form a network that is both cohesive (so that rules and acts are tightly coupled and substantively convergent) and consensual (in the sense that experiential learning takes place more or less consistently throughout the network). The argument also implies that adaptive communities, on average, occur less frequently in public than in private schools. This difference is expected, in part, because, at least at the secondary level, public schools tend to have larger enrollments than private schools and more specialized curricula and faculties. It also is expected because of the lesser ability of public schools to select their students and because of their greater propensity toward bureaucratic standardization.

Moreover, the centralizing trend in the external environment that is produced by the accountability movement should accentuate hierarchical control more sharply in public than in private schools. That is, accountability requirements, which bear more sharply on public than on private schools, demand an identifiable agent, usually an administrator who is to account for instructional performance. We expect this agent, consequently, to try to achieve and then enforce as uniform a set of instructional practices as possible within the school or schools for which he or she is responsible. This circumstance should provide a barrier to the incorporation of administrators into schools' adaptive communities, in addition to the barriers raised by large size and intensive faculty specialization.

When hierarchies are flat, agency tends to diffuse, so that a greater number of a school's faculty members may be held directly accountable to parents as well as to the school's constituents and stakeholders. When the local environment contains a heterogeneous array of interests, their competing or conflicting demands are likely to dampen a faculty's efforts to solve instructional problems or to pursue a given set of pedagogical rules consistently. However, if we are correct that organizational autonomy is more often found among private than public schools, their narrow market niches should substantially reduce the frequency with which the teachers in these schools find themselves agents who are responsible to incompatible interests.

Because the chances for the formation of adaptive faculty communities are further reduced by the concentration of textbook markets and exposure to mandated innovation, organizational form and environmental attributes have more frequent and more potent mutually reinforcing adverse consequences for instructional productivity among public than among private schools. The probability of these adverse effects becomes still higher in the public subsector because external accountability requirements increase the chances of hierarchical control within schools and districts.

Effects of Selectivity and Chartering

The degree to which a school is selective of its inputs should affect organizational learning in three ways. First, selectivity of students and materials defines the hard realities that teachers confront every day in their classrooms. These constraints on daily work arise from the degree to which students are selected according to criteria consistent with a school's mission and the degree to which texts and other materials are chosen according to similar criteria, thereby escaping the concentrated textbook market. The lower the level of student selectivity, whether by the school or by the students, the greater the likelihood that teachers will confront problems of student motivation, resistance, and capability. The lower the level of materials selectivity, the greater the likelihood that they will find themselves working with materials ill suited to what their courses require and what their students can handle.

Second, faculty selectivity, interacting with chartering and size, affects the likelihood that adaptive faculty communities will form. Smaller schools, chartered schools, and homogeneous schools make adaptation more likely because the range of activities that require consistent adaptation are narrower than in schools where lack of selectivity allows the multiplication of difficulties to occur.

Cohesion and consensus characterize adaptive communities. That is, they display dense networks of sentimentally positive ties between colleagues. These sentiments are based primarily on professional respect. In these dense collegial networks, problem-solving interaction can be frequent and relatively free of the distortions that are produced by multilinked communication. At the same time, in these networks, interpersonal influence provides the social control that grounds action on the instructional rules and conventions on which the community agrees. When a school can select its administrators and faculty, it is likely to select them on the basis of instructional outlooks and styles and technical and moral capacities that agree with the school's mission and the motives and abilities of its students. Moreover, when the school is chartered, that is, when its mission is explicit, valued, and widely known, the criteria for selection are likely to be more clear than in other schools, and faculty members are more likely to be self-selected as well as selectively recruited. In this way, selectivity and chartering should work together to produce pedagogically consensual faculties, whose members are trained in the instructional rules that characterize the school and are likely to form strong collegial ties on the basis of mutual professional respect.

When the school is small, selectivity and chartering should create conditions under which the entire faculty forms an adaptive community, whose members by virtue of training and prior experience and participation in the community's pedagogical problem solving and environment of social control follow the same rules of instructional procedure. This pedagogical agreement, realized in action, should create consistent classroom experience, crossing subject matter lines, that increases the likelihood of effective academic outcomes for the greater number of students in the school.

When the school is large and the faculty correspondingly more intensively specialized, selectivity and chartering should create conditions similarly conducive to adaptive faculty communities, but these communities are more likely to occur within subgroup boundaries produced by the division of faculty labor, in particular, the teaching fields and departments. In these schools, instructional adaptations are more likely to be subject-specific than facultywide, resulting in modes of instruction that themselves vary by subject matter and that produce correspondingly varying trajectories of academic attainment according to students' subject-specific capabilities and interests.

Third, when a school can select its staff, what it wishes to accomplish in its courses and how it conducts them are likely to align with the interests of parents and other external actors. This alignment should lead these actors to trust the competence of the staff, that is, it should increase their willingness to grant them the pedagogical leeway required to set their own rules for teaching. Chartering should strengthen trust in teachers' pedagogical competence, to the degree that explicitness of purpose and clarity about the nature of the schooling to be provided makes clear to both staff and external actors the criteria on which staff selection has occurred.

Because private schools more often than public schools are selective of faculty and of students and because they are chartered and small, their faculties should more often form facultywide adaptive communities with beneficial effects on the value that they add to students' learning. However, private high schools, no less than public schools, are usually larger and more heterogeneous than the elementary schools in their subsector, so that differential learning trajectories should be observed more often in high schools in both subsectors, but should describe more elevated learning curves among the private high schools. However, no small number of public schools, in particular academically oriented and other special-purpose high schools, are chartered and can be selective of faculty, so that the trends that we have posited for the formation of adaptive faculty communities and for students' learning should characterize these schools as well.

Conclusion

Our review of the institutional histories of the public and private subsectors in American education describes a process of institutionalization in which the subsectors became increasingly distinct. In this process, state versus private ownership has come to denote differences in the way in which citizens' entitlements to and obligations for schooling are balanced. As a consequence, the public, by contrast with the private subsector has become more vulnerable to trends toward political and regulatory centralization and consequent bureaucratic formalization and standardization and to the constraints of the concentrated textbook market and the vicissitudes of the heterogeneous market for pedagogical innovation.

We identified two primary social organizational dimensions along which schools vary: the degree to which their control environments are centralized or decentralized (so that schools are more heteronomous or autonomous organizations), and the degree to which they occupy broad or narrow niches for the provision of educational services. Dichotomizing each of these dimensions yields a fourfold property space. Schools in decentralized environments and broad niches are highly vulnerable to multiple interests of local external actors, those in centralized environments and broad niches somewhat less vulnerable, those in decentralized environments and narrow niches still less vulnerable, and those in centralized environments and narrow niches the least vulnerable of all.

At present, the larger number of public schools are in the first of these cells, but recent trends suggest that they may be moving toward the second, becoming somewhat less exposed to the interests of multiple local actors. Schools in the private subsector occupy the third cell, for the most part, although some (e.g., Catholic diocesan high schools) are in the fourth. Thus, at present, private schools on average are likely to be more autonomous than public ones. However, as our historical review suggests, they may be moving toward greater exposure to regulatory control that is external to any educational system of which they may be a part. If so, they, like the public schools, may experience pressures toward standardization and possibly also toward dependence on the textbook market and on mandated innovation.

Moreover, a common consideration for all schools is the viability of pedagogical practice, with respect in particular to schools that pose the most intransigent problems of learning and student conduct. The viability question cuts across all schools, regardless of subsector. Selecting students is a device that enables a school to reduce its exposure to such intractable problems, a device to which private schools, on average, have greater access.

Our discussion of the conditions that foster organizational learning among faculties centered on relationships between degrees of organizational autonomy and niche width, the occurrence and scope of adaptive communities within faculties, and the interaction of these conditions with faculty size and specialization. This discussion led to the conclusion that the fostering conditions occur more often in private than in public schools, a conclusion that gained further strength when we also considered the interaction of forms of selectivity with chartering.

However, our treatment of the relationships between organizational learning, heteronomy-autonomy, and niche width should make it clear that some private schools are in less favorable situations, while some public schools are in very favorable situations indeed. The former include private schools that are not well placed in the market for students or that, like many inner-city Catholic schools, serve disparate clienteles. The latter include public schools that enjoy narrow niches by virtue of families' residential choices. Therefore, in research on the organizational conditions and mechanisms that affect teachers' work and students' learning, the public-private distinction is of secondary importance to more analytically fundamental dimensions along which school organization may vary. That is, the public-private distinction seems to be analogous to the idea of urbanism. Like urbanism, it is a significant feature of the institutional landscape and thus worth close analysis. The urban-rural dichotomy is of limited use because it obscures significant particularities of urban and rural life and institutions, both similarities and differences. In the same way, the public-private dichotomy obscures key social organizational dimensions along which schools differ. In the historical portion of our essay, we showed how the public-private distinction has acquired the denotation of governmental versus nongovernmental control. However, as the remainder of our essay demonstrates, this meaning maps badly onto analytical dimensions that are central to understanding how schools work. These dimensions cut across the boundary between schools that are under formal governmental control and those that are not.

Note

The authors are grateful for the comments of participants in the conference "Effects of School Sector on Educational Outcomes," November 9–10, 2002, University of Notre Dame, at which an earlier version of this essay was presented.

References

Aldrich, H. E., & Pfeffer, J. (1976). Environments of organizations. *Annual Review of Sociology* (Vol. 2). Palo Alto, CA: Annual Review Inc.

Bailyn, B. (1960). *Education in the forming of American society: Needs and opportunities for study.* New York: Vintage Books.

Baker, D. P. (1992). The politics of American Catholic school expansion, 1870–1930. In B. Fuller & R. Rubinson (Eds.), *The political construction of education: The state, school expansion, and economic change* (pp. 189–206). New York: Praeger.

Beadie, N. (2001). Academy students in the mid-nineteenth century: Social geography, demography, and the culture of academy attendance. *History of Education Quarterly, 41,* 251–262.

Bidwell, C. E. (2001). Analyzing schools as organizations: Long-term permanence and short-term change [Extra Issue]. *Sociology of Education,* 100–114.

Bidwell, C. E., & Kasarda, J. D. (1980). Conceptualizing and measuring the effect of school and schooling. *American Journal of Education, 88,* 401–430.

Bidwell, C. E., & Yasumoto, J. Y. (1999). The collegial focus: Teaching fields, collegial relationships, and instructional practice in American high schools. *Sociology of Education, 72,* 234–256.

Brown, J. S., & Duguid, P. (2000). *The social life of information.* Cambridge, MA: Harvard Business School Press.

Clemens, E. (2002). Invention, innovation, proliferation: Explaining organizational genesis and change. *Research in the Sociology of Organization, 19,* 1–48.

Cohen, D., & Prusak, L. (2001). *In good company.* Cambridge, MA: Harvard Business School Press.

Coleman, J. S., & Hoffer, T. (1987). *Public and private high schools: The impact of communities.* New York: Basic Books.

Coleman, J. S., Hoffer, T., & Kilgore, S. (1982). *High school achievement: Public, Catholic, and private schools compared.* New York: Basic Books.

Cremin, L. A. (1970). *American education: The colonial experience, 1607–1783.* New York: Harper & Row.

Cuban, L. (1993). *How teachers taught.* New York: Teachers College Press.

Demos, J. (1970). *A little commonwealth: Family life in Plymouth Colony.* London: Oxford University Press.

DiMaggio, P. J., & Powell, W. W. (1983). The iron cage revisited: Isomorphism and collective rationality in organizational fields. *American Sociological Review, 48,* 147–160.

Dreeben, R. (1996). The occupation of teaching and educational reform. In K. K. Wong (Ed.), *Advances in educational policy 2: Rethinking school reform in Chicago* (pp. 93–124). Greenwich, CT: JAI Press.

Etzioni, A. (1996). *The new golden rule.* New York: Basic Books.

Fischer, D. H. (1989). *Albion's seed: Four British folkways in America.* New York: Oxford University Press.

Greeley, A. M., & Rossi, P. H. (1966). *The education of Catholic Americans.* Chicago: Aldine.

Gusfield, J. (1955). Social structure and moral reform: A study of the Women's Christian Temperance Union. *American Journal of Sociology, 61,* 221–232.

Herbst, J. (1989). *And sadly teach: Teacher education and professionalization in American culture.* Madison: University of Wisconsin Press.

Kaestle, C. F. (1973). *The evolution of an urban school system: New York City, 1750–1850.* Cambridge, MA: Harvard University Press.

Lave, J., & Wenger, E. (1991). *Situated learning.* Cambridge, Eng.: Cambridge University Press.

Leslie, B. (2001). Where have all the academies gone? *History of Education Quarterly, 41,* 262–270.

March, J. G., Schulz, M., & Zhou, X. (2000). *The dynamics of rules: Change in written organizational codes.* Stanford, CA: Stanford University Press.

McLaughlin, M. W., & Talbert, J. (2001). *Professional communities and the work of high school teaching.* Chicago: University of Chicago Press.

Meyer, J. W. (1977). The effects of education as an institution. *American Journal of Sociology, 83,* 55–77.

Meyer, J. W. (1983). Centralization of funding and control in educational governance. In J. W. Meyer & W. R. Scott (Eds.), *Organizational environments: Ritual and rationality* (pp. 45–67). Beverly Hills, CA: Sage.

Meyer, J. W., Kamens, D. H., & Benavot, A. (1992). *School knowledge for the masses: World models and national primary curricular categories in the twentieth century.* Washington, DC: Falmer Press.

Meyer, J. W., & Rowan, B. (1977). Institutionalized organizations: Formal structure as myth and ceremony. *American Journal of Sociology, 83,* 340–363.

Meyer, J. W., & Scott, W. R. (1994). *Institutional environments and organizations: Structural complexity and individualism.* Thousand Oaks, CA: Sage.

Morgan, E. S. (1944). *The Puritan family: Religion and domestic relations in seventeenth-century New England.* New York: Harper & Row.

Parsons, T. (1951). *The social system.* Glencoe, IL: Free Press.

Perlmann, J., & Margo, R. A. (2001). *Women's work? American schoolteachers, 1650–1920.* Chicago: University of Chicago Press.

Perrow, C. (1961). The analysis of goals in complex organizations. *American Sociological Review, 26,* 854–866.

Pfeffer, J., & Salancik, G. R. (1978). *The external control of organizations: A resource dependence perspective.* New York: Harper & Row.

Ravitch, D. (1974). *The great school wars: New York City, 1805–1973: A history of the public schools as a battlefield of social change.* New York: Basic Books.

Reese, W. J. (1995). *The origins of the American high school.* New Haven, CT: Yale University Press.

Rossi, A. S. (1954). *Determinants of reliance on religious leaders and their effect upon school attitudes and participation.* Unpublished manuscript, Harvard Graduate School of Education Center for Field Studies.

Rossi, P. H. (1954). *The publics of the local schools.* Unpublished manuscript, Harvard Graduate School of Education Center for Field Studies.

Rowan, B. (2002a). Teachers' work and instructional management, Part 1: Alternative views of the task of teaching. In W. K. Hoy & C. G. Miskel (Eds.), *Theory and research in educational administration: Vol. 1* (pp. 129–149). Greenwich, CT: Information Age.

Rowan, B. (2002b). *The new institutionalism and the study of education: Changing ideas for changing times.* Paper presented at a conference on Advancing the Institutional Research Agenda in Education: From Analysis to Policy, State University of New York at Albany.

Selznick, P. (1957). *Leadership in administration: A sociological interpretation.* Evanston, IL: Row, Peterson & Co.

Seybolt, R. F. (1935). *The private schools of colonial Boston.* Cambridge, MA: Harvard University Press.

Siskin, L. S. (1994). *Realms of knowledge: Academic departments in secondary schools.* Washington, DC: Falmer Press.

Stinchcombe, A. (1965). Social structure and organizations. In J. G. March (Ed.), *Handbook of organizations* (pp. 142–193). Chicago: Rand-McNally.

Tolley, K. (2001). The rise of the academies: Continuity or change? *History of Education Quarterly, 41,* 225–239.

Tolley, K. (2002). Mapping the landscape of higher schooling, 1727–1850. In N. Beadie & K. Tolley (Eds.), *Chartered schools: Two hundred years of independent academies in the United States, 1727–1925.* New York: Routledge Falmer.

Tyack, D., & Cuban, L. (1995). *Tinkering toward utopia.* Cambridge, MA: Harvard University Press.

Weber, M. (1978). *Economy and society: An outline of interpretive sociology* (G. Roth & C. Wittich, Eds. and Trans.). Berkeley: University of California Press.

Yasumoto, J. Y., Uekawa, K., & Bidwell, C. E. (2001). The collegial focus and student achievement. *Sociology of Education, 74,* 181–209.

Zald, M. N. (1970). *Organizational change: The political economy of the YMCA.* Chicago: University of Chicago Press.

2 | Innovation in Educational Markets

An Organizational Analysis of Third Sector
Private Schools in Toronto

Scott Davies and Linda Quirke

This chapter offers an organizational analysis of *third sector* private schools in Toronto, Canada. Third sector schools are private schools that are neither religious nor elite. While private schools have long served religious and elite communities in Canada, they are becoming increasingly differentiated. Indeed, one in five Ontario private school students attends third sector schools. These schools are typically small, with enrollments of less than fifty, and are located at humble sites such as office buildings, old houses, or shopping plazas. They distinguish themselves with specialized pedagogy that attracts clients who do not seek prestigious name-brand education or religious orientations.

Do markets encourage schools to be innovative? Today, many market advocates decry the paucity of invention in public schools and celebrate the entrepreneurial dynamism of the private sector. Yet, such claims are rarely empirically grounded and often ignore the diversity of private schools. Established elite schools, as an example, embrace long-standing school forms and derive their prestige from tradition, not innovation. Likewise, religious private schools have historically mimicked mainstream public schools in order to secure legitimacy (Baker, 1992). Private schools are most likely to be innovative in relatively new markets. In the United States, charter schools would meet this requirement. However, in Ontario, where there is no charter school legislation, third sector private schools best exemplify such a market.

This sector offers a strategic vantage point for studying educational markets. While elite schools conform to historic images of patrician education, and while religious schools mix standard school forms with the doctrines of their respective communities, third sector schools are free to build their own identity and mandate. Lacking an established legacy, they are arguably the most likely to embrace innovations. Attracting parents who seek neither religion nor entrée into elite networks, these schools may be motivated to embrace novel pedagogies. Moreover, they are closer to the market than are charter schools or magnet schools, since they are not organized through a public bureaucracy. Needing to comply only with bare-bones health and safety and curricular guidelines and the most minimal of inspections, these schools can innovate as they choose. Bound by few regulations, they represent a purer expression of market forces than do charter, voucher, or magnet schools.

Advocates of educational markets claim that private schools are more innovative and responsive than are public schools (e.g., Chubb & Moe, 1990; Clinchy, 2000; Hepburn, 2001; Lawton, Freedman, & Robertson, 1995). They trace these traits to private schools' freedom from central controls. Relying on public funding pushes schools to conform to legal conventions rather than to provide effective service. Unions demand the hiring of certified teachers, boards force compliance with curricular guidelines, and governments leverage teaching with standardized tests. These bureaucratic shackles make public schools unresponsive to their clients, according to private school advocates, who cite choice, small size, and self-governance as magic traits for successful schools (Meier, 2000). Since private schools evade most hierarchical regulations, they are said to "bust bureaucracy" and devise ingenious forms of pedagogy. Further, markets are seen to encourage schools to adopt a different organizational character. Since private schools charge fees to survive, they must be more responsive to their clients; otherwise, those dollars will go elsewhere. Markets thus reward pedagogical success and punish failure, and thereby motivate schools to have well-defined missions, to demonstrate their effectiveness, and to satisfy customers. These hypothesized effects beg the question, however: In organizational terms, how do schools adapt to market forces? Institutional theory is applied to this question in order to better explain the relation between school organizations and their environments.

THEORETICAL FRAMEWORK: UPDATING THE NEW INSTITUTIONALISM

The *new institutionalism* developed by John Meyer and his colleagues over twenty-five years ago (Meyer, 1977; Meyer & Rowan, 1977, 1978) sets the tone for organizational analyses of modern school systems. They described two pervasive trends. First was the institutionalization of the *schooling rule*, the ever-widening use of certified teachers, standardized curricular topics, registered students, and other accreditation procedures. They noted how this school form has become increasingly legitimate in modern society, due to the use of educational credentials in labor markets and to the spread of norms of individual rights, citizenship, and economic goals. According to the institutionalists, isomorphism across different types of schools is a stark fact as well as one of the most noteworthy aspects of educational organizations. Subsequent work in this tradition has documented the diffusion of this standard school form throughout the world (Meyer & Ramirez, 2000).

Second, Meyer and associates highlighted the peculiar nature of this school form. Distinguishing between organizations operating in institutional (i.e., governmental and nonprofit) sectors versus for-profit sectors, they traced schools' legitimacy to their compliance with accepted rules and structures, not to their efficiency. The result, according to the new institutionalists, is *loose coupling*, the hallmark trait of school organization. Public schools adapt to their environments by elaborating their formal structures (categories of students, grades, courses, credentials, and certification) while leaving their technical core (actual classroom instruction and learning) relatively unmonitored. Instead of continually ensuring that they maximize instruction by inspecting teaching or measuring learning, schools expend more energy conforming to the evolving school form. This practice is justified by schools' *logic of confidence* that delegates instruction to the professional prerogatives of teachers in secluded classrooms. Instruction is guided only by broad theories that resemble vaguely specified platitudes more than detailed rules, and it is not backed by tight inspection, agreed-upon measures of performance, or consequent sanctions. The irony is that this loose coupling is actually adaptive for schools, simultaneously bringing legitimacy while avoiding exposure of problems.

Since the advent of this theory, some important trends have emerged in North American education. The major reform initiatives since 1980—standardized curricula, measurable goals, and testing—have placed schools under more centralized control in the name of quality and accountability. These initiatives serve to recouple schools' formal and technical structures by indirectly controlling classroom content and holding schools accountable for minimal outcomes (Rowan, 2002). Further, more control of public schools is accompanied by a movement for school choice. This choice movement is creating a market environment for different types of schools. School choice in varying guises—charter schools, vouchers, home schooling, magnet schools, and tax credits for private schools—is being touted as a lever to challenge the *one best way* model of organizing schools and to create grounds for innovation.

These changed conditions have at least two implications for institutional theory. Whereas that theory presumed that schools are governed by public bodies and stressed their need to comply with rationalized myths, schools of choice are freer of regulations. Relying on paying customers rather than government funds, they ought to be concerned less with conforming to legalistic categories than with pleasing clients. Moreover, the bottom-line emphasis of the private sector ought to make those schools more *tightly coupled* like technical organizations, presuming parents choose schools based on their performance. In the language of institutional theory, since private schools need not comply with a regulatory environment but are instead subject to market imperatives, they should exhibit less collective isomorphism, have thinner formal structures, and be more tightly coupled than public schools.

Context: Trends in Ontario Education

Ontario has recently witnessed both of these educational trends toward more centralized control and standardization of public schools alongside a flourishing private school sector. Since taking power in 1995, its Conservative government has introduced a series of regulations that have brought much turmoil. To boost quality, accountability, and public trust, the province has established standardized tests in several grades, forced re-accreditation for teachers every five years, reported school test scores in *league tables*, tightened budgets, and toughened curricula. These initiatives have strengthened provincial control of public schools, centralizing much power in the process. However, the government has simultaneously left private schools largely unregulated and does not require that they comply with these initiatives.

During this time, private schools have enjoyed a growing popularity. Over the past decade, the number of Ontario students in private schools has grown by 40 percent, while the number of private schools rose by 44 percent (Davies, Aurini, & Quirke, 2002). Currently, about 5 percent of Ontario school children are in private schools. Catholic schools are fully funded by the province and are not deemed to be private. Even though only a few have direct contact with private schools, most parents appear to hold them in esteem. In a 1997 survey, 46 percent of Canadian parents said that they would "prefer to send their child to a private school if they could afford it," an increase from 39 percent only four years earlier (Environics, 1997). In 1999, 61 percent of Canadians agreed that "private school students receive much better education than public school students," while in 2000, 66 percent of Ontarians agreed with the same statement (Angus Reid, 1999, 2000). Clearly, private schools do not suffer from an image problem. Perhaps capitalizing on this popularity, the provincial government recently introduced a small tax credit to assist the burgeoning number of families who desire but cannot afford private school tuition.

This situation has created a key paradox (for an elaboration of this argument, see Aurini, 2002). Ontario private schools are gaining popularity even though they can evade the very initiatives (i.e., standardized tests, curricular standards, teacher accreditation) that have been imposed on public schools in the name of public confidence. Further, the province is allowing public funds to go to private schools without any corresponding accountability measures, a move that critics have seized upon. Ontario's private schools, thus largely unregulated, have an opportunity to become an even starker alternative to public schools. As such, they offer a strategic setting for examining processes in educational markets.

Research Questions

This paper tests claims about educational markets, using new institutional theory to identify key features of school organization. The literature suggests three possible effects of markets on school organization.

The first research question is whether markets reverse pressures for isomorphism. Market advocates see parental desires for more personalized treatment and higher quality as fueling the demand for private schools, and thus they would expect new private schools to offer smaller scale instruction and to diversify their curricula into special themes, creating a series of market niches. Hence, market theorists would envision the third sector as comprised of small schools that offer personalized treatment in a diverse, multiniche market.

New institutional theory offers a very different prediction. One of its major tenets is that organizations become more similar to one another as a result of coercive, normative, and mimetic forces (DiMaggio & Powell, 1991). But are such forces strong among private schools? Institutional theory has rarely examined isomorphism in private education. Importantly, the third sector schools in Ontario face only weak coercive pressures because they are largely untouched by provincial policies. Partly because their lobbying organizations have successfully fended off attempts at interference, they are not required to hire certified teachers. Elementary private schools must simply enroll five students and pass a health and safety inspection. Private high schools meet these requirements and must also use the mandated curriculum, but otherwise they are free to operate as they wish. Given this lack of regulation, the existence of normative and mimetic pressures for isomorphism is an open question. Institutional theory predicts that new schools will face a strong normative environment set by established public and elite private schools and that they will be compelled to mimic successful organizations. Recently, Rowan (2002) has noted that deregulation and choice have led to some differentiation among religious, magnet, and charter schools, though he deems such differences to be marginal, reasoning that these schools emulate their public counterparts when facing similar consumer pressures.

The second question addressed in this research is whether private schools have weaker formal structures. Market theory suggests that since private schools are in weak regulatory environments, they will place less emphasis on external legitimacy and will dilute formal structures such as standard physical plant and formal teacher qualifications if needed. However, new institutional theory suggests that any such innovations will be limited, reasoning that the standard image of *school* has diffused so deeply through society that even private schools now conform to it to secure legitimacy. As a consequence, standard school forms shape the demand for private education, informing the criteria, reasoning, and rationale by which parents choose schools. Formal structures, in this view, generate trust in markets as well as in public bureaucracies and hence remain good for business.

The third question is whether markets encourage schools to regulate their instruction and learning. If parents seek instructional excellence, and choose schools accordingly, then it is reasonable to expect private schools to closely monitor their teaching effectiveness. According to market logic, private schools should eschew the logic of confidence that prevails in public schools and develop some systematic practice to demonstrate their effectiveness to parents. This line of thinking has produced a research tradition that has compared standardized test scores between public and private schools (e.g., Coleman, 1990; Bryk, Lee, & Holland, 1993; McEwan, 2000; Witte, 2000), with an implicit assumption that parents make choices at least partly on the basis of such scores (see also Schneider, Teske, & Marschall, 2000).

Again, new institutional theory offers a contrasting expectation. The theory holds that any close monitoring of instruction and learning only exposes problems and causes disruption, with the effect of undermining public trust (Meyer, 1977; Meyer & Ramirez, 2000; Meyer & Rowan, 1977, 1978). This is a key issue for private schools, which depend on consumer confidence for survival. Hence, a reasonable counter-prediction is that private schools will evade direct monitoring by evolving new, nonmeasurable goals, distinct mandates, and consumer-satisfaction measures, or they will borrow norms of teacher professionalism from the public sector. In other words, they will retain a loose coupling between instruction and assessment.

Data and Methods

Over the past four years, data have been collected through site visits and interviews at private schools in Toronto. A sample of schools was drawn from a government registry of private schools in the Greater Toronto area. Third sector schools are defined as neither religious, nor listed on the elite independent registry, nor run as language or reform schools. According to this definition, the city has 64 third sector schools. To witness market forces at work, it was reasoned that young schools are less established and hence subject to more market pressures. As such, the sample of schools was limited to schools that were less than fifteen years old. Among third sector schools, 49 have been established between 1988 and 2003. Of these schools, 22 have been surveyed thus far. Because this sample has not been randomly drawn, statements about predominant patterns are speculative. Nonetheless, the range and diversity of school types and practices within these schools are very suggestive. What these data may now lack in representativeness is compensated for by their richness gained from lengthy interviews and site visits.

These schools were contacted by phone, and an interview with the principal was requested. Representatives from only one school declined to be interviewed. The researchers visited 21 of the 22 schools, toured their premises, and conducted interviews with their principals that lasted between 45 to 120 minutes. Principals were asked about their school's history, practices, and goals as well as about their own perceptions of parental demands and preferences. Responses were coded regarding each school's niche, governance, physical plant, use of certified teachers, and methods of demonstrating effectiveness. This information is found in Appendices A and B (note that each school has been given a pseudonym). In addition, several other informants were interviewed, including the head of a private school organization, an educational consultant, and a representative of an independent regulatory organization.

Findings

Reversing Isomorphic Pressures

Niches. Decades ago, private education in Ontario largely consisted of religious schools and elite institutions, but today an entrepreneurial third sector of private schools is expanding the range of choice. Each year, many new private schools emerge, making the third sector a diverse assortment of organizations (see Appendix A). Through this research, three types of niches are identified.

The first type of niche is based on curricular focus. Third sector schools offer a variety of unique pedagogical themes. Schools specialize in academic intensive studies; woman-centered studies; liberal arts; social justice and environmental issues; museum-based studies; Russian-based multiple language studies; an accelerated learning concentration; and core knowledge studies, modeled after the ideas of professor and author E. D. Hirsch (1987). These varied approaches differ markedly from most local public or elite private schools. For instance, one school uses local museums to guide its problem-based learning. Another supplements the standard curriculum with several foreign languages, including French, Spanish, Russian, and Hebrew. One high school re-creates a classical liberal arts experience, requiring students to study ancient languages, art, and drama. Other schools focus on intensive academics, attracting parents in search of advantages that may boost their children's odds of attending university.

A few distinguish themselves as *alternative schools*. Several principals openly reject the "frenzied" drive for advantage and opt for a more supportive, nurturing, and compassionate educational environment. One elementary school bills itself as building self-esteem by not issuing grades or homework until the seventh grade. Its principal categorizes her clients as "people that are more on a spiritual path. Alternative, you know, that kind of group.... We're not New Age per se. But that market certainly would be attracted to us" (Wilson Academy). Similarly, one principal explains that her well-educated and artistic clients give priority to encouraging their children's creativity (Sheppard Academy). Likewise, a liberal arts principal notes that his clients are not "uptight" about university and value a classical education for itself (Christie High).

A second type of niche is distinguished not by the content of its curricula but by its special services. Some schools offer alternate hours, such as a high school that operates from 10 A.M. until 5 P.M., because, as its principal explains, "there are so many studies that say that the teenage body doesn't start functioning until 10 in the morning" (Bay High). This school also boasts 3-hour classes, reasoning that they allow students more time to focus: "Half the problem with the 75-minute class is by the time you get the class settled, do a lesson, the class is done. Kids have to shift gears, go somewhere else, whereas we'd rather just give them a 3-hour block of time, so you can get into something, and focus. And that's what a lot of these kids are lacking, too, the ability to concentrate and focus for long periods of time" (Bay High). Eight schools offer high school courses on a per-credit basis. Catering to part-time students who are preparing for university entrance, these schools extend daily classes so students can complete required instructional hours more quickly. In contrast, one elementary principal, a former day-care owner with no teaching experience, has the reputation of "making it easy for parents." Her school offers free hot lunches, snacks, and before- and after-school day care, even on holidays and school breaks. She explains that working parents are willing to spend private tuition fees for the convenience of dropping off their children at 7 A.M. and picking them up at 6:30 P.M. Such schools are examples of innovative niches that emerge through special services.

A third type of niche is generated by diverse student populations. Several schools cater to gifted students, athletes, dancers, or students with learning disabilities or special needs. One school grew out of a nearby dance studio, offering a flexible schedule that accommodates practice hours. Other schools clearly express a desire to enroll enriched and gifted children, whom one principal identified as "ignored" in public schools (Christie High). And because most established private schools will not admit students with learning or behavioral problems, several schools have emerged that specifically address attention deficit disorder or related disabilities.

Class size: The personal touch. All principals report that private schools are growing in appeal because parents are looking for personalized treatment for their children. Consistent with market theory, third sector schools provide keen customer service. Evidence for this is found in their structure: third sector schools are small. Only 7 of 22 schools enroll more than 50 students, while 8 enroll fewer than 30 students. Class sizes range from 3 to 20, with an average of 9 students. Site visits confirm that limited physical space simply cannot accommodate large classes. Most so-called classrooms are the size of offices, with a large table surrounded by chairs. Only those few schools that rent school buildings have conventional classrooms large enough for more than 10 students.

Respondents emphasize that these classes are markedly smaller than the public school norm of 25 to 30 students and thereby offer a more attentive, individualized education. Principals claim to know each student by name, to answer the phone themselves, and to meet personally with parents. One principal contrasts her availability to the bureaucracy found in public schools and cites it as a business advantage: "If I ran this school like the [public] board runs their schools, we would be out of business. I spend a lot of time with people who come into the school. I had two sets of parents in this morning, for instance. Parents could hardly get into a public school to observe and get an hour with the principal" (Private school leader). Another principal notes that parents want "the best possible service for their kids" (Spadina High).

Third sector principals link their individualized attention to parental demands and claim to be better equipped than the beleaguered public schools. Their websites and brochures proclaim that they recognize students as unique individuals.

According to one principal, parents "want their kids to be treated as individuals.... Kids today are very micro-managed. They have their whole day planned for them. And when they come to a school they expect their kid to be micro-managed as well" (Dundas Academy). Almost all interviewees, regardless of their history or circumstance, see customized attention as the backbone of their school, hailing intimate class sizes as a major selling point because, as one principal put it, students "can't just slip through the cracks . . . there's no hiding. It's pretty personal and interactive" (Christie High). Since most of these schools lack established reputations and celebrated alumni, they reassure parents by providing superior customer service. Rather than being governed with an air of bureaucracy or adhering to convention, they espouse informality, strive to be responsive to parents, and champion their small classes as the trait that distinguishes them from overcrowded public schools.

However, since third sector schools occupy a variety of market positions, they generate a variety of consumer ethics. Establishing oneself in the educational marketplace takes time. A consequence is that the age of the school shapes its willingness to readily respond to parental demands. Young schools in precarious market positions are most likely to focus on satisfying customers. Early in their life span, schools must make good on claims to be responsive. For one principal, when her school opened initially, parents could expect to meet with her anytime. But since her school has gained a reputation, she limits visits to certain days and hours, without exceptions. Similarly, the operator of a successful private school for twenty years now caters less to parents' demands: "I can say with confidence, too bad, I'm sorry, if you want to withdraw, fine, because I have a very healthy waiting list. But a younger private school will not be able to do the same thing because they're in survival mode . . . if they're operating close to the mark" (Private school leader). Another principal of a five-year-old school describes new private schools as "very vulnerable . . . because when parents pay, they feel the right to demand." She recalls: "The first two years we had to sell the school to attract parents, to give discounts, to promise this and that. Sometimes I didn't even make people pay because we needed students. But in the fourth year we had graduates, and everyone got into university, and got scholarships, not only entrance scholarships, but second-year scholarships. . . . That's what shows that it works" (Union Academy). Thus, third sector schools claim to be more accommodating to parents relative to public schools, but the degree of this responsiveness is mediated by their market position. New schools that lack standing in the community must be responsive or risk losing students. But as they gain reputations and waiting lists, principals can then rest on their laurels and ease their strong consumer-oriented push.

For-profit status, the instability of markets, and innovation. In addition to their niche character and small sizes, another organizational trait that distinguishes third sector schools is their governance structure. Fully 17 of 22 third sector schools surveyed operate as for-profit organizations. All are independently owned; none is an educational management organization (EMO). Most of their principals opt for for-profit status, pointing to the greater latitude gained from not having a board of directors. By adopting this governance form, third sector schools claim greater freedom and flexibility. A principal explains this advantage:

> If I have a class that should be kept smaller, or we have a child who needs help, we don't have to go through a lot of red tape, we're able to provide it. . . . My feeling from talking to principals from public schools around this neighborhood is that they're constantly juggling their needs . . . there's a slowness to the process. Their system is more encumbered . . . and you can't independently make these decisions. So I think cutting through the red tape is an advantage of the private sector. In the public sector they may be more encumbered by union restrictions and things like that (Wellesley Academy).

For instance, one for-profit high school principal avoids provincial regulations by simply cutting a grade from his school. In Ontario, ninth grade students are required to take a comprehensive selection of courses, including physical education, computers, and French. This principal explains: "When we had grade nines, you have to have music, art and phys. ed. in grade nine. You must. So we set up an art room and a music room. We taught phys. ed. offsite. But it honestly just wasn't worth it. I had to hire specialists" (Pape High). Lacking such resources, this principal simply excluded grade nine from his school the next year. Being unencumbered by local school boards or boards of directors, for-profit schools can sidestep such constraints rather easily.

While for-profit status offers flexibility, it makes schools wholly dependent on the fees paid by parents. A consequence is that private schools often go out of business. Amidst net growth is substantial instability. While 461 private schools were opened in Ontario between 1990 and 2000, 258 schools shut down during that same period (Ontario Ministry of Education, 2001). Local experts trace this failure to management problems. One claims that "most of the schools close because of poor management, poor promotion—all administrative types of things. It's not necessarily that there are bad things happening in the classroom" (Private school leader). Similarly, another argues that while these schools may have intriguing pedagogies, they suffer from inexperienced operators and limited client markets:

> It's nice to have a sparkling thing to offer, and there are some kids like that, but are there enough to fill a school? So you get these people with an idealistic notion, but without any experience. And finally, the bottom line for any of these schools is financial balance. You want to charge enough so that you can pay your teachers enough.... At the same time you don't want to charge so much that you put yourself out of business. The feeling I have is that the private schools are just at the edge of putting themselves out of business (Private education consultant).

Third sector principals are acutely aware of their precarious position. At least two schools, both established in the late 1990s, may soon shut their doors. Several discuss the difficulty of attracting parents in their first few years of operation. One principal recalls: "There is that hesitancy when you're new. Our first year, we only had five kids in our first year. Because parents said, 'oh, we'll wait until next year.' They want to see if you're still going to be around next year" (Dundas Academy).

A challenge that schools face is to provide an education that is sufficiently unique to draw students from the mainstream but that is not overly offbeat. One consequence of a volatile marketplace is that parental demand can be a conservative force on schools. For instance, some alternative school personnel admit that they dilute their aspirations to attract parents. Though their teachers had "totally torn down the walls" in their own minds, aiming to "revolutionize" students, they soon found they were "beating their heads against the wall," encountering reluctant parents: "[We] wanted this mandate, this alternative philosophy, to really educate, culturally and socially. But we didn't have the kids... it took a year for us to go out there and find five students who wanted to be revolutionized" (Bay High). Other schools also want to try more *de-schooling* initiatives such as banning grades or not seeking provincial accreditation, but they admit that their market would probably not bear such alternatives (Dundas Academy, York Mills Academy, Wilson Academy). Most principals doubt that parents want something that is necessarily innovative. A private school leader comments:

> I would ask, "'do they need to be truly innovative'"? The answer is, 'probably not.' ... My sense is that parents are not very interested in the innovative, offbeat thing. They are looking for a guarantee of good academics... to be sure their kids know how to read and write and do math, the basics. And they don't get a sense that this is happening for their child in the public schools (Private school leader).

Another principal notes of her school: "No. I think not, I think the only innovative thing is how to put it together, the curriculum, the pedagogy. I don't think I teach any differently than the way I taught in [a local public school]. . . . I'm very fortunate to have a solid background in terms of pedagogy. But I don't think there's anything *innovative*" (Davisville Academy).

In summary, third sector schools are in a near-perfect market situation, subject to little governmental regulation and run mostly as for-profit enterprises. These conditions produce multiple niches, a norm of small classes, a varying ethos to provide personalized treatment, and a substantial amount of instability. In some cases, market vulnerability limits the innovations that some educators wish to offer. To address issues of innovation further, how these schools deviate from standard organizational forms is explored in the following section.

Weaker Formal Structures

In this section three aspects of schools' formal structures are examined: their physical plant, their extracurricular structures, and their use of credentialed teachers.

Physical plant and use of resources. The most immediate way in which third sector schools deviate from both public and elite private schools is in their physical plant (see Appendix B). Only 6 of 22 enterprises rent standard floor space from public schools; none owns a proper school building. The others typically lease rooms in office buildings, shopping plazas, and old houses, or in former churches, fire stations, and banks. Because of their sensitivity to the cost of rent, many third sector schools are established in commercial space, and rarely in prime residential real estate.

Their unorthodox locations force most schools to either improvise their extracurricular activities or to forgo them altogether. With enrollments of less than fifty, most of these schools lack resources for playing fields, gyms, pools, or music instruction. To provide physical education, several make use of local facilities, such as nearby YMCAs, private health clubs, public parks, or tennis courts (e.g., Chester High, Dundas Academy, Davisville Academy, Lawrence Academy, Christie High, Castle Frank High). A principal of a school operating in an old house exemplifies this entrepreneurship:

> The city gave me that field over there, so I use that field. I use a lot of the neighborhood facilities. I use the Jewish Community Centre over here. There's the Tai Kwon Do centre down a little bit further, and a yoga studio. So they do little modules in each of those places. I use the Gardiner Museum for ceramics and of course the Royal Ontario Museum (Davisville Academy).

As these schools compete against public and elite schools that enjoy superior resources, do they lose some legitimacy? A private school assessor articulates this issue clearly: "Public education is cyclical, funding will go up again, and all of a sudden people will start asking, 'why am I spending all of this money for this church basement school when I have a nice public school right here with great facilities, computers, library, all qualified staff, a gym . . . why am I paying?'" (Private school assessor).

Many interviewees admit that students are initially hesitant because an office or renovated house "doesn't look like a school" (Sherbourne High). Some principals are frank about their lack of extracurricula: "There's some disadvantages to coming here, social disadvantages. Have you seen the pool? The gym? The badminton court? Have you watched our rowing club? We face that head-on, because we do not make any claims to be a school that has a total, balanced program, all the arts, phys. ed., and so on. It's an academic high school" (Pape High). Another says: "'School' is more than just delivering credits. School is a whole socialization procedure. This is for kids who have been through that and are willing to walk away from it and are old enough to say, 'I just want to get my credits'" (Spadina High). One principal notes that his students, being dependent on a nearby park for physical education classes, are out of luck if it rains or snows on a given day (Dundas Academy).

How do these schools survive despite the lack of many of the physical trappings of a traditional school? Many schools seek to regain legitimacy by channeling their resources to their specialized pedagogy. A resounding theme among principals is that strong academics compensate for humble settings. One of them notes:

> [At first] I said, who's going to want to come to a shopping plaza to put their grade 6 kid in school? Well, that class was soon full. It goes to show that if you provide a quality education, people will come, even if it's in a hole-in-the-wall like this. For most parents who are coming here, it's the academics that's A-number one for them. Extracurriculars? They take care of the extracurriculars, Brownies, Scouts, whatever. But we take care of the academics, so they don't have to worry about that. That's the A-prime number one (Dundas Academy).

Asked if parents are willing to forgo music or gym classes, a leader of a private school association argues: "Yes. They will make do. . . . Parents *are* prepared to forgo the frills" (Private school leader).

One principal believes that because many children attend preschool in similar locations, parents are increasingly used to informal settings: "So as long as their child is learning, they don't need all the accessories, or the accompanying hoopla" (Wellesley Academy). In comparing her pay-by-the-credit school to elite private schools, a principal elaborates: "We don't even pretend to do the same thing. They offer the full gamut of a school. I do one thing. I offer credits. All of those other extra things that high schools have historically offered, I can't offer. I've taken education down to the most common denominator, and that is delivering credits" (Spadina High). Another principal says of his students: "They've made a decision to come here, which means they're motivated for academics. That's basically all we offer. We don't have any sports. At the end of the day, students don't care about that stuff. They want the best possible academic education. We know there are shortcomings. There's not a scholastic community, there's not this rah-rah-rah. If they want it, they can go somewhere else" (Bay High).

Importantly, many schools draw from affluent populations that are already highly involved in extra activities, epitomizing a child-rearing culture described by Lareau (2002). As one teacher puts it: "They all have their outside lives. A lot of them do so many extra lessons, competitive stuff, that it's not a big deal. A lot of them realize that when they're here, they're not here to be social. They're here for school." (Bay High). Another principal reasons: "I guess we're a niche, not for people who want the art program, the dance, the drama, the rest of it. That's why we tell the parents for one year, keep that socializing on hold, put them in an after-school club, put them in baseball, softball, whatever your child is interested [in], swimming. They can get their socializing from there" (Osgoode Academy). By restricting their resources, markets force these schools either to improvise their extracurricula or to define them as a "frill" and trade them off for intensive academics. While there may be some loss of legitimacy, this trade-off is accepted because so many clients are engaged in private extracurricular activities and have the resources to get frills elsewhere.

Teacher credentials. Running small enterprises in competitive markets, third sector principals speak of their tight budgets relative to elite or public schools. This reality is most keenly felt in the area of staffing. Teacher salaries are a large expense for schools. As businesses, third sector schools often need to be flexible to deal with costs, such as hiring instructors on a temporary or part-time basis. However, their hiring is embedded in a larger context. Public schools and elite private schools generally hire certified teachers and pay them a fairly high rate. New graduates from teachers' colleges use public school wages as a benchmark.

In this context, most third sector schools are relaxing their hiring requirements (see Appendix B). However, the new tax credit is highlighting issues of teacher certification, with the provincial government facing criticism for placing so few regulations on private schools. Less than half (10 of 22) of the principals interviewed are themselves accredited Ontario teachers (members of the Ontario College of Teachers, or OCT), and two have no teaching background at all. Only three schools are staffed entirely with OCT teachers. Most schools mix accredited with nonaccredited instructors.

Hiring decisions are thus very pragmatic. Almost all principals want to pay teachers well but find it difficult to offer competitive wages to credentialed teachers (Pape High, Dundas Academy, Private school leader, Spadina High). As one puts it, "This is a very small place. Usually the certified teachers are asking for more money. . . . At the moment I cannot afford all of them to be certified" (Sherbourne High). One principal hires recent university graduates who have not yet found jobs: "They're lucky to get $10 an hour here. If they are qualified, maybe $15, $18. You can't compete with $30 an hour [i.e., the rate of a certified teacher]. Everybody wants to get in the public school system, but they can't" (Chester High). Another principal reports: "I feel more comfortable knowing that the teachers are qualified, but then again, the flexibility it gives when it's hard to find a qualified person . . . staffing is a big issue" (Castle Frank High).

How, then, do third sector schools attract quality instructors? Almost all principals view themselves as offering prospective teachers a trade-off: lower wages for better working conditions, in particular, smaller classes and fewer discipline challenges. As one puts it" [O]bviously we don't have a lot of the things that the public system has—the benefits, the same wages—and we work a little more. But our teachers love it. All the teachers are here, working through the summer" (Christie High). Another principal emphasizes that his staff get "tremendous exposure" from his small classes (Broadview High).

Given these trade-offs, most third sector principals staff their schools in creative ways. Many hire uncertified teachers from among the ranks of graduate students or recent M.A. graduates without jobs (Chester High, Sherbourne High). Others assemble ad hoc staff by utilizing talented yet uncertified people in their social networks, such as local musicians and actors. One principal hires an "actor slash teacher" to conduct drama classes consisting of Monty Python comedy skits for struggling eighth grade students, with music curricula including "some good Gershwin tunes" (Davisville Academy). One school brings in dancers, martial arts experts, and performance artists to offer physical education and art (Sheppard Academy).

While creative, this practice raises a key issue: If legitimacy stems from hiring formally certified teachers, how do third sector schools regain that legitimacy? The answer comes from the personalized relationships between teachers and clients.

For teaching, personal characteristics matter more than credentials. One (uncertified) principal elaborates on the loose relationship between teaching skills and credentials:

> [T]here are people who can teach, and there are people who can't teach. I think that there are a lot of great teachers who have gone to teachers' college, and there are a lot of great teachers who haven't gone to teachers' college. There are a lot of poor teachers who have gone to teachers' college, and a lot of poor teachers who haven't gone to teachers' college. I'm not sure if that process makes a significant difference in the end result. If they're not a good teacher they'll always struggle, regardless of whether they went to teachers' college or not (Christie High).

Another (certified) principal says, "I've taught next door to many teachers who were certified whom I personally wouldn't want if I had children. So I really look at the individual more than the accreditation." (Wilson Academy).

Many emphasize personal characteristics as paramount. A (certified) principal describes her relationship with parents: "They want *me*. They send their kids here so that *I* will teach them" (Davisville Academy). One principal describes an uncertified teacher: "The parents love him, the kids love him, that's what really counts. The kids let you know whether there's a good teacher in there or not" (Wilson Academy). Another teacher declares, "When parents find someone who's willing to listen to their problems and who connects with them . . . they feel that bond, that you're able to help them. That counts for more than the formal credential." (York Mills Academy). A teacher in a museum-based school reasons: "My teaching background is entirely informal. I think that despite all our attempts, pedagogy is more art than science at this point. A lot of teaching is a matter of personality. . . . People who've been through OCT, they might not have a great view of us, but I think it's a cultural difference. . . . Teaching is like a vocation" (Sheppard Academy). Another principal worries: "I'm so afraid that they're going to make a law that private schools are going to have certified teachers only. That will be a catastrophe . . . There are so many good teachers not certified . . . Personal qualities are very important, as long as they have at least a B.A., or B.Sc. . . . A lot depends on his desire, and on his passion, and on his devotion. You know, I prefer not to hire teachers from public school, because they are used to a very uncaring approach" (Union Academy).

This emphasis on personal characteristics is linked to the nature of parental demand. Far from fretting about their legitimacy, most school operators state that few parents seek information about credentials. Asked if parents care about teacher certification, a representative of a private school association sharply replies: "No. They don't. It's all in the product, okay? They [uncertified teachers] are gaining parents' respect through other means. Is a person a good teacher or not? The parents, when they go into the school, they can tell whether that teacher is doing a good job or not—they can get into the classroom" (Private school leader). According to another principal: "Never. . . . It's much more important to them how professional is the teacher than if he has some paper from OCT. Not all the parents are aware of Ontario College of Teachers" (Union Academy). Likewise, another administrator claims that parents do not care if all teachers are certified (York Mills Academy), while others say that parents are more interested in a teacher's experience than credentials (Sherbourne High). Even those who prefer certified teachers emphasize results: "What I'm really looking for is performance, because productivity is what we produce with youngsters' skill sets" (Pape High). A few operators are overtly hostile to certified teachers, faulting their training as stifling creativity, imposing a "transmissive" style of pedagogy, and encouraging students to merely regurgitate material rather think independently (York Mills Academy, Sheppard Academy, Chester High).

Several claim to be up front with parents on this issue. One principal remarks, "I don't hide the fact that one of our teachers is uncertified. And I tell them to just ask the parents. They love him. The proof is in the pudding, so to speak" (Wilson Academy). Similarly, a special education principal discusses her own lack of formal teaching credentials: "I'm up front about that with every one of my parents. It's one of the first things I tell them. It's never been an issue for anybody. I think after I've spent an hour and a half with a parent, and I can get into the issues and I'll ask them a question, and they'll say, how did you know my child was like that?" (Finch Academy).

Overall, uncertified teachers are a common feature of the third sector landscape. Most have some higher educational background, but many lack teaching credentials. Principals like the flexibility of hiring whomever they choose, regardless of credentials, and emphasize personal qualities and results over formal qualifications. They rationalize this practice by proclaiming qualifications to be irrelevant to most parents. The implication is that markets create both pressures and freedoms that weaken formal structures. Intense competition restricts budgets and creates the need for flexible hiring, making it difficult to attract fully certified teachers. Yet principals can hire whom they please, since their schools are largely unregulated. Small size and personal relationships allow consumer preferences to nullify some of the legitimacy lost from weaker formal structures.

Tighter Coupling

If the third sector is about anything, it is about variety. Recent provincial reforms that tighten curricula, impose tests, and report scores in league tables all promote standardization. Private schools are not required to participate in these initiatives, but market logic suggests that parent demand will compel them to do so. This section focuses on whether the emerging *testing culture*, which has sent a shock wave through the public system over the past eight years, has spilled over into the third sector. To the contrary, few schools are participating in this culture, and their operators emphasize customer satisfaction as their method of establishing their accountability (see Appendix B).

Weak participation is found among schools in terms of the new standardized testing initiatives. Only three schools actually write the provincial tests. The rest do not, even those who boast of lofty academic standards. Some principals favor the testing, but they are in the minority. One of the three principals notes that no parents have inquired about her school's test score standing (Glencairn Academy). Only a few principals want the government to regulate the private sector more closely, mainly because they worry that bad private schools would sully their own image. Half of the principals are critical of those reforms, indicating that the testing culture is hardly the unifying ethos of this sector. A representative of nonelite private schools flatly told the government that her schools "would have nothing to do with those tests." Like most interviewees, she opposes the tests for practical reasons: "I don't think they're good tests to begin with, I don't put a lot of value in them. I don't think province-wide testing helps improve the standards at all. In fact, it almost distracts from the standards, because teachers start teaching to the test. And they also have to spend so much time doing the darn testing" (Private school leader).

Similarly, another principal faults those tests for measuring "what we're *not* teaching, what we're *not* doing," noting that if private schools had to pay for their own testing, "a lot of us would go bankrupt. It would be financially devastating" (Wilson Academy). One school tried the tests but has since stopped: "We don't like the testing. We did [it] the first year. It was a nightmare! They're [administered] in May and they refer back to something you've done in September, October. This is ridiculous! Because of the amount of time I said, 'no,' we are not devoting an entire year to this" (Wellesley Academy). Another school principal criticizes the testing culture, depicting it as "a tail that's wagging the whole pedagogical dog" and reasoning that many parents are afraid that their children will only know content, rote work, and memorization (Sheppard Academy).

This reluctance toward standardized tests echoes concerns that have been voiced by educators for several decades. Interviewees worry that standardized tests would narrow the scope of education, that they are unfair to some types of students, and that they promote a rigid *teaching to the test*. However, what is perhaps unanticipated is that these complaints are being aired in the market-driven private sector, since commentators usually associate them with progressive pedagogues and a public sector ethos.

These views highlight a key characteristic of the niche-driven, third sector market: a tension between its emerging specialties, particularly alternative and special education, and the uniformity promoted by standardized testing. As a result, the testing culture is not yet shaping market demand in the third sector. Few principals feel compelled to participate in standardized testing because they consider that parents do not use test scores when they choose schools, nor do they care about such formalisms. Many parents, especially those with children in younger grades, reportedly have a more holistic approach. Asked if parents inquire about her school's average test scores, one principal states: "No, I think parents are really very realistic, more realistic than we give them credit for, more than society gives them credit for. . . . They're seeing it more holistically than how many kids met the provincial guidelines. They're savvy" (Davisville Academy). In fact, the testing culture may be creating a reaction. The principals of three alternative schools believe that their market is being fueled by the testing culture, which is seen as creating too much stress and pressure for many students and parents who want a more nurturing environment (e.g., York Mills Academy, Wilson Academy, Sheppard Academy). Some report that they now issue grades only reluctantly and would like to move away from letter or number grading altogether (e.g., Dundas Academy).

If most third sector schools eschew testing, how do they demonstrate their effectiveness to parents? Third sector schools have access to three methods, none of which is emphasized in the literature on educational markets and all of which embody the niche-like character of these schools. First, some organizations are leading a movement toward collective self-assessment. Some private school organizations, along with an independent, nonprofit organization, are encouraging schools to be assessed voluntarily. However, leaders of these organizations maintain that their assessments allow for flexible, multiple goals and avoid test scores or any type of league table comparison: "All we're interested in is reflective self-practice. Are they able to justify why they're not doing this or that? We're not trying to tell them what to do. We're just trying to make sure that there's a certain level of expectation for parents when they send their child, that they'll get an appropriate education, and money is not being squandered" (Private school assessor). A private school organization leader adds: "There is a desire on the part of schools to be well run. But they're very, very nervous about any kind of evaluation process that could be perceived to interfere with their philosophical position in the classroom.... And that's why we're setting up an administrative type of criteria. Those are things that are still broad enough that they are nonthreatening to schools" (Private school leader). In other words, this form of monitoring allows schools to retain a loosely coupled structure within a market niche.

While this type of assessment is being pitched to third sector schools, only older and elite schools are participating thus far (Private school assessor). None of the third sector schools visited participates in these evaluations. A few third sector schools have a second type of monitoring. Two feeder schools explicitly point to their graduates' high acceptance rates into elite high schools and universities and thus deem themselves successful (Dupont Day School, Eglinton Day School).

Mostly, however, a third method is common. All schools, particularly newer ones exposed to intense market competition, are developing a consumer-oriented form of accountability. They claim to demonstrate their effectiveness not with test scores but by offering detailed and/or open reporting to parents. These schools satisfy consumers by their open availability to parents and offer students close contact with teachers as well as immediate feedback.

Most schools champion their personalized, detailed, and sometimes informal reports to parents. Only 3 of 22 schools use the standard one-per-term Ontario report card; most use more intensive methods. One school issues report cards every half term. That principal adds, "if the parents ever need to see anybody, they can just come on in and we're right here" (Christie High). Another school issues ten report cards and parent-teacher interviews annually. As its principal explains, "Lots of communication. Is it mandatory? No. But if you're paying $11,000 or $12,000 for your kid to come here, you'll consider it pretty mandatory" (Pape High).

This principal, like several others, emphasizes that parents can directly observe her classrooms, and she sees this openness as a product of market competition:

> [Parents] know what's happening in the school, and we make sure they know. We're very much under a microscope. And we want to be under a microscope. It's a microscope of our own making. We're competing with some pretty high-powered schools. Parents look at what they're getting for their money, and they should. They're aware because we've made them aware (Pape High).

Another principal reasons: "They can always come in. I spent an hour with a parent this morning. They don't get that kind of attention from a public school principal. One of the reasons that people select independent schools is because of the attention that they and their child will get" (Private school leader). Still another principal recalls: "The first month the school was open, I spoke to every single parent, every week. They feel so close to us that they can call. They come here or they talk to us because they feel that we have some kind of relationship with their students. It's very demanding. But it's a good indication that what we're doing is working" (Bay High).

One special education principal describes her methods:

> My parent-teacher interviews are fifty minutes long. Ten-minute interviews [as in the public system] are useless. We close the school for 2 days and we run interviews Thursday after school, all day Friday, all day Monday, and Tuesday after school, and I'll probably have to extend that next year. But parents have to know. Our report cards are very comprehensive. If I showed you a template, you wouldn't believe it (Finch Academy).

One school even offers parents free one-week trials to observe their child in class before paying tuition. The principal explains:

> They'll get to meet the teacher, they watch them right in the classroom, and can stay as long as they want. I had one parent who had her son here for the one-week trial, and she stayed for the whole week. I just carried on. We want them to stay as long as they need to, to feel comfortable about their choice. Pick up a chair and enjoy yourself. So then they can see everything that goes on (Wilson Academy).

This consumerist form of accountability allows some schools to develop alternate goals and thus other criteria to gauge their success. Some cite their ability to bolster involvement and enthusiasm among students who were formerly disgruntled in public schools. One teacher of boys with behavioral problems claims success if "parents are saying, 'hey, he wants to come to school, he's happy, he's not hanging out with his druggie friends anymore, he actually finished the book last night!'" (Davisville Academy). Similarly, the principal of an alternative pedagogy school reports: "A lot of kids who come [from the public system] missed forty classes. And they had 5 percent in a course. . . . They don't skip [class] here. They never skip. Because we're so small. One way of evaluating ourselves, is this instant feedback" (Bay High).

A major conclusion, then, is that market forces do not necessarily create pressures for tighter coupling, at least in the form of the testing culture. Few third sector schools participate in Ontario's test initiatives. Instead, most develop alternate goals, which vary by niche, use qualitative assessments, or understand accountability and effectiveness in consumerist terms, using individualized interactions with parents and students. Principals claim that parents want open, personal communication, not test scores. Indeed, some third sector niches are buoyed by progressive philosophies that do not sit well with the testing culture. By emphasizing their openness to parents, these schools are weakening the logic of confidence in teachers' professionalism that prevails in public schools. Reflecting their need to attract consumers, these schools instead adopt a more consumer-friendly logic.

Conclusion: Implications for Market Theory

Are third sector schools innovative? Most are for-profit ventures in an unregulated market and depend on a customer base to survive. Market advocates presume that such pressures will spark innovative responses. Some such innovations are indeed present. The third sector is characterized by a variety of niches, individualized care via small classes, unorthodox physical plants, and some deviation from public school norms, such as hiring uncertified teachers.

In organizational terms, market competition encourages these schools to resist many isomorphic pressures via a series of trade-offs. They can weaken their formal structures by emphasizing an ethos of customer service. While some of these practices may have questionable legitimacy within the larger institutional environment, these schools compensate by appealing to alternative sources of legitimacy derived from market values and movements for parent choice. By catering to their constituencies, schools sidestep some isomorphic pressures. Niches also nullified pressures for mimetic isomorphism. Only 3 of 22 schools are fashioning themselves as feeder schools for the elite. The rest avoid competition with those schools, conceding to be not in their league. Instead of adopting tried and true elite practices, they are reducing their class sizes and are developing unique themes and services. The result is a heterogeneous collection of schools that serves needs not met by existing schools. No single school offers an educational experience to appeal to everyone but instead caters to a particular clientele.

In other ways, however, markets are a brake on innovation. Several schools want to provide more experimental pedagogy but are constrained by the demands of parents, whose trust is premised on the standard school form. Most parents have a threshold for innovation and are generally conservative. Schools can deviate only so far until parents balk and look elsewhere for something more familiar with recognized credentials. The most upscale markets for private education, the elite schools, tend to prize the most traditional of school forms. These pressures constrain educational providers who are more receptive to innovative ideas.

More important, third sector schools do little to directly monitor their own effectiveness. Only the most established elite schools are embracing the test culture and related forms of regulation. Their willingness is likely a product of their secure, semi-monopoly position, aided by long waiting lists, selective student bodies, and resourceful alumni networks. Being in weaker market positions, third sector schools instead provide accountability through their customer relations, not by measuring learning. Schools that are vulnerable to market competition are most hesitant about testing and most welcoming of consumer satisfaction norms. Loose coupling is therefore reinforced in segmented and unstable educational markets.

Markets thus encourage some forms of innovation but not others. They promote consumer-friendly innovations such as small classes and tailored curricula, which have a high market value because they are not matched by mainstream public schools that cannot select students or offer small classes. But direct competition also encourages new schools to be averse to tight coupling and to develop consumerist forms of accountability.

These findings offer several contributions to the sociology of education. The detailed studies of educational organizations complement existing research on public and private school comparisons that tend to focus only on tracking and achievement. The diversity of private education is highlighted by the third sector, a population of schools that differs from those most often researched, such as Catholic schools (which are fully funded in Ontario and are very similar to their public counterparts), and charter, magnet, and voucher-receiving schools (none of which exists in Ontario). This empirically grounded qualitative study helps further to develop institutional theory, which has been built on large-scale surveys or theoretical thought-pieces, not on site visits or in-depth interviews. Further, it responds to calls to update institutional theory in light of emerging realities over the past two decades (Rowan, 2002).

This research also has implications for market theory. It suggests that parental demand does not necessarily push schools toward the test-score maximization style of demonstrable effectiveness if the test culture does not inform parent choice. That presumption may be a product of a particular institutional context, namely, the deep diffusion of standardized test scores in American K-12 public education. But as Rowan (2002) points out, this culture has not diffused into other sectors of American education, such as preschool and postsecondary levels, which have developed other norms for evaluation. Similarly, Canadian education lacks a strongly institutionalized test-score culture; though growing, it is new and relatively weak in Ontario. Consequently, consumer demand assumes a different shape and adopts other, more informal methods of accountability. Market theory errs if it equates consumer demand with test score maximization and if it fails to recognize how markets can instead accentuate the multidimensional nature of educational goals.

Appendix A. School Characteristics, Pedagogical Theme or Niche

School	Year Est.	Governance Status	Class Size	School Size	Pedagogical Theme or Niche
Bathurst High	2000	For-profit	5	50	Caters to ethnic/immigrant community, grades 11-12; enriched, university bound; not only providing opportunity for high marks but also good academic foundation necessary for university success; allows by-the-credit
Bay High	2000	For-profit	3	15	Alternative school to prepare students for university, core academics, flex Fridays (each Friday is spent out on a field trip), schedule accommodates teenage time-clock, 10 A.M.–5 P.M., two 3-hour classes a day; allows by-the-credit
Broadview High	1997	For-profit	12–17	120	English as a second language, international high school students, meeting their specific needs to prepare for university; allows by-the-credit
Castle Frank High	1998	Non-profit	8	22	Tutorial approach, grades 11 and 12; catering to dancers, athletes; flexible timetabling; allows by-the-credit
Chester High	2002	For-profit	6–8	50	Accelerated learning; allows by-the-credit
Christie High	1997	Charitable	6–10	45	Classical, broad-based, enriched/gifted liberal arts focus, i.e., ancient languages; academics without competitive edge; students also do volunteer work
Davisville Academy	2002	For-profit	8	8	Rescue mission school for grades 7–8 students on the cusp of learning disability
Dundas Academy	1998	For-profit	12	32	Tutoring-style elementary school

Appendix A. School Characteristics, Pedagogical Theme or Niche (*cont.*)

School	Year Est.	Governance Status	Class Size	School Size	Pedagogical Theme or Niche
Dupont Day School	1995	Charitable	15–16	85	Feeder school for elite schools; located in downtown core
Eglinton Day School	1998	Non-profit	16–20	198	Feeder school for elite schools; niche is gifted, enriched; core knowledge
Finch Academy	1995	For-profit	10	30	ADHD, ADD learning disabled; "pit-stop" school—students come here for few years for support, then return to larger public or private school
Glencairn Academy	1995	For-profit	14	170	Schooling plus day care, 7 A.M.– 6 P.M.; snacks, hot lunches; accelerates children one year ahead of public system
Lawrence Academy	1999	For-profit	7	7	Well-known principal offers individual attention, grade 8 only; small class; takes students on outings, swimming, golf, tennis, etc.; helps prepare students for high school
Osgoode Academy	1996	Charitable	5	5	Intense remediation; learning-disabled intervention school for learning-disabled students with language problems
Pape High	1991	For-profit	12	55	Tutorial approach, grades 10–12, core academics, small classes, safe environment; allows by-the-credit

Appendix A. School Characteristics, Pedagogical Theme or Niche (cont.)

School	Year Est.	Governance Status	Class Size	School Size	Pedagogical Theme or Niche
Sheppard Academy	2001	For-profit	12	40	Museum-based schooling; grades 7–9; museum collections used as base for problem-based learning; want kids with interesting hobbies, i.e., filmmaking, volunteer work, etc.
Sherbourne High	2002	For-profit	8	45	Caters to ethnic/immigrant community, grades 11–12; enriched, university-bound; offers core academics, math and sciences; allows by-the-credit
Spadina High	1999	For-profit	8–10	130	Tutorial approach; core academics; grades 10+; by the credit; get credit in 44 days; some students have slight learning disabilities
Union Academy	1998	For-profit	16	300	European-style schooling, accelerated; focus on core academics, languages
Wellesley Academy	1988	For-profit	12	130	Elite school for special ed; feeder school to elite schools; early intervention to ward off academic problems; Plan B for students who cannot get into elite schools
Wilson Academy	2001	For-profit	8	16	Focus neither religious nor academic; focus on nurturing whole child, for children who learn differently than mainstream; 60 percent learning disabled
York Mills Academy	1989	For-profit	NA	7	Association for home-schooling parents

Appendix B. Physical Plant Resources, Teacher Credentials, and Schools' Demonstrated Effectiveness

School	Physical Plant	Phys. Ed. Resources	Teacher Credentials	Demonstrated Effectiveness
Bathurst High	Office space	No	Mix	Success measured by growing school enrollment; local public schools refer students, drawing high-achieving students from local public schools
Bay High	Office space	No	One-fifth OCT	Graduation rates, students gaining entry to university; accessibility, instant feedback accountability for parents, students' commitment measured by attendance rates
Broadview High	Office space	No	No	Graduation rates, students gaining entry to university
Castle Frank High	Office space	Dance studio	Mix	Graduation rates, students gaining entry to university
Chester High	Office space	No	Mix	Graduation rates, students gaining entry to university as well as to local elite private schools; also drawing students from local public schools; guarantees students will learn 400 percent faster using accelerated learning strategies
Christie High	Old house	No	One-fourth OCT	Report cards every term and half term; parents can always come in to talk; overall graduation rates
Davisville Academy	Old house	Local park	Mix	Provincial student testing as a benchmark; parents updated with weekly e-mails; parents rarely come in to complain
Dundas Academy	Office space	Local park	Yes, all OCT	High student retention rate compared to elite private schools; if concerned, parents can come in and talk to principal anytime

Appendix B. Physical Plant Resources, Teacher Credentials, and Schools' Demonstrated Effectiveness (*cont.*)

School	Physical Plant	Phys. Ed. Resources	Teacher Credentials	Demonstrated Effectiveness
Dupont Day School	Office space	Local park	No	Students gaining entry to local elite private schools; regular contact between teaching staff and parents; readily available interview times with teachers
Eglinton Day School	Rented school	Yes	Mix	Graduation rates, acceptance rates at other local elite private schools and other private schools in United States
Finch Academy	Rented school	Yes	Yes, all OCT	Statistics kept of results of student progress (i.e., skills mastered), students tested at both beginning and end of year; 50-minute parent-teacher interviews; comprehensive report cards
Glencairn Academy	Rented school	Yes	Mix	Provincial student testing and SSAT; students winning external academic awards; graduation rates, acceptance rates at local private schools
Lawrence Academy	House basement	Pool; tennis	NA	Will see students' progress through homework, progress reports periodically; report cards every 65 days; independent standardized testing at beginning and end of year; shows parents samples of students' work at end of year
Osgoode Academy	Office space	Parking lot	Yes, OCT	High turnover rate of returning students to mainstream schools
Pape High	Office space	No	Mix	10 report cards per year; 10 mandatory parent-teacher interviews; graduation rates, students gaining entry to university
Sheppard Academy	Old house	No	One-eighth OCT	Anecdotal report cards, nonstandard assessment; transparent curriculum; parental involvement encouraged

Appendix B. Physical Plant Resources, Teacher Credentials, and Schools' Demonstrated Effectiveness (*cont.*)

School	Physical Plant	Phys. Ed. Resources	Teacher Credentials	Demonstrated Effectiveness
Sherbourne High	Office space	No	No	Drawing high-achieving students from local public schools
Spadina High	Office space	No	Mix	Graduation rates, students gaining entry to university; principal very accessible to parents
Union Academy	Rented school	Yes	Mix	Students winning external academic awards; graduates' university admissions, university scholarships
Wellesley Academy	Rented school	Yes	Mix	Independent test results (not provincial tests); referrals from elite private schools
Wilson Academy	Rented school	Yes	Mix	Students are happy to go to school, not stressed with low self-esteem; anecdotal report cards; no grades assigned
York Mills Academy	NA	No	NA	Very little demonstrated effectiveness; parents are home schoolers, heavily involved; principal acts largely as consultant

Note

This project was funded by the Social Science and Humanities Research Council of Canada's "Initiative for the New Economy." The authors would like to thank Janice Aurini for her helpful ideas and assistance with data collection.

References

Angus Reid. (1999). *Canadians' attitudes regarding the public school system*. Retrieved August 31, 2003, from www.angusreid.com/search/pdf/media/pr990621%5ft1.pdf

Angus Reid. (2000). *A failing grade for Ontario's public school system*. Retrieved August 31, 2003, from www.angusreid.com/search/pdf/media/mr000303%5f1.pdf

Aurini, J. (2002). *Public versus private logics to schooling: Paradoxical trends in educational reform*. Unpublished manuscript.

Baker, D. P. (1992). The politics of American Catholic school expansion, 1870–1930. In B. Fuller & R. Rubinson (Eds.), *The political construction of education: The state, school expansion, and economic change* (pp. 189–206). New York: Praeger.

Bryk, A. S., Lee, V. E., & Holland, P. B. (1993). *Catholic schools and the common good*. Cambridge, MA: Harvard University Press.

Chubb, J. E., & Moe, T. M. (1990). *Politics, markets, and American schools*. Washington, DC: Brookings Institution.

Clinchy, E. (2000). Introduction: The educationally challenged American school district. In E. Clinchy (Ed.), *Creating new schools: How small schools are changing American education* (pp. 1–16). New York: Teachers College Press.

Coleman, J. S. (1990). *Equality and achievement in education*. Boulder, CO: Westview.

Davies, S., Aurini, J., & Quirke, L. (2002). New markets for private education in Canada. *Education Canada, 42*(3), 36–41.

DiMaggio, P. J., & Powell, W. W. (1991). The iron cage revisited: Institutional isomorphism and collective rationality in organizational fields. In W. W. Powell & P. J. DiMaggio (Eds.), *The new institutionalism in organizational analysis* (pp. 63–82). Chicago: University of Chicago Press.

Environics. (1997). *Focus Canada, 1997-2*. Toronto, Ontario, Canada: Author.

Hepburn, C. (Ed.). (2001). *Can the market save our schools?* Vancouver, British Columbia, Canada: The Fraser Institute.

Hirsch, E. D. (1987). *Cultural literacy: What every American needs to know*. Boston: Houghton Mifflin.

Lareau, A. (2002). Invisible inequality: Social class and childrearing in black families and white families. *American Sociological Review, 67*(5), 747–776.

Lawton, S. B., Freedman, J., & Robertson, H. (1995). *Busting bureaucracy to reclaim our schools*. Montreal, Quebec, Canada: Institute for Research on Public Policy.

McEwan, P. J. (2000). *Comparing the effectiveness of public and private schools: A review of evidence and interpretations* (Occasional Paper #3). New York: National Center for the Study of Privatization in Education, Columbia University.

Meier, D. (2000). Can the odds be changed? What will it take to make small schools ordinary practice? In E. Clinchy (Ed.), *Creating new schools: How small schools are changing American education* (pp. 183–190). New York: Teachers College Press.

Meyer, J. W. (1977). The effects of education as an institution. *American Journal of Sociology, 83*(1), 55–77.

Meyer, J. W., & Ramirez, F. (2000). The world institutionalization of education. In J. Schriewer (Ed.), *Discourse formation in comparative education* (pp. 111–132). Frankfurt: Peter Lang.

Meyer, J. W., & Rowan, B. (1977). Institutionalized organizations: Formal structure as myth and ceremony. *American Journal of Sociology, 83*(2), 340–363.

Meyer, J. W., & Rowan, B. (1978). The structure of educational organizations. In M. W. Meyer & Associates (Eds.), *Environments and organizations* (pp. 78-109). San Francisco: Jossey-Bass.

Ontario Ministry of Education (2001). *Private school openings and closings as of July 2001.* Ottawa, Ontario, Canada: Author.

Quirke, L. (2002). *Strategic myth creation and organizational segmentation: Institutional theory and the case of Ontario private schools.* Unpublished manuscript.

Rowan, B. (2002, September). *The new institutionalism and the study of education: Changing ideas for changing times.* Paper presented at a conference on Advancing the Institutional Research Agenda in Education, Albany, NY.

Schneider, M., Teske, P., & Marschall, M. (2000). *Choosing schools: Consumer choice and the quality of American schools.* Princeton, NJ: Princeton University Press.

Witte, J. F. (2000). *The market approach to education: An analysis of America's first voucher program.* Princeton, NJ: Princeton University Press.

3 | Public and Private School Differences

The Relationship of Adolescent Religious Involvement to Psychological Well-Being and Altruistic Behavior

Barbara Schneider, Lisa Hoogstra, Fengbin Chang, and Holly Rice Sexton

Research has shown that religion plays an important role in adolescents' lives, positively impacting their academic performance, educational aspirations, worldview, and optimism about the future (Regnerus, Smith, & Fritsch, 2003). Being religious has also been associated with adolescent psychological well-being, positive self-concept, and good physical health (Ellison, 1991; Oleckno & Blacconiere, 1991; Donahue & Benson, 1995). In addition, adolescent religiosity has been related to a reduced likelihood of engaging in risky behaviors such as smoking, drugs, and alcohol use (Hays, Stacy, Widaman, DiMatteo, & Downey, 1986; Rohrbaugh & Jessor, 1975; Woodroof, 1985). While researchers have investigated the relationship between religiosity and various outcomes, few studies have examined the mechanisms through which these relationships develop. Using data from the first and second follow-ups of the National Education Longitudinal Study of 1988–2000, this chapter examines the relationship between adolescent religiosity and positive psychological and behavioral outcomes in various school contexts (specifically, public vs. private schools), controlling for individual characteristics and family and peer influences.

Although a great deal of attention has been devoted to public and Catholic school differences in academic achievement and educational attainment, less attention has been paid to psychological and behavioral outcomes. Research conducted in the 1980s found that Catholic schools had lower dropout rates and higher college matriculation rates than public schools. Researchers attributed these differences to the emphasis placed on academic achievement in Catholic schools and to shared norms and values that emphasized hard work, responsibility to others, and the religious and moral development of students (Coleman & Hoffer, 1987; Bryk, Lee, & Holland, 1993). The supportive environment of Catholic schools might also be expected to positively affect psychological and social outcomes such as self-esteem, self-efficacy, and participation in altruistic activities. To explore this question, a more recent data set is used to examine the effects of public and private schools, as well as families and peers, on these outcomes.

Adolescents and Religiosity

Adolescence is a period of personal and religious identity formation. Between the ages of 13 and 18, teenagers begin to explicitly articulate their sense of who they are, including how they relate to their parents and their peers (Erikson, 1958; Csikszentmihalyi & Larson, 1984). Adolescence is also the time when young people are perhaps most vulnerable with respect to their sexual identity, since they are adjusting to dramatic changes in their physical development (Csikszentmihalyi & Schmidt, 1998). While these emotional and physical changes are occurring, many adolescents are trying to clarify their spiritual beliefs and determine what values are important to them and what moral principles should guide their behavior. Sometimes this can be difficult due to societal and peer pressures that challenge family and religious beliefs. Adolescents often receive conflicting messages from their families, friends, and the media about what should be valued and how one should act. Increasingly, research suggests the importance of providing young people with opportunities to develop moral judgments and ethical behaviors that will lead them to become responsible, caring, and civic-minded adults (Wilson, 2001; Damon, 2002).

Having a religious identity can help teenagers develop a more positive sense of self as they move through adolescence to adulthood. Research indicates that religious identification provides adolescents with an inner strength, sometimes referred to as resilience, that may be especially helpful for coping with personal adversity. The stresses and pressures of peer groups often place adolescents in a precarious position, where they are presented with difficult choices. Religion becomes a spiritual resource to draw upon when facing social problems, ambiguities in relationships, and personal, moral, and ethical decisions.

Belonging to a religious group, especially for adolescents who are becoming more socially and ethically conscious, can offer opportunities for moral growth and personal responsibility. Religious participation (e.g., attending religious services) is viewed as a form of social integration that reinforces values and attitudes upheld by the family and the religious community with which one affiliates, thus encouraging positive goals and behaviors (King & Elder, 1999; Regnerus & Elder, 2001). This seems particularly important since many public institutions such as schools have adopted a code of "moral relativism and ambivalence" (Damon, 2002, p. xii), where standards of honesty, fairness, compassion, and responsibility are rarely articulated or discussed.

The majority of teenagers report that they are religious to some extent (Smith, Denton, Faris, & Regnerus, 2002; Regnerus, Smith, & Fritsch, 2003). Studies that examine religiosity among adolescents indicate that for some, being religious refers to direct participation in an organized religious group, whereas for others, it refers more generally to spirituality or a belief in a particular deity. Measures of how religious adolescents feel are also somewhat imprecise. Many studies that examine religiosity use survey items with response categories that typically range from "Not at all" to "Very religious" (see, e.g., Muller & Ellison, 2001; Schmidt, 2005). When these responses are analyzed, categories are often collapsed, thus making it difficult to distinguish those who are somewhat religious from others who are more or less religious. Regardless of what being religious means to different individuals, it is generally seen as important to the lives of American adolescents.

Religiosity can refer to a variety of factors, including religious beliefs, religious participation, and religious involvement in secular activities, such as volunteering with a church-sponsored youth group in a soup kitchen (Hill & Hood, 1999). Several scholars have attempted to define religiosity in terms of different aspects of religious commitment (Ellison, Gay, & Glass, 1989) or through a more social-psychological frame of religious identity (Horowitz, 1999). Dimensions of commitment tend to include personal faith, participation in organized religious activities, and identification with a particular religious denomination. Similarly, researchers emphasizing components of religious identity refer to the subjective assessment of spirituality in one's life, religious practice, and communal affiliation. The overlap between these two conceptions suggests that in defining religious commitment or identity, it is important to consider both subjective and objective aspects of religious involvement (i.e., viewing oneself as religious as well as participating in religious activities). Merely examining participation or affiliation tends to underestimate the importance that religious identity has in an individual's life.

For most adolescents, religious identity develops within the context of the family. Religion is a family activity, and religious participation is highest among families with school-age children (Stolzenberg, Blair-Loy, & Waite, 1995). It is therefore not surprising that religious practice and family processes are often associated with each other (Wilcox, 2001). Religious practices within the family can help parents guide their behaviors with each other and their children. In a recent study of adolescent religiosity, Schmidt (2005) finds that, compared to those who consider themselves nonreligious, adolescents who report higher levels of religiosity perceive their families as being more involved in their lives and as having higher expectations for them. It may be that being a good parent involves not only providing an environment that is supportive, nurturing, and goal directed, but one that is also influenced by beliefs deeply rooted within a particular religious tradition. Religious affiliation may strengthen a young person's sense of self by conferring a sense of belonging and group identity that is more stable than the fluidity of teenage peer groups (Schneider & Stevenson, 1999; Steinberg, Brown, & Dornbusch, 1997). Based on previous research we would expect adolescent religiosity to be associated with positive parenting practices, and for both to be associated with adolescent well-being and altruistic behavior.

Religiosity, Psychological Well-Being, and Altruistic Participation

The links between religiosity, in the form of religious participation, and school-related outcomes, such as academic achievement, have tended to be modest (Muller & Ellison, 2001; Regnerus, Smith, & Fritsch, 2003). It may be that religious involvement is linked to other positive outcomes such as psychological well-being and participation in altruistic activities. Churches routinely sponsor projects such as food and clothing drives for the poor and visits to the elderly and encourage their members to take part. Schools also offer opportunities for such participation through school-sponsored service clubs. Increasingly, critics are urging public schools to promote adolescent development through programs and activities that are designed to enhance cooperation, responsibility, and caring for others (see, e.g., Wilson, 2001; Damon, 2002; Schneider & Stevenson, 1999). Community service, student government, and other forms of extracurricular participation are thought to foster adolescent identity formation. Beyond what is taught in the classroom, extracurricular activities are often seen as the appropriate place to teach students about fairness, responsibility to others, and ethnic and religious tolerance. Much like religious involvement, participation in extracurricular activities has been shown to shape how adolescents define themselves (Guest & Schneider, 2003). Research indicates that students who are involved in extracurricular activities are more likely to have a positive self-image (Eccles & Barber, 1999). It is therefore not surprising that participation in these activities is being promoted in all types of schools.

The psychological benefits of such activities appear to derive in part from the positive peer relationships that adolescents develop through their participation. As Schneider and Stevenson (1999) have noted, activity-based groups, including service clubs and church-sponsored youth programs, help adolescents to develop relationships around common values and interests. In contrast to the fluidity that characterizes most adolescent relationships, activity-based groups generally provide a more stable context for identity development; although the membership of such groups changes, it does so less frequently than social groups. One might expect that adolescents who view themselves as religious would be more likely to participate in such groups, particularly in service clubs, and to form peer relationships that reinforce religious beliefs and values.

The question of causality is inconclusive, however, for some adolescents may take part in activities for reasons that are unrelated to their religious beliefs, such as portfolio-building for college. Others may do so because they are genuinely interested in helping others, such as altruistic endeavors that stem from parents' concerns and values and that may be dependent on or independent of family religious affiliation, practice, or spirituality. To understand the relationship between religiosity and adolescent development, it is important to examine school and community factors, independent of religion, that may be affecting adolescents' values and relationships to others.

Public/Private School Differences: A Focus on Psychological Outcomes

Since the 1980s there has been a great deal of interest in differences in student outcomes between Catholic and public schools (Coleman & Hoffer, 1987; Bryk et al., 1993; Neal, 1997; Grogger & Neal, 2000). Findings from several studies have consistently shown that among disadvantaged students—minorities, those from lower economic strata, and those from less supportive family environments—academic achievement and high school graduation rates are higher in Catholic than in public high schools. This "Catholic school advantage" has been attributed to a more rigorous academic curriculum and to shared norms and values that emphasize hard work, academic achievement, and responsibility to others. Bryk et al. (1993) found that Catholic high schools exhibited higher levels of communal organization, as defined by shared values and activities, and more caring relationships among faculty and students. This communal organization was in turn associated with greater teacher commitment and student engagement.

This research suggests that there also may be a Catholic school advantage with respect to psychological and behavioral outcomes. Students who attend Catholic high schools may especially benefit from the overlap in the values and norms of the school and religious community, particularly if they are religious themselves, and they may be more likely to develop a positive self-image. Catholic high school students are also more likely than students in public schools to participate in community service, which has a long tradition in these high schools (Bryk et al., 1993).

Recent research, however, indicates that Catholic high schools have changed substantially since the 1980s, when much of the research on Catholic school effects was conducted, raising questions about whether these high schools offer the same advantages to students that they once did. As Baker and Riordan (1998) have noted in examining trends in Catholic school attendance over the past few decades, the composition of Catholic schools is changing. Whereas less than 2 percent of students in Catholic secondary schools were non-Catholic in 1972, today between 20 and 30 percent of students are non-Catholic. In addition, these students are more likely than those in the past to be nonwhite, to come from wealthier families, and to pay higher tuitions. These changes appear to be affecting the priorities of Catholic schools, with more emphasis being given to academic excellence. In light of these changes, students at Catholic schools may more closely resemble students at nonreligious private schools than they once did.

Some Assumptions

Previous research suggests that religiosity positively contributes to adolescent identity formation. Research on public/Catholic school differences in turn suggests that attending a private religious school may strengthen the relationship between adolescent religiosity and positive psychological and behavioral outcomes by reinforcing religious norms and values. To investigate the strength of these influences on adolescent psychological and behavioral outcomes, we examine differences in self-esteem, self-efficacy, and altruistic participation in public versus private schools, particularly private religious schools. While it is assumed that adolescent religiosity will be positively associated with these outcomes, regardless of the type of school attended, students who go to private religious schools are expected to have higher ratings on measures of self-esteem, self-efficacy, and altruistic participation than those who go to public schools. However, the psychological benefits of attending private religious schools may be greater for students who have higher levels of religious involvement. For these students, the norms and values emphasized by the school are likely to reinforce the norms and values found at home and within the larger religious community, which may positively influence students' self-esteem and self-efficacy. This is less likely to be the case for students who have low levels of religious involvement. In other words, adolescent religious involvement may interact with religious (vs. public) school attendance in influencing adolescent psychological well-being.

Much like religious practice, involvement in extracurricular activities such as service clubs and community volunteer groups requires self-discipline and adherence to particular rules. During adolescence, when young people are seeking new identities and understandings of themselves and their worlds, these activities, much like the consistent actions of their parents, help to set benchmarks of acceptable behavior and social responsibility; such activities can also help adolescents to form relationships with peers who share similar interests and values. Participation may increase adolescents' self-esteem and sense of self-efficacy. This is likely to be the case in both public and private schools.

Families who are religious in orientation are more likely to place a high value on community service and to encourage their children to participate. Such families are also more likely to send their children to private religious schools. Levels of religious involvement and extracurricular participation, especially in activities that are altruistic in nature, are thus expected to be higher for students in private religious schools than for those in public high schools. However, private schools, regardless of whether they are religious or secular, view extracurricular participation as an important component of a student's high school portfolio. Consequently, these schools are likely to expect their students to engage in extracurricular activities that have a community-service orientation. Thus, student participation in community service is expected to be higher in private schools, whether religious or not, than it is in public schools.

Although parents with strong moral and ethical principles may also be religious, this is not necessarily the case for all families. Parents may set high standards of conduct for their children and practice good parenting regardless of their religious involvement. However, for those who are religious, the influence of religiosity on adolescent well-being and altruistic behavior may be transmitted through good parenting practices (having high expectations combined with guidance of and support for the child's academic and social development). Previous research has shown that positive parenting practices are related to adolescent psychological well-being and positive behavioral outcomes. It is assumed that these same relationships will be evident in this population, regardless of the type of school attended. Overall, it is expected that there will be independent effects for adolescent religiosity, family and peer influences, and school sector on adolescent psychological well-being and altruistic participation.

DATA AND METHOD

Analyses for this chapter are based on data from students and their parents who took part in the National Education Longitudinal Study of 1988–2000 (NELS), a nationally representative sample of eighth graders who were first surveyed in 1988, with follow-ups in 1990, 1992, 1994, and 2000. The NELS sample includes 24,599 students in its base year. Data from the base year, first, and second follow-ups are used in analyses, supplemented with information drawn from the base-year parent survey. Descriptive analyses are based on the sample of students who participated in NELS in 1988, 1990, and 1992 and for whom data were available on self-esteem, self-efficacy, and altruistic participation, measured at both tenth and twelfth grade, and religious involvement, measured at tenth grade (N's range from 13,184 to 14,529 for these measures). Subsequent multivariate analyses are based on a subsample of these students for whom complete data were available on all variables included in analyses (N's for these analyses range from 8,670 to 8,725). Analyses were conducted to determine if there were selection effects for the subsample. Results from a Heckman procedure (Heckman, 1976, 1979) revealed that selection effects were negligible (results available from the authors).

Parent measures are based on items from the base-year parent survey (completed when students were eighth graders); parents did not complete surveys during the first follow-up (when students were tenth graders). Student measures are based on items taken from the first and second follow-up student surveys (completed when students were in tenth and twelfth grade). As tenth graders, students who participated in the first follow-up were asked to complete a survey in which they provided information about their background, relationships with parents and peers, schoolwork, attitudes, psychological well-being, and religious involvement. Students were resurveyed two years later, when most were high school seniors.

Adolescent Outcomes: Psychological Well-Being and Altruistic Participation

The first dependent variable, psychological well-being, consists of two constructs—self-esteem and self-efficacy. Self-esteem is based on seven items that were taken from Rosenberg's (1979) self-esteem scale: "I feel good about myself"; "I feel I am a person of worth, the equal of other people"; "I am able to do things as well as most other people"; "On the whole, I am satisfied with myself"; "I feel useless at times" (reverse coded); "At times, I think I am no good at all" (reverse coded); and "I feel I do not have much to be proud of" (reverse coded). Response options for each item range from 1 to 4 ("Strongly disagree" to "Strongly agree"). Responses were summed to form a composite variable (Cronbach's *alpha* = .82).

Self-efficacy, the second measure of psychological well-being, is based on six items that comprise a locus of control scale: "I don't have enough control over the direction my life is taking" (reverse coded); "In my life, good luck is more important than hard work for success" (reverse coded); "Every time I try to get ahead, something or somebody stops me" (reverse coded); "My plans hardly ever work out, so planning only makes me unhappy" (reverse coded); "When I make plans, I am almost certain I can make them work"; and "Chance and luck are very important for what happens in my life" (reverse coded). Responses again range from 1 to 4, indicating level of agreement with the statement, and were summed to create a composite variable (Cronbach's *alpha* = .74). High scores on this measure indicate that the student has a greater sense of self-efficacy (a sense of being in control of events in one's life, and the ability to set goals and meet them).

The second dependent variable, altruistic participation, assesses the extent of a student's involvement in school- or community-sponsored service activities and is based on the following items: "In the first half of the school year, did you receive any community service awards?" (1 = Yes; 0 = No); Service club participation during the current school year (0 = School does not offer or Did not participate; 1 = Participated; 2 = Participated as an officer); Frequency of volunteering or performing community service outside of school (Responses range from 1 to 4, with 1 indicating "Rarely or never" and 4 indicating "Everyday or almost everyday"). Because response options vary across items, responses to each item were standardized to a mean of zero and a standard deviation of one. The three standardized scores were then summed to create a composite measure. Responses to these items were not expected to be highly correlated since the items assess involvement in different contexts (school and community) and few students received community service awards. The composite measure serves as a general indicator of community service involvement.

All dependent measures are based on items that were included in the NELS Second Follow-up Student Survey when students were in twelfth grade. Prior measures of the three dependent variables are included in regression analyses. Because self-esteem, self-efficacy, and altruistic participation are correlated with each other over time, all three lagged variables are entered in regression models. For example, in the regression model estimating twelfth grade self-esteem, tenth grade measures of self-efficacy and altruistic participation are included as independent variables in the model along with the lagged variable for self-esteem. Thus, in regression analyses, what is being modeled is the effect of the other independent variables on the change in these measures between tenth and twelfth grade. The lagged measures are the same as the dependent measures described above and are based on similar items that were included in the First Follow-up Student Survey (Cronbach's *alpha* for the tenth grade self-esteem and self-efficacy measures is .81 and .71, respectively).

Student, Family, and Peer Influences on Adolescent Well-Being

Because religious involvement encompasses objective and subjective dimensions, a composite measure of religious involvement that includes both dimensions was constructed, following Muller and Ellison (2001). This measure of religious involvement was based on tenth graders' responses to the following items from the First Follow-up Student Survey: (1) frequency of attending religious services; (2) frequency of participating in religious activities; and (3) perception of oneself as religious ("Do you think of yourself as a religious person?"). Responses for the first item range from 1 ("Not at all") to 6 ("More than once a week"); those for the second item range from 1 ("Rarely or never") to 4 ("Every day or almost every day"); and those for the third item range from 1 ("Not at all") to 3 ("Very"). Standardized scores were created for each item with a mean of zero and a standard deviation of one. The three standardized scores were then summed to create a composite measure of religious involvement (Cronbach's *alpha* = .78).

Two measures of family involvement are used in analyses: parent social support, and family challenge. Although parent involvement measures have been shown to be modestly related to academic achievement, it is assumed that for psychological well-being and social behaviors such participation may enhance adolescent self-esteem, self-efficacy, and altruism. The parent social support measure is designed to examine the extent to which parents are actively involved in their teenager's school. If a parent is present and visible at school, an adolescent may feel more secure and attached to the school and its activities. The five survey items on which this measure is based assess the extent to which parents are involved in parent-teacher networks: whether they belong to a parent-teacher organization (PTO), attend meetings of the PTO, take part in activities of the PTO, belong to any other parent organization, or act as a volunteer at the school (1 = Yes and 0 = No for each item; summed responses range from 0 to 5).

The family challenge measure is designed to assess parents' involvement in providing academic guidance to their adolescents. In previous studies, family challenge was measured using items developed by Rathunde (see Rathunde, 1996; Csikszentmihalyi, Rathunde, & Whalen, 1993; Csikszentmihalyi & Schneider, 2000) to assess the extent to which parents stimulate and guide their children. These specific items were not included in NELS; however, the NELS parent survey does include items that assess the extent to which parents provide some form of educational guidance to their adolescents. Three of these items were used to construct the family challenge measure: the frequency with which parents had discussions with their eighth graders about experiences at school, plans for high school, and plans after high school. Response categories for these three items range from 1 ("Not at all") to 4 ("Regularly"). Responses were summed to form a composite measure (Cronbach's *alpha* = .73).

Several student and family background variables are used as controls in analyses. These include the student's gender, race and ethnicity, whether the student lives with both parents (biological or adoptive), number of siblings, and family socioeconomic status (as measured by parents' highest level of education). Race and ethnicity categories include White, African American, Hispanic, and Asian. Additionally, parents' educational expectations for their adolescent is included as a control variable. This measure is based on an item in the tenth-grade student survey, which asks how far in school students think that their father and mother want them to go. Specific response options were collapsed to create four categories: high school or less, some college, a four-year degree, and a graduate or professional degree. The highest level of education reported for either the mother or the father was used in creating this variable.

Two measures are used to assess peer values relevant to students' religious involvement and participation in altruistic activities: the importance to the student's friends of taking part in religious activities, and doing community work or volunteering. Responses to each of these items range from 1 ("Not at all important") to 3 ("Very important").

School Influences on Adolescent Well-Being and Altruistic Behaviors

The schools attended by tenth grade students were coded to reflect both school sector (public/private) and religious affiliation. Because of the small number of schools in the NELS sample with a religious affiliation other than Catholic, identifying information about these schools, including their denomination, is not available in the data set for reasons of confidentiality. Non-Catholic religious schools were therefore coded only as "private, other religious." The other coding categories for schools were Catholic, nonreligious private, and public. Dummy variable coding was used, with public schools serving as the reference category in multivariate analyses. (See Appendix A for a summary of variables included in analyses and their means and standard deviations; see Appendix B for the correlation matrix for key variables used in analyses.)

Results

Descriptive Analyses

To determine whether adolescent religious involvement and the three outcome measures varied significantly by type of school attended, a one-way analysis of variance (ANOVA) was conducted. As shown in Table 3.1, there are significant differences by school sector for these measures. Students at nonreligious private schools report higher self-esteem and higher self-efficacy at twelfth grade than students in all other types of schools. In contrast, students in public schools have lower ratings on these measures at twelfth grade than private school students. The self-esteem ratings of students in Catholic and "other religious" schools fall in the middle. Self-esteem and self-efficacy ratings appear to change only slightly over the two-year period; self-efficacy ratings increase significantly for students in private nonreligious schools.

As expected, students who attended private schools, whether religious or nonreligious, rated themselves significantly higher on measures of altruistic participation and religious involvement compared to students at public schools. Among students at nonreligious private schools, levels of altruistic participation increased substantially between tenth and twelfth grade, which suggests that students may be motivated by "portfolio building" for college (at tenth grade, participation at these schools does not differ significantly from that at public schools). Although Catholic students' involvement in community service also increases between tenth and twelfth grade, this increase is not as dramatic, suggesting that Catholic students may take part for reasons other than portfolio building.

While religious participation is higher among students at private versus public schools, students who attend "other religious" schools have significantly higher ratings on this measure than students at either Catholic or nonreligious private schools. To better understand the reasons for this difference, the religious affiliation of students at "other religious" schools was examined, using information available in student surveys (analysis not shown). In general, the results of this analysis suggest that most of the students in "other religious" schools in the NELS

Table 3.1. Analysis of Variance for Psychological Well-Being, Altruistic Behavior, and Religious Involvement (NELS: 1988–2000)[a]

Variables	(1) Public Mean	(SD)	(2) Catholic Mean	(SD)	(3) Private, Other Religious Mean	(SD)	(4) Private, Nonreligious Mean	(SD)	Total Mean	(SD)
Self-esteem (Grade 12)	21.96	3.43	22.34	3.52	21.97	3.73	23.19	3.60	22.01	3.45
N	11081		833		371		764		13049	
Self-esteem (Grade 10)	21.31	3.37	22.02	3.48	21.26	3.86	22.54	3.61	21.38	3.40
N	12426		850		393		844		14513	
Self-efficacy (Grade 12)	18.02	2.88	18.28	2.62	19.12	2.90	19.16	2.90	18.09	2.87
N	11147		839		371		770		13127	
Self-efficacy (Grade 10)	17.75	2.80	18.38	2.78	18.95	2.93	18.46	2.50	17.83	2.80
N	12440		844		397		848		14529	
Altruistic participation (Grade 12)	-.13	1.99	.48	2.32	.20	1.99	.43	2.27	-.07	2.03
N	11242		817		362		763		13184	
Altruistic participation (Grade 10)	-.05	1.97	.30	2.21	.30	2.00	.10	1.98	-.02	1.99
N	11513		808		370		821		13512	
Religious involvement (Grade 10)	-.02	2.5	.58	2.03	2.47	2.25	.75	2.96	.08	2.51
N	12308		856		397		832		14393	

[a] Data are weighted to produce results generalizable to the population of U.S. high school students. The panel weight applies to sample members who were participants in 1988, 1990, and 1992.

Source: National Education Longitudinal Study of 1988–2000, National Center for Education Statistics, U.S. Department of Education.

sample attend conservative Protestant, "other Christian," or Jewish schools. These schools typically emphasize religious development (McLaughlin, 1997) and may have less diverse student populations than Catholic schools, which accept young people from other religious backgrounds. Among the Catholic schools in the sample, 26 percent of students indicated that they were non-Catholic.

In summary, the ANOVA results indicate that there are significant school-sector differences in adolescent psychological and behavioral outcomes. To further examine the effects of school sector on these outcomes, a series of multivariate regression and hierarchical linear models were estimated.

Student, Family, Peer, and School Influences on Adolescent Well-Being

Results of the multivariate regression analyses, presented in Table 3.2, indicate that adolescent religious involvement has significant independent effects on all three outcomes, suggesting that religion matters with respect to adolescent identity formation. There are also significant school effects, even when controlling for student, family, and peer influences. Attending a private, nonreligious school (vs. a public school) is positively and significantly associated with self-esteem and self-efficacy at twelfth grade, whereas attending a Catholic (vs. public) school is positively and significantly associated with altruistic participation.

Turning to the specific models, the inclusion of prior measures of psychological well-being in the self-esteem model reduces the effect of adolescent religious involvement, suggesting that religious involvement is correlated with these prior measures and has indirect effects on self-esteem at twelfth grade. With the exception of gender and race/ethnicity, student family-background characteristics have little influence on self-esteem. Adolescent girls have significantly lower self-esteem compared to adolescent males; Hispanic and African American adolescents have significantly higher self-esteem than whites, findings that are consistent with previous research.

In contrast to the student variables, the parent and family variables have consistently significant and positive associations with self-esteem. Students whose parents have higher levels of education and higher educational expectations for their children rate themselves significantly higher on self-esteem than those whose parents are less educated and have lower expectations. Parent social support is also positively and significantly associated with self-esteem, even after controlling for prior psychological well-being.

Table 3.2. Religious Involvement and Its Relationship to Self-Esteem, Self-Efficacy, and Altruistic Participation[a]

Independent Variables	Self-Esteem (Grade 12)		Self-Efficacy (Grade 12)		Altruistic Participation (Grade 12)	
	Model 1	Model 2	Model 1	Model 2	Model 1	Model 2
Student Measures						
Religious Involvement	.059***	.007	.130***	.069***	.109***	.079***
Female	-.840***	-.350***	.454***	.556***	.208***	.119**
Asian	-.308+	-.238	-.341*	-.280*	.042	.033
Hispanic	.625***	.427***	.193+	.150	.122	.111
Black	1.243***	.492***	-.245*	-.445***	.022	-.100
Prior Well-Being (Grade 10)						
Self-esteem	___	.503***	___	.140***	___	.012
Self-efficacy	___	.091***	___	.330***	___	.015
Altruistic participation	___	-.003	___	.028*	___	.329***
Family and Peer Measures						
Parent social support	.093***	.047*	.050*	.019	.045**	.025+
Family challenge	.081**	.024	.080***	.032+	.027+	.016
Nontraditional family	.018	.050	-.210**	-.175**	.067	.116*
Number of siblings	-.048	-.035	-.033	-.025	.013	.016
Parent educational attainment	.089*	.068*	.041	.007	.290***	.249***
Parent educational expectations (Grade 10)	.361***	.144***	.281***	.099**	.288***	.200***
Peer relationship						
Religious activity is important	-.126+	-.069	-.044	.001	-.127**	-.045
Volunteer work is important	.051	-.031	-.171**	-.240***	.614***	.278***
School Sector Measures (vs. public)						
Catholic	-.308*	-.303*	-.174	-.160	.329***	.264**
Private, other religious	-.974*	-.531	.147	.268	-.613*	-.510*
Private, nonreligious	1.067***	.609**	1.089***	.862***	.192	.189
Interaction Terms						
Religious involvement * Catholic	.270***	.209***	.101+	.033	.068+	.058
Religious involvement * Private, other religious	.430***	.210*	.274**	.131	.058	.028
Religious involvement * Private, nonreligious	.296**	.233**	.054	.060	.000	.028
Constant	20.297***	9.004***	16.602***	8.743***	-2.696***	-2.338***
Observations	8670	8670	8724	8724	8725	8725
Adjusted R-squared	.05	.32	.05	.24	.10	.19

+p < .10; *p < .05; **p < .01; ***p < .001 (two-tailed tests)
[a] Data are weighted to produce results generalizable to the population of U.S. high school students. The panel weight applies to sample members who were participants in 1988, 1990, and 1992.
Source: National Education Longitudinal Study of 1988–2000, National Center for Education Statistics, U.S. Department of Education.

The school sector effects are particularly noteworthy. Attending a Catholic school (vs. a public school) has a significant negative effect on self-esteem. This effect should be interpreted with caution, however. The self-esteem ratings of Catholic (vs. public) school students vary by level of religious involvement, as shown by the interaction coefficient for these variables. For students who attend Catholic (vs. public) schools, a one-unit increase in religious involvement results in a one-fifth-unit increase in self-esteem in the full model. Similar interaction effects are found for students who attend private nonreligious and "other religious" schools (vs. public schools), with religious students rating themselves significantly higher on self-esteem. These findings suggest that students who are religious are more likely to benefit psychologically from religious school attendance.

Looking at the self-efficacy model, adolescent religious involvement has a significant positive effect on this outcome, even when controlling for other variables in the model. There are also significant positive associations between self-efficacy at twelfth grade and prior psychological well-being, including altruistic participation. The effect for prior participation in community service suggests its importance for adolescent well-being. An inspection of standardized coefficients (not shown) for this model confirms that student characteristics have a relatively greater influence on self-efficacy than they do on self-esteem. In contrast, parent and family variables tend to have little influence on this outcome. Parent educational expectations is a significant positive predictor of self-efficacy, as it was for self-esteem, but apart from nontraditional family structure, which has a significant negative relationship to twelfth grade self-efficacy, the other parent and family measures are not significantly related to this outcome in the full model.

Notably, peer values have a significant negative association with self-efficacy. Students who say that their friends view participation in community service as important rate themselves significantly lower on measures of self-efficacy than those whose friends place less importance on such activities, net of other variables in the model. This suggests that students whose friends value involvement in service activities may feel pressured to conform to peer expectations; such expectations may extend to participation in other types of social activities such as hanging out with friends and going to parties.

In the altruistic participation model, the effects for religious involvement and school sector are noteworthy. The standardized coefficients for this model (not shown) indicate that religious involvement is one of the strongest predictors of altruistic participation, confirming the emphasis placed on such participation by many religious denominations. There is also a significant positive effect for Catholic (vs. public) school students, even when controlling for the effect of adolescent religious involvement, which may be attributable to the long tradition of community service in Catholic schools. The significant negative effect for "other religious" (vs. public) schools should be interpreted with caution. Supplementary analyses indicate that this variable is highly correlated with other variables in the model. As shown in ANOVA results, students at "other religious" schools have particularly high levels of religious involvement, and the inclusion of this variable may suppress the effects of religious school attendance. In addition, supplementary analyses suggest that schools within this category are affiliated with several different denominations and may vary in the emphasis that they place on community service.

These results show that there are significant school-sector effects on these three outcomes. As expected, religious involvement and altruistic participation are higher among students in private schools (whether religious or nonreligious) than they are in public schools. However, when other variables are controlled for, only Catholic (vs. public) school students have significantly higher levels of community service participation at twelfth grade. Students at Catholic and other religious schools who had high levels of religious involvement also had significantly higher self-esteem ratings than public school students. A similar interaction effect was found for students in private nonreligious (vs. public) schools, with religious students rating themselves significantly higher on self-esteem than students in public schools. Compared with public school students, teenagers in nonreligious private schools also had significantly higher self-efficacy ratings.

Regardless of the type of school attended, adolescent religious involvement was positively associated with all three outcomes, with direct effects on self-efficacy and altruistic participation and indirect effects on self-esteem. Prior participation in community service activities was found to be positively associated with self-efficacy, independent of adolescent religious involvement, type of school attended, or family and peer influences, suggesting the importance of such activities for adolescent well-being. There is also indirect evidence indicating that community service provides a context for forming stable peer relationships. Students who indicated that their friends valued participation in community service had higher levels of participation in these activities two years later.

Although parent social support and family challenge were positively associated with these three outcomes, the effect of these measures was reduced when prior measures of psychological well-being and altruistic participation were included in the models, suggesting that positive parenting practices influence these outcomes earlier in adolescence but have less direct influence by the end of high school. As might be expected, given the importance placed on educational attainment by most parents and teachers, parents' educational expectations for their children remains a significant predictor of self-esteem, self-efficacy, and altruistic participation, even when controlling for prior measures of psychological well-being.

Distinguishing School Effects from Student, Family, and Peer Influences

From the analyses presented above it is unclear what the contribution of school sector is to the explanation of variance in the three outcome measures. To investigate this question, a two-level hierarchical linear model (HLM) was developed. Model development followed standard protocol by beginning first with the simplest model (unconditional) followed by the addition of predictors at both level 1 and level 2. For each of the three outcomes, the initial unconditional model indicated that there was sufficient variance to justify a two-level model. Hierarchical Linear Modeling (Raudenbush, Bryk, & Congdon, 2000) was used in constructing these models.

In the HLM models, student, family, and peer variables are entered at level 1, and the school sector variables are entered at level 2. Because we were primarily interested in assessing the average differences by school sector, level 2 variables include school sector, and these variables only affect the intercept. In all models, both individual-level and school-level variables are centered on the sample mean (grand-mean centered).

Results of the three HLM models, presented in Table 3.3, make it clear that school sector contributes substantially to the explanation of variance in these models. Looking at the variance components for the self-esteem model, we see that 14 percent (1.60/(9.50+1.60)) of the total variance in the unconditional model for this outcome is between schools. In the conditional model school variance is 1.02, reduced from 1.60 in the unconditional model. The school sector variables explain 36 percent ((1.60−1.02)/1.60) of the variance between schools. In the self-efficacy model, the contribution of the school-level variables is less substantial. In the unconditional model, 13 percent (.90/(6.19+.90)) of the total variance in self-efficacy ratings is at the school level, and the school sector variables account for 16 percent ((.90−.76)/.90) of the between-school variance. The model for altruistic participation is the most interesting since between-school variance accounts for a larger proportion of the total variance: 22 percent (.94/(3.41+.94)) of the total variance in the unconditional model, compared to 13-14 percent in the other models. The school sector variables account for one-third ((.94−.63)/.94) of this variance.

Overall, the HLM results confirm the results of the regression models. Adolescent religious involvement remains a significant predictor of self-esteem, self-

Table 3.3. Two-Level HLM Analysis for Self-Esteem, Self-Efficacy, and Altruistic Participation[a]

Independent Variables	Self-Esteem (Grade 12)	Self-Efficacy (Grade 12)	Altruistic Participation (Grade 12)
Individual-Level			
Intercept	22.109***	18.349***	.107**
Student Measures			
Religious involvement	.039*	.084***	.090***
Female	-.421***	.507***	.168**
Asian	-.362	-.332*	.097
Hispanic	.243	.018	.055
Black	.363*	-.581***	-.049
Prior Well-Being (Grade 10)			
Self-esteem	.490***	.133***	.014
Self-efficacy	.100***	.352***	.014
Altruistic participation	.001	.013	.313***
Family and Peer Measures			
Parent social support	.027	.013	.038
Family challenge	.018	.027	.017
Nontraditional family	.046	-.170*	.076
Number of siblings	-.013	-.008	.002
Parent educational attainment	.083*	.026	.189***
Parent educational expectations	.135*	.126**	.182***
Peer relationship			
Religious activity is important	-.054	.016	-.049
Volunteer work is important	.014	-.136*	.258***
School-Level			
School Sector Measures (vs. public)			
Catholic	-.160	-.130	.304*
Private, other religious	.041	.649*	-.336
Private, nonreligious	.574**	.736***	.150
Variance Components			
Unconditional:			
Within Schools	9.50	6.19	3.41
Between Schools	1.60	.90	.94
Conditional:			
Within Schools	6.62	4.62	2.87
Between Schools	1.02	.76	.63
Percent of variance explained:			
Within Schools	30%	25%	16%
Between Schools	36%	16%	33%

*$p < .05$; **$p < .01$; ***$p < .001$ (two-tailed tests)

[a] Data are weighted to produce results generalizable to the population of U.S. high school students. The panel weight applies to sample members who were participants in 1988, 1990, and 1992. Sample size: Self-esteem (level-1=8670; level-2=1212); Self-efficacy (level-1=8724; level-2=1208); Altruistic participation (level-1=8725; level-2=1208). Both student-level and school-level variables centered.

Source: National Education Longitudinal Study of 1988-2000, National Center for Education Statistics, U.S. Department of Education.

efficacy, and altruistic participation in the three models. In essence, the HLM results show that psychological characteristics and altruistic behavior are influenced by school sector, especially in the case of altruistic participation. Catholic schools, regardless of student background characteristics and family and peer influences, have an independent effect on altruistic participation. For Catholic (vs. public) school students, the significant relationship between the importance that peers place on community service at tenth grade and students' altruistic participation at twelfth grade in turn points to a common school effect (Bryk et al., 1993).

Discussion

A major finding of this study is that religion matters to adolescent psychological and social development. Students who have higher levels of religious involvement tend to have higher self-esteem, a greater sense of self-efficacy, and higher levels of participation in community service activities, regardless of the type of school attended. Students who view themselves as religious may particularly benefit from religious school attendance, an effect that may be due to the overlap in norms and values between the school and the larger religious community. For these students, religious schools may provide a consistent framework of beliefs, values, and practices that serve as a positive context for identity development. Results indicate that students who have low levels of religious involvement are less likely to benefit psychologically when they attend religious schools.

It seems that one of the benefits for students who attend private nonreligious schools is that they feel better about themselves than public school students. This effect is somewhat magnified in private schools that have more resources (private nonreligious schools); such schools appear to do a better job of helping students to feel successful and to realize their educational goals. This is particularly important for adolescent development, since adolescents are psychologically vulnerable and are confronted with the tasks of defining themselves, their goals, and their values. These private schools appear to promote in their adolescents a feeling of confidence and a sense of accomplishment.

In contrast to private nonreligious schools, Catholic schools seem to be more successful in involving their students in community services. Compared to students in all other types of schools, those in Catholic schools have significantly higher levels of altruistic participation at twelfth grade, an effect that is independent of students' levels of religious involvement or family and peer influences. One explanation for this finding may be the long tradition of community service in Catholic schools (Bryk et al., 1993). Catholic schools may view this participation as a way to reinforce communal values, instill a sense of social responsibility, and initiate cooperative and caring relationships among community members.

Many Catholic high schools have community service requirements. To account for this, prior participation in community service was controlled for in the models presented in this chapter. If students are required to engage in such activities at the beginning of high school, then controlling for tenth grade participation takes into account such requirements. One explanation for increased levels of community service involvement from tenth to twelfth grade in Catholic (vs. public) schools may be that greater emphasis is placed on service participation as students progress through high school. Even if participation is required, students may be expected to devote more time to such activities as they get older. They may take on additional responsibilities or leadership roles within service groups and develop commitments to other participants and to members of the community. Students may in turn become invested in such activities, find them rewarding, and see them as making a positive contribution to the community. It seems that Catholic students would be more likely to develop such investments compared to students in public and private nonreligious schools, given the value placed on such community service in Catholic schools and within the Catholic community more generally.

Compared with public schools, Catholic and nonreligious private schools appear to more effectively promote positive adolescent psychological and social development. Private nonreligious schools seem to excel in instilling adolescents with a sense of confidence in themselves. On the other hand, Catholic schools appear to be more likely to involve students in community service. More generally, the findings of this study point to the importance of looking at psychological and behavioral outcomes, as well as at academic outcomes, when examining public/private school differences. In designs for models for reforming public schools, private schools may offer insights for enhancing not only academic achievement but also adolescent psychological and social development.

Appendix A. Description of Variables[a]

Variables	Description	Mean	S.D.
I. Dependent Variables			
Self-esteem (Grade 10, Grade 12)	Sum of seven items (1-4) of self-esteem at 10th (12th) grade: I feel good about myself; I feel I am a person of worth, the equal of other people; I am able to do things as well as most other people; On the whole, I am satisfied with myself; I feel useless at times (reverse coded); At times, I think I am no good at all (reverse coded); I feel I do not have much to be proud of (reverse coded).		
	Grade 10	21.38	3.40
	Grade 12	22.00	3.45
Self-efficacy (Grade 10, Grade 12)	Sum of six items (1-4) comprising locus of control scale at 10th (12th) grade: I don't have enough control over the direction my life is taking (reverse coded); Good luck is more important than hard work for success (reverse coded); Every time I try to get ahead, something or somebody stops me (reverse coded); My plans hardly ever work out, so planning only makes me unhappy (reverse coded); When I make plans, I am almost certain I can make them work; Chance and luck are very important for what happens in my life (reverse coded).		
	Grade 10	17.83	2.80
	Grade 12	18.09	2.88
Altruistic participation (Grade 10, Grade 12)	Sum of standardized score for three items for altruistic behavior at 10th (12th) grade: Whether adolescent received a community service award; Frequency of participation in service club; Frequency of time spent on volunteering or performing community service.		
	Grade 10	-.02	1.99
	Grade 12	-.07	2.03
II. Independent Variables			
Student and Family Characteristics			
Religious involvement (Grade 10)	Sum of the standardized score for tenth-graders' reports of (a) frequency of attendance at religious services, (b) participation in religious activities, and (c) religiosity ("Do you think of yourself as a religious person?")	.08	2.52
Female	Student is female.	.50	.50
Race/Ethnicity			
Asian	Student is Asian or Pacific Islander.	.04	.19
Black	Student is Black.	.13	.34
Hispanic	Student is Hispanic, non-white.	.11	.31
	White student (the omitted category). (Native Americans are excluded from analyses due to their small numbers in the sample.)	.73	.45

Appendix A. Description of Variables[a] *(cont.)*

Variables	Description	Mean	S.D.
Family composition (Grade 8)	1 = Nontraditional family; 0 = Mother-father family (including adoptive parents).	.35	.48
Number of siblings (Grade 8)	Parent report of number of siblings 8th grader has in the home. Range 0 to 6.	1.48	1.27
Parent educational attainment (Grade 8)	Highest level of parental education attained: 1 = HS or less; 2 = Some postsecondary; 3 = B.A.; 4 = Graduate or professional degree.	2.09	.99
Parent educational expectations (Grade 10)	Student reports of parents' educational expectations for their adolescents: How far in school does student think parents would like him/her to get? Coding same as parental education.	2.91	.81
Parent social support (Grade 8)	Sum of five parent-reported items for participating in school activities: Belong to a parent-teacher organization; Attend meeting of parent-teacher organization; Take part in the activities of a parent-teacher organization; Act as a volunteer at the school; Belong to any other organization with other parents. For each item, 1 = Yes, 0 = No. Range 0 to 5.	1.39	1.53
Family challenge (Grade 8)	Sum of three parent-reported items for frequency of discussion with 8th grader about: Experiences in school; Plans for high school; Plans for after high school. For each item, 1 = Not at all, 2 = Rarely, 3 = Occasionally, and 4 = Regularly. Range 3 to 12.	10.31	1.64
Peer relationship (Grade 10)	Among your close friends, how important is it to them that they: Participate in religious activities (Range 1 to 3); Do community work or volunteering (Range 1 to 3).	1.63 1.44	.67 .58
School Sector (Grade 10)			
Public school	Public school. 1 = Yes, 0 = Others (the omitted category).	.90	.30
Catholic school	Catholic school. 1 = Yes, 0 = Others.	.06	.23
Private, other religious	Private school with other religious affiliation. 1 = Yes, 0 = Others.	.02	.14
Private, nonreligious	Private nonreligious school. 1 = Yes, 0 = Others.	.02	.14

[a] Data are weighted to produce results generalizable to the population of U.S. high school students (N=16,253). Number of cases used to calculate means and standard deviations varies because of item-specific missing data.

Source: National Education Longitudinal Study of 1988–2000, National Center for Education Statistics, U.S. Department of Education.

Appendix B. Bivariate Correlations for Key Variables Used in Analyses[a]

	(1) Self-esteem (G10)	(2) Self-esteem (G12)	(3) Self-efficacy (G10)	(4) Self-efficacy (G12)	(5) Altruistic participation (Grade 10)	(6) Altruistic participation (Grade 12)	(7) Religious involvement	(8) Parent educational attainment	(9) Parent educational expectations	(10) Parent social support	(11) Family challenge	(12) Peers' religious activity importance	(13) Peers' volunteering importance
(1) Self-esteem (G10)	1.00												
(2) Self-esteem (G12)	.55	1.00											
(3) Self-efficacy (G10)	.59	.37	1.00										
(4) Self-efficacy (G12)	.35	.58	.46	1.00									
(5) Altruistic participation (G10)	.06	.04	.06	.07	1.00								
(6) Altruistic participation (G12)	.06	.05	.09	.08	.38	1.00							
(7) Religious involvement	.10	.08	.18	.15	.17	.18	1.00						
(8) Parent educational attainment	.06	.07	.13	.09	.10	.18	.15	1.00					
(9) Parent educational expectations	.11	.10	.15	.13	.15	.17	.12	.31	1.00				
(10) Parent social support	.09	.08	.12	.10	.11	.13	.23	.29	.15	1.00			
(11) Family challenge	.09	.08	.10	.07	.09	.08	.07	.14	.13	.22	1.00		
(12) Peers' religious activity importance	.05	.04	.06	.06	.15	.12	.48	.02	.05	.10	.04	1.00	
(13) Peers' volunteering importance	.03	.02	.01[N/S]	-.01[N/S]	.27	.17	.21	-.04	.03	.04	.03	.52	1.00

Note: Unless otherwise noted (N/S) all correlations are significant at the .05 level (two-tailed tests).
[a] Data are weighted to produce results generalizable to the population of U.S. high school students. The panel weight applies to sample members who were participants in 1988, 1990, and 1992.
Source: National Education Longitudinal Study of 1988–2000, National Center for Education Statistics, U.S. Department of Education.

NOTE

This paper was written with support from the Alfred P. Sloan Center on Parents, Children, and Work at the University of Chicago. The opinions are those of the authors and should not be attributed to the Alfred P. Sloan Foundation.

REFERENCES

Baker, D. P., & Riordan, C. (1998). The "eliting" of the common American Catholic school and the national educational crisis. *Phi Delta Kappan, 80,* 16–24.
Bryk, A. S., Lee, V. E., & Holland, P. B. (1993). *Catholic schools and the common good.* Cambridge, MA: Harvard University Press.
Coleman, J. S., & Hoffer, T. (1987). *Public and private high schools: The impact of communities.* New York: Basic Books.
Csikszentmihalyi, M., & Larson, R. (1984). *Being adolescent: Conflict and growth in the teenage years.* New York: Basic Books.
Csikszentmihalyi, M., & Schmidt, J. (1998). Stress and resilience in adolescence: An evolutionary perspective. *Yearbook (National Society for the Study of Education), 97,* 1–17.
Csikszentmihalyi, M., & Schneider, B. S. (2000). *Becoming adult: How teenagers prepare for the world of work.* New York: Basic Books.
Csikszentmihalyi, M., Rathunde, K., & Whalen, S. (1993). *Talented teenagers: The roots of success and failure.* New York: Cambridge University Press.
Damon, W. (2002). *Bringing in a new era in character education.* Stanford, CA: Hoover Institution Press.
Donahue, M. J., & Benson, P. L. (1995). Religion and the well-being of adolescents. *Journal of Social Issues, 51*(2), 145–160.
Eccles, J. S., & Barber, B. L. (1999). Student council, volunteering, basketball, or marching band: What kind of extracurricular involvement really matters? *Journal of Adolescent Research, 14*(1), 10–43.
Ellison, C. G. (1991). Religious involvement and subjective well-being. *Journal of Health and Social Behavior, 32*(1), 80–99.
Ellison, C. G., Gay, D.A., & Glass, T. A. (1989). Does religious commitment contribute to individual life satisfaction? *Social Forces, 68*(1), 100–123.
Erikson, E. H. (1958). *Young man Luther: A study in psychoanalysis and history.* New York: Norton.
Grogger, J., & Neal, D. (2000). Further evidence on the effects of Catholic secondary schooling. Pp. 151–191 in *Brookings-Wharton papers on urban affairs: 2000,* W. G. Gale and J. R. Pack (Eds). Washington, DC: Brookings Institution Press.
Guest, A., & Schneider, B. (2003). Adolescents' extracurricular participation in context: The mediating effects of schools, communities, and identity. *Sociology of Education, 76,* 89–109.

Hays, R. D., Stacy, A. W., Widaman, K. F., DiMatteo, M. R., & Downey, R. (1986). Multistage path models of adolescent alcohol and drug use: A reanalysis. *Journal of Drug Issues, 16*(3), 357–369.

Heckman, J. (1976). The common structure of statistical models of truncation, sample selection, and limited dependent variables and a simple estimator for such models. *Annals of Economic and Social Measurement, 5*, 475–492.

Heckman, J. (1979). Sample selection bias as a specification error. *Econometrica, 47*, 153–161.

Hill, P. C., & Hood, R. W. (1999). *Measures of religiosity*. Birmingham, AL: Religious Education Press.

Horowitz, I. L. (1999). The cultural context of the privacy v. publicity debates. *St. Croix Review, 32*, 52.

King, V., & Elder, G. H. (1999). Are religious grandparents more involved grandparents? *Journals of Gerontology Series B–Psychological Sciences and Social Sciences, 54*, S317–S328.

McLaughlin, D. (1997). *Private schools in the United States: A statistical profile, 1993–94* (NCES 97-459). U.S. Department of Education, NCES. Washington, DC: U.S. Government Printing Office.

Muller, C., & Ellison, C. G. (2001). Religious involvement, social capital, and adolescents' academic progress: Evidence from the National Longitudinal Study of 1988. *Sociological Focus, 34*, 155–183.

National Center for Education Statistics (NCES). (2002). *CD-ROM: NELS:88/2000 public use data files and electronic codebook—base year through fourth follow-up*. Washington, DC: U.S. Department of Education.

Neal, D. (1997). The effects of Catholic secondary schooling on educational achievement. *Journal of Labor Economics, 15*, 98–123.

Oleckno, W. A., & Blacconiere, M. J. (1991). Relationship of religiosity to wellness and other health-related behaviors and outcomes. *Psychological Reports, 68*(3, Pt. 1), 819–826.

Rathunde, K. (1996). Family context and talented adolescents' optimal experience in school-related activities. *Journal of Research on Adolescence, 6*, 605–628.

Raudenbush, S., Bryk, T., & Congdon, R. (2000). *HLM 5: Hierarchical linear and nonlinear modeling* [Computer software]. Lincolnwood, IL: Scientific Software International, Inc.

Regnerus, M. D., & Elder, G. H. (2001, August). Staying on track in school: Religious influences in high- and low-risk settings. Paper presented at the annual meeting of the American Sociological Association, Anaheim, CA.

Regnerus, M. D., Smith, C., & Fritsch, M. (2003). Religion in the lives of American adolescents: A review of the literature. A research report of the National Study of Youth and Religion, number 3. Chapel Hill: University of North Carolina Press.

Rohrbaugh, J., & Jessor, R. (1975). Religiosity in youth: A personal and social control against deviant behaviour? *Journal of Personality, 43*, 136–155.

Rosenberg, M. (1979). *Conceiving the self*. New York: Basic Books.

Schmidt, J. (2005). Religiosity, emotional well-being, and family processes in working families. Pp. 303–324 in B. Schneider & L. Waite (Eds.), *Being Together, Working Apart: Dual-Career Families and the Work-Life Balance*. Cambridge, Eng.: Cambridge University Press.

Schneider, B., & Stevenson, D. (1999). *The ambitious generation: America's teenagers, motivated but directionless.* New Haven, CT: Yale University Press.

Smith, C., Denton, M. L., Faris, R., & Regnerus, M. (2002). Mapping American adolescent religious participation. *Journal for the Scientific Study of Religion, 41*(4), 597–612.

Steinberg, L. D., Brown, B. B., & Dornbusch, S. M. (1997). *Beyond the classroom: Why school reform has failed and what parents need to do.* New York: Simon & Schuster.

Stolzenberg, R. M., Blair-Loy, M., & Waite, L. J. (1995). Religious participation in early adulthood: Age and family life cycle effects on church membership. *American Sociological Review, 60*(1), 84–103.

Wilcox, W. B. (2001). *Soft patriarchs and new men: Religion, ideology, and male familial involvement.* Unpublished doctoral dissertation, Princeton University. Dissertation Abstracts International, A 62/06, 2250.

Wilson, J. (2001). Shame, guilt, and moral education. *Journal of Moral Education, 30*(1), 71–81.

Woodroof, J. T. (1985). Premarital sexual behavior and religious adolescents. *Journal for the Scientific Study of Religion, 24*(4), 343–366.

4 | Religious Participation as Cultural Capital Development

Sector Differences in Chicago's Jewish Schools

Adam Gamoran and Matthew Boxer

The chapters in this volume, like most research in the sociology of schooling, focus mainly on cognitive outcomes. Following the accepted wisdom, the authors duly emphasize the contributions of families and schools to cognitive development. Yet schooling also has cultural outcomes: the practices, attitudes, and beliefs that play important roles in the transition from youth to adulthood and that provide access to particular cultural groups. Dominated by the seminal writings of Pierre Bourdieu, the literature on cultural reproduction also recognizes the dual contributions of families and schools. This chapter examines the emergence of adolescent religious identity as a form of cultural capital development, drawing on a pilot study of Jewish schools in the Chicago area. Three sectors of Jewish schools are included: Orthodox day schools, the most religiously observant and intensive group; a non-Orthodox day school, sponsored by the Conservative movement, which advocates an intermediate level of observance; and non-Orthodox supplementary schools, which are attended on weekends and/or weekday afternoons and are sponsored by the Conservative, Reform, and Reconstructionist movements, with the latter two as the most religiously liberal of the Jewish denominations. The analysis considers the roles of both family affiliation and practices, and school type and curriculum, as potential influences on young persons' Jewish cultural capital, as represented by their commitment and capacity to engage with the traditions and practices of the Jewish people.

The focus on cognitive outcomes of education to the exclusion of other outcomes has been heightened by the current emphasis on high standards for students' academic performance, but cultural outcomes also deserve attention. Although generally overlooked in today's debates about standards as a means to improve the quality of schooling, cultural outcomes also contribute to the development and future opportunities of young persons. In the case of religious identification and activities, research on adolescents is sparse, but a recent review concluded that greater religious participation among teenagers is positively associated with a variety of indicators of health and well-being (Bridges & Moore, 2002). The question of whether and how schools and families reproduce cultural outcomes, including religious practices and attitudes, is thus of broad interest.

Past survey research on education and cultural transmission has been limited by two shortcomings: cross-sectional data, and inadequate measures of cultural capital (Nagel & Ganzeboom, 2003). This study is also cross-sectional, so the findings must be considered speculative rather than conclusive. However, the study uses new, richer measures of Jewish affiliation, practices, and commitment than are commonly found either in research on Jewish identity or in studies of cultural capital more generally. The contributions of the study thus lie in framing the problem of Jewish identity development as a matter of cultural capital transmission and in providing evidence on the associations among family, school, and young persons' religious expressions.

Jewish Religious Identification as Cultural Capital Development

Research on American Jewish identity has always reflected a concern with cultural transmission, though not explicitly so. Through the centuries, Jewish distinctiveness was preserved through an *us-them* mentality, a sense that Jews were different and isolated from other social groups. This worldview has deep roots in Jewish tradition (for example, a daily prayer praises God for setting *us* apart from other nations) and was thoroughly reinforced by government restrictions on the rights and activities of Jews. By contrast, the pluralism and relative tolerance of American society have eliminated most of these external pressures for group identification. In this context, what mechanisms will preserve the Jews as a distinctive cultural and religious group?

Conceptions of Jewish Identity

As early as the 1950s the American Jewish Committee (a cross-denominational Jewish advocacy organization) commissioned a number of studies of the social and religious character of American Jewry. The most important of these early studies was led by Marshall Sklare (Sklare & Greenblum, 1967), focusing on a Midwestern suburb referred to as "Lakeville." While the Lakeville study addressed a number of potential measures of Jewish identity, the key areas of focus related to ritual practices. Most of the research emphasized ritual practices, education, organizations, and synagogue life. Home life was seen through the lens of observance of *mitzvot* (Jewish commandments). In this research tradition, Jewish identity was viewed largely as a matter of belonging to a synagogue, affiliating with a particular denomination, and engaging in ritual practices.

As the Jewish population became more dispersed throughout America, some writers argued that measures of association with Jewish organizations, including but not limited to synagogues, were more important indicators of Jewish identification than ritual observance (Elazar, 1976). Although rituals, denominational preference, and synagogue membership continued to serve as key indicators of Jewish identity, membership in community groups and informal Jewish networks were also noted (Cohen, 1988; Goldscheider, 1986; Kobrin & Goldscheider, 1978). One can also observe a shift in thinking about Jewish identity by comparing the National Jewish Population Surveys of 1970, 1980, and 1990, which moved from a focus on religious and synagogue-based items to wider areas of Jewish activity and affiliation (Kosmin et al., 1991; Massarik & Chenkin, 1973).

According to Horowitz (2002), this shift occurred for two reasons. First, under the traditional view that religious ritual observance is the key marker of Jewish identity, when a person acts in a way that he or she perceives as Jewishly motivated (e.g., volunteering in a soup kitchen), but the action does not fit standardized notions of Jewish action (such as performing a ritual), conventional surveys miss an important element of Jewish identity. Second, Jews have not fit the classical model of assimilation in that they retained group cohesion even as they attained higher levels of economic status, became further removed from the immigrant generation, and became less religiously observant. Clearly, something other than religious ritual observance was the cause (Horowitz, 2000, 2002). Horowitz (2000) also pointed out that Jewish identity is not static, but may change over the life course in connection with life-cycle events or other critical moments (see also Schoenfeld, 1998).

These considerations led Horowitz (2000) to postulate a broader conception of Jewish identity, in which ritual practice is only one dimension and not necessarily the most important one for a given individual. She characterizes the dimensions of Jewish identity as:

- Religious activities (e.g., ritual practices)
- Cultural affiliation (e.g., displaying religious symbols, membership in religious organizations)
- Subjective attitudes (e.g., centrality of religious identity)

The present study adapts Horowitz's scales by distinguishing affiliations and practices of the *family* from affiliations and practices of the *young person* him- or herself. Subjective attitudes are measured only for the young person. The aim of the present analysis is to examine the associations between family and adolescents' affiliations and practices as well as to explore the role of Jewish schools in contributing to Jewish affiliation, observance, and commitment among adolescents. These attitudes and activities are regarded as markers of cultural capital.

Conceptions of Cultural Capital

In his classic work, *Distinction: A Social Critique of the Judgment of Taste*, Bourdieu (1984) studied members of French society, examining their preferences for and familiarity with various types of music, art, and cinema. He found that an individual's taste is conditioned strongly by his or her social status, in that members of higher social strata are more likely to prefer and be familiar with the music, art, and cinema associated with high culture and less likely to prefer and be familiar with more popular productions; similarly, the reverse is found for members of lower social classes. Because social elites set societal standards for what constitutes high culture and what is relegated to the realm of popular culture, it would be expected that the preferences of the social elites would be established as cultural ideals of high culture.

Bourdieu argued that members of different social classes are taught to appreciate culture differently through their varied structural locations, such as families, schools, acquaintances, and public institutions. In short, members of different social classes acquire preferences that closely resemble the preferences of those people and social structures with which they associate in their formative years. Thus, members of higher social classes tend to develop preferences and familiarity with high culture, whereas members of lower social classes will tend to develop preferences and familiarity with more popular culture (Bourdieu, 1977a). Bourdieu (1977b) further argued that the effect is cumulative, with greater impact for individuals for whom exposure to cultural experiences occurs early and frequently in their formative years. Moreover, the greater resources of the higher social classes ensure greater access to cultural events and items, and therefore greater opportunities for exposure to high culture, which tend to reinforce the developed preference of social elites for high culture and enable them to differentiate themselves from members of lower social classes (Bourdieu, 1984; Kraaykamp, 2003; Weber, 1978).

The end result of differential socialization is that social elites tend to pursue and attain higher levels of various cultural markers. As such, socialization produces a form of capital, measured in terms of an individual's ability to engage in the culture of his or her society. Bourdieu called this *cultural capital*, and he defined it as the general cultural knowledge, skills, and background pertaining to the culture of a social elite. Appreciation of and ability to participate in high society, therefore, are developed by accumulating cultural capital through exposure to various cultural events and items. The more an individual immerses him- or herself in society, the more he or she can develop cultural capital.

Bourdieu's *Distinction* (1984) focused on the greater cultural capital of social elites compared with nonelites in France, but other scholars have applied the concept to other populations as well; indeed, any culture or subset of a culture could be said to have its own cultural capital. Just as Bourdieu defined cultural capital in French society in terms of taste in music, art, and cinema, other societies may have different measures. It is in this respect that Jewish practices, affiliation, and commitments are considered as a form of cultural capital for the community of Jews.

Cultural Capital and Education

Much of the literature on cultural capital focuses on the contributions of family cultural capital to young people's educational attainment (e.g., de Graaf, 1986; DiMaggio, 1982; DiMaggio & Mohr, 1985), but our interest is in the reverse: How do families and schools produce cultural capital? A few studies have addressed this question. Bourdieu and Darbel (1990) focused on the relation between arts education and a facility with high culture in the arts. They found that family differences were much more important than school differences in cultivating a taste for the arts, but they speculated that in the field of literature, school instruction may play a larger role in developing cultural capital. A key difference between arts and literature instruction was that arts was a marginal subject, whereas literature was taught systematically and with the same principles of classification that were reflected in prominent cultural distinctions. Building on these ideas, Nagel and Ganzeboom (2003) developed three hypotheses about the relations between families, schools, and cultural capital. First, following Bourdieu and Darbel, they argued that school differences are more powerful than family differences. Second, they suggested that family influences would remain stable throughout childhood, but school influences would become stronger as the young person moved toward adulthood. Third, they hypothesized that school influences on cultural capital would be stronger among young persons who had a stronger foundation of cultural capital based in the family. That is, family and school effects would compound one another in generating cultural capital.

This study of Jewish cultural capital also proposes three hypotheses, which are modified from those proposed by Nagel and Ganzeboom (2003) to fit the case of Jewish schools in the United States:

- Hypothesis 1: Families and schools are independent sources of cultural transmission, as reflected in adolescent Jewish identity. Families are the site of most ritual activities, but schools are the site at which formal knowledge is generated.
- Hypothesis 2: Family effects are stronger than school effects. Despite the role of schools in generating formal knowledge, the family remains the earliest and most powerful source of cultural transmission. This is especially likely in the case of Jewish cultural capital because most of a young Jew's religious activities occur in the context of family and community.
- Hypothesis 3: Schooling effects depend on family effects, but not in the manner depicted by Bourdieu and Darbel (1990) and Nagel and Ganzeboom (2003). Whereas they saw family and school effects as mutually *reinforcing*, it seems likely that Jewish school experiences may compensate for the lack of family religious practices and affiliations among the least Jewishly active families. Thus, this study hypothesizes that school effects will be more powerful when family conditions are least conducive to cultural capital development.

To explain the basis for these hypotheses, details are provided about the varieties of Jewish family life and Jewish schooling in the United States.

Family life, school knowledge, and cultural capital. What sorts of school knowledge may foster cultural capital (religious activities, affiliation, and commitment) among American Jewish youth? An individual with knowledge of a social group's ideas, traditions, texts, and practices is able to participate as a member and identify with the group for which these cultural tools have value. Considered in this way, Jewish learning is a clear example of cultural capital development. Knowledge of religious texts, for example, is a precondition for understanding Jewish theology. Knowledge of Hebrew, the traditional Jewish language, allows one to read Judaism's religious texts and begin to understand them. In turn, understanding of the texts renders them meaningful to the reader. Understanding the texts and associating them with Jewish history and heritage may promote identification with Judaism as a whole. Furthermore, Jewish education has historically been group centered. Holtz (1984) argued that the social context in which Jewish study has traditionally occurred encourages identification with the Jewish community by establishing peer groups: "Most traditional Jewish 'reading' occurs in a social context—the class, or the study session. . . . Reading thus becomes less an act of self-reflection than a way of communal identification and communication. One studies to become part of the Jewish people itself" (p. 18).

At the same time, family and communal life provides the contexts in which Jewish practices take place. The home is the site of many important rituals, including those related to the observance of the Sabbath, which is celebrated every week with family meals. The Sabbath and other holidays are also observed by synagogue attendance. Judaism is a communal religion: A quorum of ten adults (adult males, for the Orthodox) is required to recite certain prayers, and many rituals require the involvement of several people. When a child is born, for example, he or she is traditionally named before a gathering of friends and family. A marriage ceremony requires an officiant and two witnesses to sign the marriage contract. Each of these events is typically accompanied by a celebratory feast. Even when one dies, Jewish law dictates that the body must be accompanied at all times until burial. The person accompanying the body traditionally recites psalms to honor the memory of the deceased. Virtually all rituals associated with life-cycle events are based on family and communal participation.

Jewish rites are usually performed in Hebrew. Thus, one who has knowledge of Hebrew is better equipped to participate. Furthermore, with the development of Zionism as a political ideology, the founding of the State of Israel, and the establishment of Hebrew as one of its official languages, Jews can express their desire for a return to their ancestral homeland and support for Israel through reading and speaking Hebrew. The Hebrew language is typically learned through formal instruction in a Jewish school, along with much of Jewish lore and tradition, so schooling and family life are intertwined as they transmit the cultural capital of Judaism. However, a young person whose family engages in minimal Jewish practice may still have an opportunity to participate in rituals and engage in Jewish communal activities if he or she is enrolled in a Jewish school.

The formal curriculum of Jewish schools.   Traditionally, Jewish study has meant the study of Judaism's sacred texts. These begin with the *Torah*, or the five books of Moses, and the remainder of the Hebrew Bible, which consists of two additional sections called *Nevi'im* (Prophets) and *Ketuvim* (Writings). The Bible is referred to as the Written Law, as contrasted with the Oral Law, a set of rabbinic commentaries on the Bible including the *Mishna* and *Gemara*, which together constitute the *Talmud*. The Talmud began as an oral tradition—hence the name, "Oral Law"—and was codified over a period of several hundred years. It was followed by centuries of further commentaries and exegeses of the Written and Oral Law, a process that continues to this day. Today, these texts are central to instruction in Orthodox Jewish schools and in Jewish day schools, both Orthodox and non-Orthodox (Gamoran, 2001). They appear less prominently in the curriculum of non-Orthodox supplementary schools (those that meet only for a few hours on the weekend or afternoons), whose students tend to be less religiously active.

The Hebrew language is another curricular topic that may be uniquely related to cultural capital. As the traditional language of the Jewish people, Hebrew study may stimulate a special sense of cultural affiliation and belonging as well as provide a critical tool necessary for the full expression of most ritual practices. Whereas Hebrew is universally featured in the curricula of Orthodox and non-Orthodox day schools, exposure varies among supplementary schools. Beyond the sacred texts and language, Jewish schools offer instruction in a variety of Jewish topics including history, literature, philosophy, ethics, and so on.

Although this schooling may contribute to Jewish identity, the causal process may also run in the opposite direction. A person who is more involved in Jewish ritual, who affiliates culturally, and for whom Jewishness is central, may be more likely to seek out educational opportunities that address these topics. In addition, a young person from a committed Jewish family may be sent to a school with a rich Jewish curriculum and may have a strong Jewish identity, without a causal connection between schooling and identity. Our study will not sort out these causal ambiguities. Rather, it will take a first step by exploring whether an association exists between family, school, and individual aspects of Jewish identity as a form of cultural capital.

Data and Methods

To address questions about the relation between Jewish education and cultural capital among young people in Jewish schools, this study draws on data collected from nine schools in the Chicago area in 1999–2000. Response rates ranged from 64 to 83 percent of students in grades 7 through 12 in the nine schools. Six of these are supplementary schools, meeting on weekend mornings and/or weekday afternoons for between two and five hours per week. The supplementary schools included Reform, Reconstructionist, and Conservative denominations. From these schools, 321 students responded to the survey. The remaining three are day schools. Of these, one is a non-Orthodox school with 170 respondents, and two are Orthodox with a combined total of 343 respondents. Overall, 834 students responded to the survey. The data were originally collected as a pilot study to develop survey instruments for a larger and more representative study (Schneider, 2003), but the diversity of the sample and the new indicators of family, school, and adolescent religious identification offered a unique opportunity to explore the issues raised in this chapter, despite the limited scope of the sample.

Indicators of Jewish Cultural Capital

Students were asked questions about several religious rituals and cultural affiliations that are commonly used as indicators of Jewish identity. These items were separated into four categories that refer to the students' personal practices and affiliations and those of their families. The student-specific items are used as indicators of young persons' Jewish cultural capital, and the family items as indicators of Jewish cultural capital residing in the family.

- Student's ritual practices (times in past year attended Jewish worship services, fasted on Yom Kippur, avoids handling money on Sabbath, keeps kosher)
- Family's ritual practices (family attends Passover seder, family lights Hanukkah candles, family lights candles on Friday nights, family keeps separate dishes for dairy and meat)
- Student's cultural affiliations (times in past year followed news from Israel, times in past year listened to tape/CD for Jewish content, times in past year read book for Jewish content, times in past year used Internet for Jewish content, wears or displays Jewish sign, times in past year performed volunteer work with a Jewish organization, important to student to marry a Jew, important to student to continue Jewish education past high school, number of Jewish friends)
- Family's cultural affiliations (family observed Israel Independence Day, family had Christmas tree, family has relatives in Israel, religion of others in neighborhood, important to parents for student to marry a Jew, parents have definite rules about Friday night dinner)

For each item, students were asked whether they or their families engaged in the described Jewish ritual activities and cultural affiliations and, in some cases, the extent to which they did so. For ease of comparison and index construction, each item score was converted into a z-score. Missing items were imputed as the mean values for the student's specific denominational preference and school type (supplementary school, non-Orthodox day school, or Orthodox day school). The four scales, constructed as the means of the z-scores, have reliabilities of .76

and .68 for students' and families' ritual practices, and .83 and .74 for students' and families' cultural affiliations, respectively (see Appendix A). These indices are refinements of those developed by Horowitz (2000), who established ritual practices and communal affiliations as reliable measures of Jewish identity, without specifically distinguishing between individual and family practices.

An additional identity index was constructed based on Horowitz's research to reflect the subjective centrality of Jewishness to respondents' lives. This index incorporated the attitudes toward Judaism as reflected by the following statements: "I am proud to be a Jew," "I have a clear sense of what being Jewish means to me," "I have a strong sense of belonging to the Jewish people," "I have a special responsibility to take care of Jews in need around the world," "Overall, the fact that I am a Jew has very little to do with how I see myself," "It is important for me to have friends who share my way of being Jewish," "When faced with an important life decision, I look to Judaism for guidance," and "There is something about me that non-Jews could never understand." The centrality of Jewishness index values were determined by taking the average value of responses to items in the index. Responses ranged from "Strongly agree," coded as 4 on the survey, to "Strongly disagree," coded as 1. (Negative items were reverse-coded.) The scale for this index ranges from 1 to 4 with a mean of 2.88, and its reliability is .83.

Family Variables

Indicators of families as sources of Jewish cultural capital include the two scales described above: family ritual practices, and family cultural affiliations. In addition, the analysis takes note of students' reported denominational preferences: Orthodox, Traditional, Conservative, Reform, Reconstructionist, or "Just Jewish." Due to small numbers in the Traditional and Reconstructionist categories, combined categories were created for Orthodox/Traditional (n=302) and for Reform/Reconstructionist (n=204) along with Conservative (n=221) and Just Jewish (n=79). (Preliminary analyses revealed similar patterns of survey responses for Orthodox and Traditional respondents, and for Reform and Reconstructionist respondents.) A small number of missing cases (n=10) and students who reported another religion (n=18) were included with "Just Jewish" in the reference category for regression analyses. (Omitting these cases entirely does not affect the results in any meaningful way.)

The analysis includes two additional background measures as control variables: students' grade in school, and students' gender. Students' cultural capital is likely to increase the longer they remain in Jewish schooling, and gender has been shown in past research to be associated with Jewish identity (Cohen, 1995).

School Variables

The three types of schools in our sample—supplementary schools, Orthodox day schools, and non-Orthodox day schools—represent substantially different learning environments. Supplementary schools generally offer between two and six hours of instruction per week, while day schools may offer that much instruction per day, five days per week. Supplementary school students typically attend one day per week for Judaic studies and most attend one or two additional days per week for Hebrew study, but for the vast majority, Hebrew study is limited to grades 3 or 4 through grades 7 or 8. Day schools commonly devote the morning to Judaic studies and Hebrew and set aside the afternoon (or part of the afternoon) for secular topics. Orthodox day schools presumably give more attention to Jewish study topics than non-Orthodox schools, although this has not been documented. Overall, the difference in the intensity of Jewish study between day schools and supplementary schools is expected to be larger than the difference between the Orthodox and non-Orthodox schools, due to the substantial difference in time available for instruction.

For a more direct measure of students' opportunities to engage in Jewish study in school, the analysis draws on their responses to survey questions about several topics that are commonly covered by the curriculum of Jewish schools. These topics are grouped into four categories:

- Jewish texts (*Torah, Nevi'im, Mishna, Talmud,* and modern Jewish literature)
- Jewish ritual practices (*Shabbat, Shavuot, Tisha B'av,* how to pray, content of the *Siddur* [prayer book], marriage, and death/mourning)
- Hebrew (reading out loud, understanding what is read, and speaking)
- Other Jewish study topics (Jewish history, Israel, comparative religion, and ethics, values, and philosophy)

An additive scale was constructed for each, based on whether students responded yes or no to the question, "Have you had an opportunity to learn the following subjects in school?" Because the scales were highly correlated, they are combined into a single scale of Opportunity to Learn for the regression analyses. This scale ranges from 0–27 with a mean of 19.5 and a standard deviation of 6.6. Means for supplementary, non-Orthodox day, and Orthodox day schools are 15.4, 22.7, and 22.1, respectively, confirming our supposition that the main difference in extent of Jewish study lies between the supplementary school and both types of day schools. Our measure is not fine-grained enough to capture more precise differences in intensity, ideology, or instructional approach that likely occurred between the Orthodox and non-Orthodox day schools.

Methods

The analysis relies on ordinary least squares regression to examine patterns of association between students' family and school environments, on the one hand, and their self-reported Jewish cultural capital as reflected in ritual practices, affiliations, and centrality of Jewishness, on the other. Multilevel analyses of students within schools would have been preferred, but the sample did not contain enough schools for that approach. By introducing dummy variables for school types (Orthodox Day and non-Orthodox Day versus Supplementary School), the analysis takes school sector into account, though it does not focus on differences within sectors. In a few cases of special interest, within-sector analyses were performed; these are noted without presenting the full results because they did not yield substantially different findings from the main results.

Six regression models were estimated for each of the three dependent variables. The first two examine family associations (denominational preference and family rituals and affiliations), the second two examine school associations (school type and opportunity to learn), the fifth combines the family and school variables, and the last model adds interaction terms between family rituals and affiliations and opportunity to learn. Missing cases on the indicator of opportunity to learn, combined with a small amount of missing data on the dependent variables, reduced the sample from 834 to 635 for the analysis of ritual practices and affiliation, and 620 for the analysis of centrality of Jewishness, or about 74–76 percent of the original sample. Means and standard deviations of variables in the regression models are listed in Appendix B.

Results

Table 4.1 presents results for student's ritual practices. The first two columns show important family contributions to a young person's own participation in these signals of religious and cultural identity: Both denominational preference and family practices and affiliations are significantly related to the respondent's performance of Jewish rituals. With family practices and affiliations taken into account (Model 2), the results show no difference between Reform/Reconstructionist and "Just Jewish" respondents, whereas the practices of Conservative and Orthodox respondents are progressively greater. This is to be expected since progressively greater adherence to Jewish law is what defines Conservative and Orthodox Jews.

Table 4.1. Associations with Student's Ritual Practices

Dependent Variable: Student's Ritual Practices

Independent variables	Model 1	2	3	4	5	6
Gender (1=female)	.057 (.037)	.053 (.033)	.089* (.039)	.088* (.039)	.057 (.032)	.055 (.032)
Grade in school (7–12)	.051* (.013)	.037* (.011)	.030 (.017)	.029 (.017)	.017 (.014)	.015 (.014)
Denomination Reform/ Reconstructionist	-.155* (.064)	-.031 (.058)			.097 (.058)	.107 (.058)
Conservative	.639* (.065)	.391* (.061)			.388* (.059)	.388* (.059)
Orthodox/Traditional	1.193* (.066)	.802* (.065)			.664* (.066)	.653* (.066)
Family ritual practices		.230* (.034)			.185* (.034)	.072 (.085)
Family cultural affiliation		.268* (.038)			.208* (.038)	.166 (.096)
School type Non-Orthodox day school			.846* (.054)	.776* (.060)	.291* (.057)	.276* (.058)
Orthodox day school			1.231* (.054)	1.169* (.058)	.464* (.067)	.455* (.067)
Opportunity to learn (OTL)				.009* (.003)	-.00005 (.003)	.004 (.003)
Family ritual x OTL						.007 (.005)
Family affiliation x OTL						.002 (.005)
Constant	-1.048	-.748	-.993	-1.134	-.794	-.854
Adjusted R²	.623	.704	.582	.586	.727	.729

*p < .05

Note: Coefficients are unstandardized regression coefficients, with standard errors in parentheses.

Models 3 and 4 reveal significant associations between ritual practices and school variables (school type and opportunity to learn). Note that the significant association between learning opportunities and ritual practices holds with controls for school type, that is, it is an association that occurs within sectors. Tests for differences across sectors (not shown) indicated that the coefficient for opportunity to learn does not vary significantly across school types. Regardless of which type of school a student attended, the opportunity to learn more Jewish subjects was associated with engaging in more ritual practices.

Are these associations independent of family characteristics, or are they merely a reflection of family preferences? Model 5 shows that the school type associations persist when family background is taken into account, but the opportunity-to-learn coefficient is no longer significant, nor are the interactions reported in Model 6. This means that the association between opportunity to learn and ritual practices reflected family differences, not the effects of schooling.

The results are somewhat different for respondent's cultural affiliations, another indicator of Jewish cultural capital that is examined in Table 4.2. As in Table 4.1, Models 1-4 show that both family and school characteristics are associated with higher levels on the dependent variable. In the case of affiliation, however, unlike the results for rituals, the association with opportunity to learn remains statistically significant even after taking family conditions into account, whereas the school type indicators are nonsignificant. Another difference between Tables 4.1 and 4.2 is that whereas both family rituals and family affiliations contribute to the respondent's ritual performance, only family affiliations are associated with the young person's own affiliations (compare Model 5 in Tables 4.1 and 4.2). In Model 6, the interaction terms are again nonsignificant. Overall, Table 4.2 shows that regardless of school type and family differences, students who had opportunities to learn more Jewish subjects expressed greater affiliation with Judaism.

The coefficient for opportunity to learn, the most direct measure of school cultural capital, is statistically significant but appears small, at .010. What does this mean in substantive terms? If the association were causal, an increase of one standard deviation on the opportunity scale (6.6) would result in an increase of just over one-tenth of a standard deviation on the affiliation scale (.64), a small but nontrivial effect. Put differently, the difference between a typical supplementary school student's curricular exposure (mean of about 15) and the average for a day school student (about 22) is associated with a difference in Jewish cultural affiliations of a little over one-tenth of a standard deviation. Although this is a perceptible association, it is smaller than those of the family variables. For example, a difference of one standard deviation on the family cultural affiliations scale is associated with more than one-third of a standard deviation difference in student cultural affiliations. Thus, although the opportunity-to-learn measure is significant, it is very small compared to the more salient family factor.

Table 4.3 presents the same set of models for the third dependent variable: subjective centrality of Jewishness. Whereas Models 1–4 appear similar to the other dependent variables, a striking difference appears in Model 5: Controlling for family conditions, we find that students in supplementary schools exhibit higher

Table 4.2. Associations with Student's Cultural Affiliation

Dependent Variable: Student's Cultural Affiliation

Independent variables	Model 1	2	3	4	5	6
Gender (1=female)	.109* (.039)	.104* (.035)	.133* (.041)	.131* (.040)	.105* (.035)	.102* (.035)
Grade in school (7-12)	.078* (.014)	.061* (.012)	.078* (.018)	.077* (.017)	.053* (.015)	.050* (.016)
Denomination Reform/ Reconstructionist	.092 (.068)	.215* (.062)			.256* (.065)	.267* (.065)
Conservative	.599* (.069)	.355* (.065)			.338* (.066)	.340* (.066)
Orthodox/Traditional	.866* (.070)	.499* (.070)			.443* (.073)	.436* (.073)
Family ritual practices		.091* (.037)			.068 (.037)	-.066 (.095)
Family cultural affiliation		.395* (.041)			.361* (.043)	.383 (.107)
School type Non-Orthodox day school			.570* (.057)	.430* (.062)	.040 (.064)	.029 (.064)
Orthodox day school			.693* (.056)	.568* (.060)	.114 (.074)	.110 (.075)
Opportunity to learn (OTL)				.019* (.004)	.010* (.003)	.013* (.004)
Family ritual x OTL						.008 (.005)
Family affiliation x OTL						-.001 (.005)
Constant	-1.241	-.922	-1.166	-1.447	-1.093	-1.128
Adjusted R²	.411	.524	.364	.391	.534	.535

*p < .05
Note: Coefficients are unstandardized regression coefficients, with standard errors in parentheses.

levels of centrality of Jewishness than those in either type of day school. This association is obscured when examining school characteristics alone (Models 3 and 4), because students in supplementary schools have lower levels of family religious practices and affiliations on average. But among those with similar levels of family religiosity, supplementary school students exhibit more positive attitudes about their Jewishness. The gaps between supplementary school and other students are nearly four-tenths of a standard deviation on the centrality scale (.67), a substantial

Table 4.3. Associations with Student's Centrality of Jewishness
Dependent Variable: Student's Centrality of Jewishness

Independent variables	Model 1	Model 2	Model 3	Model 4	Model 5	Model 6
Gender (1=female)	.113* (.046)	.110* (.045)	.145* (.050)	.145* (.050)	.105* (.045)	.108* (.045)
Grade in school (7-12)	.076* (.016)	.066* (.016)	.088* (.022)	.087* (.022)	.064* (.020)	.066* (.020)
Denomination						
Reform/Reconstructionist	.418* (.079)	.490* (.079)			.423* (.082)	.421* (.083)
Conservative	.686* (.081)	.542* (.083)			.551* (.083)	.547* (.083)
Orthodox/Traditional	.919* (.081)	.700* (.089)			.764* (.093)	.755* (.094)
Family ritual practices		.080 (.047)			.101* (.047)	.141 (.120)
Family cultural affiliation		.209* (.052)			.248* (.054)	.129 (.135)
School type						
Non-Orthodox day school			.217* (.070)	.112 (.077)	-.262* (.081)	-.270* (.082)
Orthodox day school			.340* (.069)	.248* (.075)	-.255* (.095)	-.263* (.095)
Opportunity to learn (OTL)				.014* (.004)	.005 (.004)	.007 (.005)
Family ritual x OTL						-.002 (.006)
Family affiliation x OTL						.007 (.007)
Constant	1.535	1.724	1.843	1.642	1.793	1.745
Adjusted R²	.280	.313	.146	.158	.324	.323

*$p < .05$
Note: Coefficients are unstandardized regression coefficients, with standard errors in parentheses.

difference. Although day school students exhibit higher centrality of Jewishness on average, the Jewish self-assurance expressed by supplementary school students is actually higher than would otherwise be expected considering their generally less Jewishly intense family environments.

The negative coefficients for day school students compared to those in supplementary schools could reflect a ceiling on the centrality-of-Jewishness scale. Such a ceiling could prevent the day school students from expressing as much centrality as would otherwise be warranted by their religious backgrounds. However, while responses on centrality of Jewishness are highly skewed among the Orthodox day school students, they conform to a roughly normal distribution among the non-Orthodox day school and the supplementary students. At least for the comparison of supplementary to non-Orthodox day school students, therefore, evidence of higher centrality of Jewishness for supplementary students appears to be a substantive finding rather than an artifactual one. As before, neither of the interaction terms is statistically significant. Supplementary analyses (not shown) confirmed that the interactions are also insignificant when examined within each school type separately.

Looking across the dependent variables, we see that our analysis is least successful in explaining variation in centrality of Jewishness, with an adjusted R^2 of .324 for Model 5, compared with .727 for ritual practices and .534 for cultural affiliations. This may suggest that a young person's ideas and sense of self are more independent of school and family than are his or her activities. It may also reflect the fact that the analysis lacks a direct measure of family centrality of Jewishness, whereas the models for students' rituals and affiliations include more direct family-level counterparts.

Discussion and Conclusion

Overall, our results show support for two of our three hypotheses. First, school conditions and family environments are independently associated with Jewish cultural capital as reflected in young persons' ritual performances, Jewish affiliations, and centrality of Jewishness. The combined model (Model 5) revealed several significant family associations and at least one significant school indicator in each case. Second, adolescents' Jewish cultural capital appears more closely linked to their family environments than to their schooling experiences. This result, also, was anticipated. The family effects are more consistent throughout, and when they are included separately, the family variables explain more variance than the school variables. Differences between denominational preferences were invariably larger than differences between school types, and in the one case of a significant association for opportunity to learn, its effect was dwarfed by the family variables.

The third hypothesis predicted that richer school contexts would compensate for families who engage in relatively few Jewish activities, and that this would be reflected in negative interaction terms between opportunity to learn and family rituals and affiliations. This hypothesis contrasted with that of Nagel and

Ganzeboom (2003), who proposed that family and school conditions have compounding effects that are reflected in positive interaction terms. The results supported neither of these positions: Family and school associations are independent, with no interactions one way or the other. Perhaps families and schools have both compounding and compensating effects, which cancel out each other and make it appear as if there is no interaction. Or, perhaps neither process is occurring.

The finding of more powerful family than school effects is consistent with many years of research in the sociology of schooling (e.g., Coleman et al., 1966). That body of research focuses mainly on the association between socioeconomic circumstances and educational achievement, whereas the association examined here is between family religious resources and the possession of religious cultural capital, but the pattern is the same. While religious schools provide a vehicle for the transmission of religion and culture, they do not supplant families. In the case of Jewish schools, neither day schools nor supplementary schools can stand alone as forces for transmitting identity or preserving *Jewish continuity* from one generation to the next, and the results suggest that Jewish cultural capital is more a product of the family and home than of the school. As Meyer (2003) commented, "Jewish knowledge deepens Jewish commitment, but it does not create it. . . . Jewish experiences . . . create the emotional matrix within which cognitive learning can be lodged. . . . The emotional matrix is first created and then principally sustained in the home. . . . What the school can do is expand upon it" (p. 152). The findings in this study are consistent with Meyer's view, although longitudinal data will be required to sort out the causal and temporal patterns.

This study could also be extended fruitfully by examining a wider range of religious and/or cultural groups. To what extent do Catholic, other Christian, and Islamic schools, for instance, transmit the cultural capital of their respective traditions? Catholic schools typically devote far less time to formal religious instruction than do Jewish day schools. Does this mean that they play a smaller role in fostering cultural capital? One study found that Catholic supplementary education (catechesis) and Catholic parochial schools were about equally effective in promoting religious identification (Elford, 1994). Is this because formal religious instruction in Catholic schools is relatively limited? Or because family environments matter far more than schools? Or because religious schooling has different effects for students in a majority religion (Christian, in the case of the United States) than for students in religious minorities (e.g., Judaism and Islam in the United States)? Answers to questions such as these would shed light on how young persons develop their religious identities, an important but generally unacknowledged issue at a time when noncognitive growth is almost forgotten in the press for academic standards.

Appendix A. Scale Items, Means, and Reliabilities

Student cultural capital	Item range	Item mean	Scale reliability
Student ritual practices			.7574
Times attended Jewish worship services in past year	0–5	2.90	
Fasted on Yom Kippur	0–1	.81	
Avoids handling money on Sabbath	0–1	.45	
Keeps kosher	0–5	3.05	
Student cultural affiliation			.8257
Follow news from Israel	0–5	3.05	
Listen to audio recordings for Jewish content	0–5	1.53	
Read books for Jewish content	0–5	1.33	
Use Internet for Jewish content	0–5	1.32	
Wear/display Jewish sign	0–3	1.35	
Perform volunteer work through Jewish organization	0–5	1.15	
Important to respondent to marry a Jew	1–4	2.90	
Important to respondent to continue Jewish education past high school	1–4	2.56	
Number of Jewish friends	0–7	3.90	
Subjective centrality of Jewishness			.8347
Proud to be a Jew	1–4	3.57	
Clear sense of being Jewish	1–4	3.21	
Strong sense of belonging to the Jewish people	1–4	3.23	
Strong sense of responsibility to Jews in need around the world	1–4	2.88	
Being Jewish has to do with how student views self (reverse coded)	1–4	3.78	
Important to have Jewish friends	1–4	2.80	
Look to Judaism for help with important decisions	1–4	2.42	
Something about me that non-Jews cannot understand	1–4	2.37	

Family environment	Item range	Item mean	Scale reliability
Family ritual practices			.6756
Family attends seder	0–3	2.74	
Family lights Hanukkah candles	0–8	7.70	
Family lights candles on Friday night	0–3	2.14	
Family keeps separate sets of dishes for dairy and meat	0–1	.59	
Family cultural affiliation			.7374
Family observed Yom Ha'atzmaut	0–1	.52	
Family had Christmas tree (reverse coded)	0–3	.24	
Family has relatives in Israel	0–1	.64	
Religion of people in neighborhood	1–5	2.68	
Important to parents that student marry a Jew	1–4	3.17	
Parents have definite rules about Friday night dinner	0–1	.58	

Appendix A. Scale Items, Means, and Reliabilities (*cont.*)

Opportunity to learn	Item range	Item mean	Scale reliability
All subjects			.9101
Jewish texts			.8301
Torah	0–1	.87	
Prophets	0–1	.78	
Mishna	0–1	.69	
Talmud (Gemara)	0–1	.70	
Modern Jewish literature	0–1	.62	
Jewish rituals			.8604
Shabbat	0–1	.89	
Shavuot	0–1	.83	
Tisha B'av	0–1	.78	
How to pray	0–1	.79	
Content of prayer book	0–1	.77	
Customs of marriage	0–1	.70	
Customs of death/mourning	0–1	.70	
Customs of circumcision	0–1	.69	
Hebrew			.8794
Reading out loud	0–1	.88	
Reading comprehension	0–1	.83	
Speaking	0–1	.82	
Other Jewish studies			.7988
Jews in the Middle Ages	0–1	.76	
American Jewish history	0–1	.66	
Holocaust	0–1	.94	
History of Zionism and modern Israel	0–1	.73	
Jewish philosophy	0–1	.52	
Kabbalah (Jewish mysticism)	0–1	.29	
Comparative religion	0–1	.54	
Varieties of contemporary Jewish practice and thought	0–1	.58	
Tzedakah (charity)	0–1	.87	
Tikkun Olam ("repairing" the world)	0–1	.72	
Ahavat Yisrael (care about Jews around the world)	0–1	.75	

Appendix B. Means and Standard Deviations of Variables in Regressions

Variables	Mean	Standard deviation
Student ritual practice	-.034	.755
Student cultural affiliation	-.009	.643
Centrality of Jewishness	2.882	.674
Gender (1 = female)	.50	.50
Grade in school (7–12)	9.01	1.63
Reform/Reconstructionist	.287	.453
Conservative	.266	.442
Orthodox/Traditional	.332	.471
Just Jewish/other/missing	.110	.313
Family ritual practice	-.008	.702
Family cultural affiliation	-.032	.652
Non-Orthodox day school	.222	.416
Orthodox day school	.373	.484
Supplementary school	.405	.491
Opportunity to learn	19.550	6.606

Note

The authors are grateful for helpful comments from William Carbonaro, Maureen Hallinan, Annette Hochstein, and Barry Holtz on earlier versions of this paper. Research for this paper was supported by the Mandel Foundation and by the Center for Research on Educational Opportunity, University of Notre Dame. The data were collected through a cooperative research project of the Jewish Federation of Metropolitan Chicago, the Community Foundation for Jewish Education, the Associated Talmud Torahs, the Mandel Foundation, and the University of Chicago and funded by a grant from the Spencer Foundation.

References

Bourdieu, P. (1977a). *Outline of a theory of practice*. Cambridge, Eng.: Cambridge University Press.

Bourdieu, P. (1977b). Cultural reproduction and social reproduction. In J. Karabel & A. H. Halsey (Eds.), *Power and ideology in education* (pp. 489–511). New York: Oxford University Press.

Bourdieu, P. (1984). *Distinction: A social critique of the judgment of taste*. Cambridge, MA: Harvard University Press.

Bourdieu, P., & Darbel, A. (1990). *The love of art: European art museums and their public*. Stanford, CA: Stanford University Press.

Bridges, L. J., & Moore, K. A. (2002). *Research brief: Religious involvement and children's well-being: What research tells us (and what it doesn't)*. Washington, DC: Child Trends.

Cohen, S. M. (1988). *American assimilation or Jewish revival?* Bloomington: Indiana University Press.

Cohen, S. M. (1995). The impact of varieties of Jewish education upon Jewish identity: An intergenerational perspective. *Contemporary Jewry, 16,* 68–96.

Coleman, J. S., Campbell, E. Q., Hobson, C. J., McPartland, J., Mood, A. M., Weinfield, F. D., & York, R. L. (1966). *Equality of educational opportunity*. Washington, DC: U.S. Government Printing Office.

de Graaf, P. M. (1986). The impact of financial and cultural resources on educational attainment in the Netherlands. *Sociology of Education, 59,* 237–246.

DiMaggio, P. (1982). Cultural capital and school success: The impact of status culture participation on the grades of U.S. high school students. *American Sociological Review, 47,* 189–201.

DiMaggio, P., & Mohr, J. (1985). Cultural capital, educational attainment, and marital selection. *American Journal of Sociology, 90,* 1231–1261.

Elazar, D. J. (1976). *Community and polity: The organizational dynamics of American Jewry*. Philadelphia: Jewish Publication Society.

Elford, G. (1994). *Toward shaping the agenda: A study of Catholic religious education/catechesis.* Washington, DC: Educational Testing Service.

Gamoran, A. (2001). *Learning in Jewish schools: Perceptions of adolescents.* Paper presented at the annual meeting of the Association for Jewish Studies, Washington, DC.

Goldscheider, C. (1986). *Jewish continuity and change: Emerging patterns in America.* Bloomington: Indiana University Press.

Holtz, B. (Ed.). (1984). *Back to the sources.* New York: Summit Books.

Horowitz, B. (2000). *Connections and journeys.* New York: United Jewish Appeal-Federation of New York.

Horowitz, B. (2002). Reframing the study of contemporary American Jewish identity. *Contemporary Jewry, 23,* 14–34.

Kobrin, F., & Goldscheider, C. (1978). *The ethnic factor in family structure and mobility.* Cambridge, MA: Ballinger Press.

Kosmin, B. A., Goldstein, S., Waksberg, J., Lerer, N., Keysar, A., & Scheckner., J. (1991). *Highlights of the CJF 1990 National Jewish Population Survey.* New York: Council of Jewish Federations.

Kraaykamp, G. (2003). Cumulative advantages and inequality in lifestyle: A Dutch description of distinction in taste. *The Netherlands' Journal of Social Sciences, 38,* 121–143.

Massarik, F., & Chenkin, A. (1973). United States National Jewish Population Survey. *American Jewish Year Book, 73,* 264–306.

Meyer, M. A. (2003). Reflections on the educated Jew from the perspective of Reform Judaism. In S. Fox, I. Scheffler, & D. Marom (Eds.), *Visions of Jewish education* (pp. 149–161). Cambridge, Eng.: Cambridge University Press.

Nagel, I., & Ganzeboom, H. B. G. (2003). Participation in legitimate culture: Family and school effects from adolescence to adulthood. *The Netherlands' Journal of Social Sciences, 38,* 102–120.

Schneider, B. (2003). *Report on the Cooperative Research Project of Chicago Area Jewish Schools.* Chicago: The Jewish School Study Team.

Schoenfeld, S. (1998). Six methodological problems in forecasting the impact of Jewish education on Jewish identity. *Journal of Jewish Education, 64,* 87–101.

Sklare, M., & Greenblum, J. (1967). *Jewish identity on the suburban frontier: A study of group survival in the open society.* Chicago: University of Chicago Press.

Weber, M. (1978). *Economy and society: An outline of interpretive sociology* (G. Roth & C. Wittich, Eds. and Trans.). Berkeley: University of California Press.

5 | The Practice of Ability Grouping

Sector Differences in Implementation

Maureen T. Hallinan and Brandy J. Ellison

Grouping students by ability for instruction is a common practice in both private and public schools. Ability grouping is popular among many educators, parents, and students because they regard it as a way for teachers to tailor instruction to the learning level of students. They believe that by ability grouping, teachers are better able to engage student interest, ensure that students comprehend curricular instruction, and give assignments that students can complete independently and successfully. For these reasons, its proponents argue that the practice is more effective than heterogeneous grouping in promoting student learning.

Critics of ability grouping argue, however, that the practice is inequitable because it channels more learning opportunities to some students than to others. They point to the disproportionate number of lower socioeconomic status (SES) and minority students assigned to low ability groups as evidence to support their argument. Since the quality of the curriculum and pedagogy is generally regarded as inferior in low-level ability groups, student placement in these lower groups is likely accompanied by lost opportunities to learn. Moreover, low ability groups may be characterized by greater disorder, more discipline problems, and more time spent on administrative matters than higher level groups, which further deprives lower-ability grouped students of instruction.

Research examining the effects of ability grouping is fairly consistent in reporting that students assigned to higher ability groups have greater gains in achievement than those assigned to lower ones. This finding supports the claim that the practice distributes learning opportunities unequally. At the same time, studies show little evidence that school personnel rely on SES, race, or ethnicity in assigning students to ability group levels. This result counters the charge that the practice of ability grouping is inherently inequitable. Apparently, students who find learning difficult are assigned to lower ability groups because of their academic limitations rather than background characteristics. These students then fail to receive the higher quality instruction and pedagogy provided to those in higher ability groups, and they lose ground academically.

Given the strong evidence of ability group effects on student learning, how ability grouping is practiced is of central interest to educators, parents, and students. Of particular interest is whether characteristics of schools transmit the effects of ability grouping to student achievement. A characteristic of special concern in this regard is school sector. Differences in the way that ability grouping is practiced in public and private schools may help to explain differences in student outcomes across school sector.

Comparing the practice of ability grouping in Catholic and public schools is of special interest when examining the mechanisms that link ability grouping to student achievement. Catholic schools have long been regarded as institutions that provide a high-quality education to students. Catholic parents send their children to Catholic schools not only because they value the religious instruction offered there, but also because they believe that their children will receive an outstanding education. Non-Catholic parents enroll their children in Catholic schools primarily for the quality of the education.

Until the latter part of the twentieth century, little empirical research had been conducted to evaluate the quality of a Catholic education. The positive reputation of Catholic schools was based primarily on a sense that Catholic school graduates were successful in gaining admission to elite colleges, in winning academic scholarships and honors, and in attaining a high rate of college completion. It was not until the 1980s, more than 100 years after the creation of the Catholic school system, that longitudinal survey data became available to permit research examining the Catholic school reputation for excellence. These data enabled researchers to investigate whether organizational and pedagogical practices, such as ability grouping, are implemented differently in Catholic and public schools, and, if so, if this might account for the gap in academic achievement that differentiates the two sectors.

The first wave of the national longitudinal survey, High School and Beyond (HSB), became available in 1982. This data set contains information on students in 1,015 secondary public and private schools across the country. Coleman, Hoffer, and Kilgore (1982) analyzed these cross-sectional data to compare student achievement in Catholic and public schools. They found that students in Catholic schools earned higher test scores than their peers in public or other private schools. While the differences in test scores across school sector were not large, they were noteworthy in their consistency across subject area, grade, and school demographic characteristics. This result became known as "the Catholic school advantage." The study provided empirical support for the belief that Catholic schools are particularly successful in promoting academic achievement.

The Coleman et al. (1982) study was criticized on methodological and statistical grounds. The sharpest criticism stemmed from the fact that the analysis was based on cross-sectional data and hence could not establish causality. When the second wave of HSB became available, Hoffer, Greeley, and Coleman (1985) repeated the analysis. Their results, based on longitudinal models, showed the same Catholic school advantage that had been observed in the cross-sectional study. The researchers concluded that Catholic schools are engaging in practices and policies that are particularly conducive to student learning. They hypothesized that a strong curriculum, strict discipline, and a communal spirit characterize Catholic schools and account for their academic success.

In the subsequent analyses of the HSB data, Greeley (1982) and Hoffer et al. (1985) employed several analytic techniques to examine further the Catholic school advantage. These studies revealed a positive effect of Catholic school attendance on verbal and mathematics achievement gains from sophomore to senior year. The effect was equivalent to half a grade in these subjects. It was attributed to the strength of the curriculum, the number of required courses, and the amount of homework assigned. The gains were larger for African American, Hispanic, and lower SES students, leading to the claim that Catholic schools uniquely promote the common school ideal. By reducing the negative effects of race and SES on achievement, Catholic schools distribute learning opportunities more equitably across students. The research also showed that when public schools made demands on students similar to those made in Catholic schools, they produced comparable achievement results.

In the late 1980s, responding to a request from the National Catholic Educational Association to study effective Catholic schools, Bryk and Holland undertook an intensive examination of a small number of Catholic high schools, and Bryk and Lee conducted further comparative analyses of student achievement in public and Catholic high schools in the HSB data set. Their results (Bryk, Lee, & Holland, 1993) were consistent with Coleman, Hoffer, and Kilgore's (1982) work revealing a Catholic school advantage. The in-depth analysis of seven Catholic high schools provided insights into how Catholic schools attain their academic success. The researchers concluded that the strength of the curriculum in these schools is a major cause of student achievement. They observed that teachers in Catholic schools assume that all students can learn and require all students to take challenging courses. The schools also avoid offering low-level remedial courses and provide a solid curriculum for students at all ability levels.

Bryk et al. (1993) identified the climate of Catholic schools as another factor that explains the Catholic school advantage. They noted that Catholic schools are orderly environments where students feel safe and secure, because discipline is regularly and consistently enforced. Moreover, Catholic school students have a sense of shared identity. Along with their principal and faculty, students form a close community characterized by respect, caring, and service. The faith-based orientation of Catholic schools serves as a powerful force that unifies the school community and provides an additional layer of support to help students develop cognitively, emotionally, and socially. This faith-based orientation motivates teachers to pursue the goals of the school and supports their commitment to student learning.

While these major research studies offer empirical evidence of the high quality of a Catholic education, they do not analyze the mechanisms that explain the Catholic school advantage. Suggesting that a rigorous curriculum, strict discipline, and a communal spirit promote student learning identifies factors that increase achievement, but it does not explain how schools channel learning opportunities to students and engage them in the learning process. Further analysis is needed to better understand Catholic school effectiveness.

One of the primary mechanisms that schools use to promote student learning is the organization of students for instruction. How students are assigned to classes and other instructional groupings determines the curriculum to which they are exposed and the pedagogical characteristics of the teachers who instruct them. Further, the way that students are organized for instruction evokes social psychological processes that influence learning. Hence, it is likely that curricular differentiation has a direct impact on student learning and can explain differences across schools and school sectors in student academic achievement.

In most private and public middle and secondary schools in the United States, students are grouped for instruction by ability. A large body of research has accumulated evaluating the efficacy of ability grouping in public schools. The results of these studies are fairly consistent in concluding that variation in how ability grouping is practiced explains some of the within and between school differences in student achievement. For this reason, a comparative analysis of ability grouping in Catholic and public schools could determine whether the enactment of ability grouping in Catholic schools explains their academic effectiveness. This chapter identifies similarities and differences in the way that ability grouping is practiced in Catholic and public schools in order to determine whether this practice accounts for or contributes to the Catholic school advantage.

History of Ability Grouping

Ability grouping in public high schools became common around the beginning of the twentieth century, precipitated by changes in immigration patterns, the expansion of education, and the advent of intelligence tests. As the population of school-aged children grew, school size increased. This made it necessary to develop a better system for organizing students for instruction within the larger schools. Homogeneous grouping emerged as a convenient way for schools to serve the needs of a variety of students with different backgrounds and abilities (Goldberg, Passow, & Justman, 1966; Lucas, 1999). Intelligence tests facilitated the assignment of students to these groups (Mondale & Patton, 2001).

Ability grouping originated as a strict curricular assignment designed to prepare students for a career. This practice was referred to as tracking. Most schools had three tracks: vocational, general, and academic. The vocational track trained students for trades such as plumbing, mechanics, and carpentry. The general track offered students the basic knowledge needed for low-skilled jobs that would not require a college degree. The academic track prepared students for college. Assignment to one of these tracks determined the trajectory of a student's career prospects. Once assigned to a track, the student had little latitude in choosing courses and was rarely allowed to take courses outside the prescribed track. This rigid structure effectively guaranteed that the majority of students would be led into specific educational or career paths because they were constrained from exploring other vocational or academic options while in high school.

The structure of the public high school curriculum began to change during the 1950s. High school enrollment grew significantly during this time because baby boomers were reaching adolescence. Students still took required courses within their assigned track, but, in addition, they could choose from a variety of elective courses. This growth in course offerings led to the characterization of the comprehensive high school as a "shopping mall" (Powell, Farrar, & Cohen, 1985) where students were given the opportunity to choose electives that fit their specific interests. This signaled the beginning of a change in the structure of tracking (Lucas, 1999).

The public school curriculum experienced another transformation during the late 1960s and early 1970s when schools began to place greater emphasis on academic achievement and college preparation. This was due in part to pressure arising from the success of other nations in the areas of math and science (Mondale & Patton, 2001; Powell et al., 1985). In addition, many scholars and educators began to doubt the validity of intelligence tests as scientific instruments to determine curricular assignments (Scarr & Weinberg, 1976; Stodolsky & Lesser, 1967). For these reasons, schools began to prescribe a standard academic curriculum for all students. Courses in mathematics, social studies, science, and English became almost universal requirements for a high school diploma. This type of academic curriculum remains in place in most schools today.

As tracking changed and was replaced by a more academic curriculum, educators began to stratify courses by ability level. While still referred to as tracking, this method of organizing students for instruction is more accurately called ability grouping. Ability group levels generally include Basic, Regular, Honors, and Advanced courses. Basic courses are designed to offer students extra help and a less challenging curriculum. Regular courses provide a general academic foundation, while Honors classes present more material and require a somewhat higher level of involvement. Advanced courses are most challenging and prepare students for college. Placement at any course level is designed to allow students to acquire the skills necessary either to advance to postsecondary education or to obtain postsecondary employment. The number of course levels varies from school to school, depending on the size and mission of the school. While all students receive an academic education, they can take a Basic course in one subject and an Advanced course in another. This allows them to focus on subjects of particular interest or to receive extra help in a weak subject. Ability grouping is widely practiced in middle and high schools today.

Little information is available about the way that students were grouped for instruction in Catholic schools in the first half of the twentieth century. However, the history of curricular decisions in these schools is suggestive. The Catholic school system was well established as separate from the public school system at the turn of the twentieth century. Its creation arose partly as a reaction to the overarching Protestant ethos of public schools and partly as an attempt by Catholic immigrant communities to resist Americanization and maintain their ethnic identity. Catholic schools briefly considered imitating public schools by offering a more vocationally based curriculum. However, they soon rejected this form of curriculum because they believed that all Catholic school students, regardless of their social origins, must be trained to reason and given a broad body of knowledge to prepare them to assume their responsibilities in society (Bryk et al., 1993).

Catholic colleges also put pressure on secondary schools to maintain an academic curriculum by favoring college preparatory schools in their admissions policies and by initiating strict admissions requirements. The decision to focus on academic programs over vocational training set the tone for Catholic education in the coming decades (Bryk et al., 1993). Given this strong emphasis on an academic curriculum, it is likely that some Catholic schools practiced ability grouping, at least at the secondary level, by the middle of the twentieth century.

Like public schools, Catholic schools began to offer more elective choices during the 1950s (Bryk, et al., 1993). However, these changes did not persist, and Catholic schools quickly returned to a more strictly academic curriculum. The relatively smaller size of these schools and their limited facilities made an expanded curriculum inefficient. More important, Catholic schools were committed to a strong academic curriculum. They avoided introducing elective options that might dilute their academic program. Consequently, as the public schools adapted a more diverse curriculum as part of school reform efforts in the 1960s and 1970s, Catholic schools chose to limit their curriculum to predominantly academic courses. This difference in curricular offerings in public and Catholic schools continues to the present.

By the middle of the twentieth century, most Catholic high schools were practicing ability grouping in order to meet their high academic standards. Since the schools were typically smaller than public schools, they tended to have only two or three ability group levels, such as Regular and Honors, or Basic, Regular, and Honors. In contrast to their counterparts in many public schools, students in the Basic ability group in Catholic schools were given a rigorous curriculum and faced high expectations for achievement. The Basic group tended to be small, and students were encouraged to move to a higher ability group as soon as possible. The high ability group in most Catholic schools resembled the Advanced group in public schools in terms of the rigor of the curriculum and the aptitude of the students (Hallinan, 2002).

The practice of ability grouping in both the public and Catholic sectors was pervasive throughout the second half of the twentieth century. Research on the effects of the organizational differentiation of the curriculum grew rapidly. Ability grouping became a central issue in discussions of school reform. Questions about the efficacy and equity of the practice attracted the attention of politicians as well as of policymakers. Interestingly, despite the dominance of ability grouping in public discourse on schooling, Coleman et al. (1982) neglected to include a variable for ability grouping in their statistical analyses of HSB. This omission became one of the main critiques of the study (Braddock, 1981; Goldberger & Cain, 1982). Even today, despite the large amount of research on the effects of ability grouping, little research is available comparing how ability grouping is practiced in public and Catholic schools.

EFFECTS OF ABILITY GROUPING ON STUDENT ACHIEVEMENT

A large amount of research examining the effects of ability grouping on academic achievement is available. Interest in ability grouping effects may be due, in part, to the intriguing finding that more variation in achievement occurs within schools than between schools (Coleman et al., 1966; Gamoran, 1987). This variation generally takes place across ability groups, suggesting that group placement is a powerful determinant of academic achievement.

Research examining the effects of ability grouping on student achievement generally has taken one of two directions. Most studies compare student achievement across ability groups in homogeneously grouped schools. A few studies compare student achievement in homogeneously and heterogeneously grouped schools. This latter approach is not used often because most schools employ at least some form of ability grouping. Both types of studies show that ability grouping disproportionately benefits students in higher groups.

Studies that compare students across ability groups in homogeneously grouped schools consistently show that, controlling for ability, students in high and Advanced ability groups show the greatest gains in achievement (Alexander & McGill, 1976; Gamoran & Berends, 1987; Hallinan & Kubitschek, 1999; Sorensen & Hallinan, 1986). Students assigned to the low ability groups make the least gains. The findings vary by school, likely due to fluctuations in ability grouping policies and practices. Some schools impose more rigorous academic standards than others in making assignments, and schools vary in the learning opportunities provided at a given ability group level.

Researchers who compare homogeneously and heterogeneously grouped schools also find benefits to high ability group placement. These studies show that mean achievement scores across grouped and ungrouped schools are similar. However, variation in these scores is greater in homogeneously grouped schools, where students score both higher and lower than their counterparts in heterogeneously grouped schools, where scores are closer to the mean. This finding indicates that students in low groups in ability grouped schools would score higher if they were to attend an ungrouped school. On the other hand, students who are placed in high or Advanced groups in ability grouped schools would do less well in an ungrouped school. These findings reinforce the conclusion that ability grouping disproportionately benefits those in high level classes and may harm those in Basic classes (Figlio & Page, 2002; Kerckhoff, 1986; Slavin, 1990).

Betts and Shkolnik (2000) offer a challenge to this finding. They find that after controlling for teachers' perceptions of the ability of their classes in both homogeneous and heterogeneous schools, no significant negative effects of grouping on the academic achievement of students in the lowest groups occurred. Students in middle groups were disadvantaged and those in the highest ones were advantaged, but not to the extent shown in previous research. Rees, Brewer, and Argys (2000) critiqued this research by claiming that many of the supposedly heterogeneous schools in the sample actually had an informal system of tracking and that many of the heterogeneous classes actually contained students with similar ability levels. In general, the overwhelming conclusion of ability group researchers is that the practice advantages students assigned to high ability groups, disadvantages or does not help those assigned to low groups, and has little effect on students in the middle groups, compared to those in ungrouped schools.

In comparing ability group effects in one Catholic and four public schools, Gamoran (1992) found that the effect of ability group level on achievement was reduced in Catholic schools. In this study, the gap between high and low group students in Catholic schools was narrower than in public schools. Moreover, the Catholic schools raised the test scores for students in low ability groups rather than depressing the scores of students in high groups. This pattern was strongest for math outcomes but also was evidenced in tests of verbal ability.

Hallinan's (1991) results were similar to those of Gamoran. The students in the Catholic school in her study had a higher mean test score than students in the six public schools in the sample. In addition, the distribution of achievement scores in the Catholic school showed less variation than in the public schools. These two studies provide evidence that Catholic school students are not necessarily disadvantaged by assignment to low ability groups, whereas public school students often are.

Other studies note the cumulative nature of ability grouping effects on student achievement (Alexander, Cook, & McGill, 1978; Gamoran & Mare, 1989). Some students may begin school with less knowledge and preparation than others. After a cursory evaluation, these students are likely to be placed in a low ability group. As time goes on, the gap between what these students learn and what their peers in higher ability groups learn makes it increasingly more difficult for them to move up. As a result, they may never have the opportunity to realize their full potential. Alexander and Cook (1982) found that the apparent effects of high school grouping were due in large part to previous group placement and resource differences. In this way, group placement can continually reinforce and enhance initial differences among students.

The learning deficit resulting from low-ability group placement is likely to be smaller in Catholic schools than in public schools. Catholic schools typically offer quality instruction at all levels, including the low ability groups. Moreover, Catholic school students in low ability groups are less likely to be socially stigmatized than those in public schools. These factors reduce some of the negative instructional and social psychological effects of ability grouping that may prevent students from achieving their potential (Bryk et al., 1993).

Determinants of Ability Group Effects

While numerous studies have documented the magnitude and direction of ability group effects on student learning, research on the determinants of these effects is less common. This gap in the research may be due to the complexity of the learning process. A number of factors influence student learning, making it difficult to conceptualize learning and to collect data on all the variables that likely create differences in ability group outcomes. Nevertheless, sufficient studies are available to provide insight into how ability grouping influences student achievement.

Hallinan (2003) cites three factors identified in previous research as leading to inequalities in ability group outcomes: the quantity and quality of instruction, motivational factors, and academic climate. These factors are interrelated. Learning opportunities are greatest when students receive ongoing, high-quality instruction, are motivated to learn, and enjoy a supportive academic environment. If one or more of these factors is missing, student performance will be negatively affected. Previous research shows that these three factors are more likely to be present in high ability groups than in lower ones.

Several studies examine differences in the quantity and quality of instruction as a potential mechanism for creating and maintaining inequalities in student achievement (Gamoran & Berends, 1987; Hallinan, 1994; Oakes, 1985). Researchers have found that students in high ability groups tend to receive high-quality instruction from effective teachers, while their peers in lower ability groups are likely to be given a less interesting curriculum and inexperienced or ineffective instructors. This situation can create inequalities among students who might have performed equally well if they had been assigned to the same teacher and ability group (Alexander et al., 1978).

Eder (1981) points to the difficulty of teaching a class that is composed almost entirely of students who need extra help in a subject. When a class of students finds learning difficult, the number of disruptions and the general disorganization in the classroom increase. An ineffective teacher exacerbates this situation. These findings indicate that students in low ability groups are likely to receive less instruction than students in higher ability groups. Research also suggests that the quantity and quality of instruction may be higher in Catholic schools than in public schools. Hoffer et al. (1985) found that Catholic schools tend to assign students to rigorous academic courses, to require more semesters of academic course work for graduation, and to assign more homework than public schools. Students at all ability group levels, not only those in the high ability groups, benefit from these features of Catholic schools.

The second determinant of learning, student motivation, is also expected to vary by school sector. Teachers and parents influence student motivation through their expectations for student performance. Pallas, Entwisle, Alexander, and Stluka (1994) found that parents and teachers view students in high ability groups as more competent than those in lower ones. Differential expectations may lead teachers to treat students based on their ability group placement rather than on their academic performance. When low expectations are conveyed to students, their self-confidence diminishes and their motivation decreases.

All teachers, whether in public or Catholic schools, tend to have high expectations for the performance of students in high ability groups. However, teacher expectations for students in low ability groups may vary by school sector. Teachers in Catholic schools likely have a more positive view of the academic potential of students in low ability groups than teachers in public schools. Catholic school teachers see low group placement as a chance for students to improve rather than as a statement about the students' abilities (Gamoran, 1992). Catholic schools also profess a more egalitarian philosophy of learning than public schools. This attitude may help to mitigate some of the potentially negative effects of labeling and prevent a loss of student motivation (Camarena, 1990).

The third determinant of achievement is the learning climate of a classroom. Academic climate is formed by the norms that a teacher establishes for student performance as well as by the norms that students set for their behavior in the class. A strong academic climate is characterized by high standards for performance and by peer interactions that support achievement and high educational aspirations (Alexander & McGill, 1976). Research indicates that the strength of the academic climate decreases by ability group level. High ability groups tend to have a strong academic climate, while low ones have a weak academic climate.

While the high ability groups in both Catholic and public schools are likely to have strong academic climates, sector differences are expected in the academic climate of low ability groups. Research shows that low ability groups in public schools generally have a weak academic climate. However, this may not be the case in Catholic schools. The Catholic emphasis on academic achievement permeates the entire school, as does teacher determination that all students can and should learn. Moreover, the average student in a Catholic school is more likely to be exposed to peers who emphasize academic success and plan to attend college than the average public school student (Bryk et al., 1993). These factors suggest that ability groups at all levels in Catholic schools are likely to have a strong learning climate that fosters student achievement.

Assignment of Students to Ability Groups

The effect of ability group level on academic achievement highlights the importance of the process of assigning students to ability groups. If ability group level has an independent effect on student achievement, then it is critically important that students be assigned to the ability group that best facilitates their learning. Researchers have examined the assignment process to identify the criteria used by schools in making group placements. The findings show that schools vary in the criteria that they employ to determine ability group. As a result, not all schools are equally successful in making a good match between a student's learning needs and the learning opportunities provided by the group to which he or she is assigned.

When tracking was first implemented early in the twentieth century, educators relied on IQ tests to make group assignments. Viewing intelligence as a fixed and inheritable trait, they believed that intelligence tests accurately measured a student's ability to learn. As the concept of intelligence evolved, educators came to see intelligence as an aptitude for learning rather than as an innate trait. This new understanding led to a reliance on standardized tests of achievement rather than on IQ tests in making ability group assignments. Standardized achievement tests covered information that students were exposed to in school.

Over the course of the twentieth century, educators further broadened their view of intelligence. Today, intelligence is seen as a multifaceted and variable trait that includes thinking processes, knowledge structures, higher order thinking skills, and metacognitive strategies (Gardner, 1983; Stodolsky & Lesser, 1967). A student's ability to learn is no longer thought of as a fixed trait but rather as the result of his or her effort in interaction with opportunities to learn (Sorensen & Hallinan, 1986). This new understanding of intelligence has not precluded reliance on standardized tests to measure ability, but it has led to the inclusion of other academic criteria in making placement decisions. Moreover, a growing realization that standardized achievement tests may be culturally biased is reducing the paramount importance given to these tests in the past in assigning students to ability groups (Scarr & Weinberg, 1976). Most contemporary schools rely on some measure of student achievement in making decisions about curricular placement. Most frequently, they use either standardized achievement test scores or prior grades or both. Some schools also seek recommendations from teachers and counselors. Increasingly, schools take into account parent and especially student preferences. When several criteria are used in the placement decision, the homogeneity of ability groups is reduced, at least as measured by achievement test scores.

Critics of ability grouping argue that school officials use student demographic characteristics in deciding assignments. They point to research studies showing a disproportionate number of minority and economically disadvantaged students in low ability groups to support their claim. Descriptive data do show a high number of minority and low SES students in low ability groups. However, when student ability is controlled in multivariate analyses, the effects of race, ethnicity, and gender are markedly reduced or disappear.

Several studies of the assignment process in public schools reveal demographic effects on ability group assignment. In a study of six public high schools, Kubitschek and Hallinan (1996) found gender effects but no race effects on the assignment of students. Slight preference was given to females in the assignment to higher ability groups in English. Hallinan (1992) found that low SES, older, and female students are more likely to be assigned to lower groups in middle schools. Gamoran and Mare (1989) reported that after controlling for SES, African Americans and females are more likely to be assigned to college preparatory math courses than whites and males. They also showed that students with high SES are more likely to be assigned to high ability groups. Because African American students are disproportionately from low SES backgrounds, they may be underrepresented in high ability groups and overrepresented in low ones. Based on these and similar studies, Gamoran (1992) and Useem (1992) concluded that the influence of background characteristics, especially SES, on the assignment process in public schools is one of the ways that ability grouping perpetuates inequalities in learning opportunities.

Studies of the effect of student demographic characteristics on ability group assignment in Catholic schools are not available. However, case studies reveal the importance that Catholic school counselors attach to assigning all students to challenging courses (Bryk et al., 1993; Gamoran, 1992). This policy suggests that student race, ethnicity, and gender are unlikely to effect ability group placement. Similarly, the commitment of Catholic schools to social justice and equity would suggest that SES is not a factor in the assignment process.

Ideally, the process of assigning students to ability groups results in their placement at a level that is congruent with their capabilities. In practice, the assignment criteria used in some schools may make this goal difficult to achieve. In public schools, guidance counselors are primarily concerned that students meet graduation requirements. This is the first consideration in assigning students to courses. Once counselors ensure that students are taking courses on track for graduation, they rely on a variety of factors to make additional course determinations.

In public high schools, each counselor is typically responsible for assigning hundreds of students to courses in a short space of time. This heavy student load creates the need to make simple assignment rules to increase efficiency. Using quantitative criteria such as standardized test scores and grades enables the counselor to achieve this end. However, counselors occasionally seek teacher recommendations, especially in ambiguous cases or for political reasons. They also consider parental requests, though parents seldom make such requests. Finally, many counselors allow students to have input into placement decisions, both for required and elective courses. As a result, students whose test scores indicate that they belong at one group level may be placed at a different level to accommodate their preferences. Moreover, given the complexity of the public school course schedule, counselors occasionally have to assign students to a different course level or to a different course altogether, to avoid a scheduling conflict (Hallinan, 1991)

Catholic schools differ somewhat from public schools in the way that they assign students to ability groups. In Catholic schools, counselors are guided primarily by their goal of assigning students to the most academically challenging courses consistent with their abilities. Bryk et al. (1993) report that Catholic students in the 1980 HSB survey were twice as likely as public school students to be assigned to an academic track and twice as likely to have been placed in that track by a school official rather than selecting it themselves. They also found that the college aspirations of students in Catholic schools matched their course assignments better than those of students in public schools. Moreover, the data revealed that students who graduate from a Catholic elementary school and then attend a public high school are less likely to be assigned to an academic track than similar students who continue their Catholic education in a Catholic school. These findings demonstrate some of the ways in which ability grouping acts as a mechanism for raising student achievement in Catholic schools.

In an empirical study examining curricular assignments in one Catholic and four public high schools, Gamoran (1992) found that the Catholic school attached greater weight to the process of making ninth-grade ability group assignments than the public schools. The Catholic school assigned a teacher to act as an adviser and discuss course placements with the students and their parents. Interestingly, the recommendations of teachers from prior courses were emphasized less by the Catholic school advisers than they were in the public schools. This reduced the impact of students' eighth-grade group assignment on their ninth grade placement. Consistent with Bryk et al.'s (1993) analysis, Gamoran's research indicates that

Catholic schools attach considerable importance to the assignment process and use curricular structure to maximize learning opportunities for all students.

In a study of ability grouping in one Catholic and six public high schools, Hallinan (2002) found that the public school students in the ninth grade were more likely to be assigned to the Honors or Advanced ability groups than the Catholic school students. New analyses of these data presented here elaborate on this finding and reveal additional ways in which Catholic and public schools differ in the practice of ability grouping.

Table 5.1 presents the distribution of students across ability groups in two courses—English and Mathematics—for all the public and Catholic students in the ninth through twelfth grades in the study. The analysis includes only those students who were taking classes at their grade level. Table 5.1 shows that in English, a higher percentage of students were assigned to Honors or Advanced groups in the public schools than in the Catholic school at every grade level. In Mathematics, more public school students were placed in Honors and Advanced groups in tenth and twelfth grades than in the Catholic school. However, in ninth grade, fewer public school students were assigned to the Honors group than Catholic school students; and in eleventh grade, fewer public school students were assigned to the Honors and Advanced groups than in the Catholic school.

At the other end of the ability group hierarchy, Table 5.1 shows that a higher percentage of public school students were placed in the Basic English class in ninth and tenth grades than in the Catholic school. In eleventh and twelfth grades, only a small percentage in either school sector were in the Basic class. Similarly, in Mathematics, significantly more public school students were assigned to Basic Mathematics in ninth, tenth, and eleventh grades than in the Catholic school. No Basic Mathematics is offered in either sector in twelfth grade.

These results indicate that in the public schools, students are more widely distributed across ability group levels in English and in Mathematics than in the Catholic school. In English, and to a lesser extent in Mathematics, more public school students are assigned to Honors and Advanced groups than Catholic school students. This pattern suggests that public school administrators are trying to provide challenging courses for higher ability students. The relatively higher percentage of public school students assigned to the Basic and Very Basic courses compared to Catholic school students shows that a larger number of public school students are performing poorly in English and Mathematics. In the Catholic school, most students in both subjects are assigned to the Regular ability group. This finding is consistent with the Catholic school philosophy that all students can learn and should be offered a challenging curriculum. Catholic school teachers may see less of a need for Honors and Advanced groups than public schools since

Table 5.1. Distribution of Students across Ability Groups by School Sector and Grade for English and Mathematics

	English					Mathematics			
	Public (N=3632)		Catholic (N=432)			Public (N=3700)		Catholic (N=429)	
	9th						9th		
					Very Basic	930	25.1%	43	10.0%
Basic	527	14.5%	41	9.5%	Basic	819	22.1%	43	10.0%
Regular	1945	53.6%	273	63.2%	Regular	1205	32.6%	206	48.0%
Honors	981	27.0%	118	27.3%	Honors	520	14.1%	111	25.9%
Advanced	179	4.9%			Advanced	226	6.1%	26	6.1%
	Public (N=2928)		Catholic (N=422)			Public (N=2566)		Catholic (N=378)	
	10th						10th		
					Very Basic	431	16.8%		
Basic	225	7.7%	23	5.5%	Basic	549	21.4%	45	11.9%
Regular	1568	53.6%	286	67.8%	Regular	961	37.5%	262	69.3%
Honors	945	32.3%	113	26.8%	Honors	435	17.0%	71	18.8%
Advanced	190	6.5%			Advanced	190	7.4%		
	Public (N=2567)		Catholic (N=382)			Public (N=1360)		Catholic (N=343)	
	11th						11th		
Basic	113	4.4%	24	6.3%	Basic	236	17.4%	28	8.2%
Regular	1272	49.6%	295	77.2%	Regular	472	34.7%	98	28.6%
Honors	980	38.2%	63	16.5%	Honors	465	34.2%	155	45.2%
Advanced	202	7.9%			Advanced	187	13.8%	62	18.1%
	Public (N=2119)		Catholic (N=385)			Public (N=789)		Catholic (N=264)	
	12th						12th		
Basic	88	4.2%	27	7.0%					
Regular	1001	47.2%	327	84.9%	Regular	310	39.3%	115	43.6%
Honors	666	31.4%	31	8.1%	Honors	309	39.2%	91	34.5%
Advanced	364	17.2%			Advanced	170	21.5%	58	22.0%

in the Catholic school, the Regular group is given a curriculum that is sufficiently rigorous to engage high ability students. They also appear to be more reluctant to assign students to a Basic or Very Basic ability group lest they not be sufficiently challenged academically.

While Table 5.1 compared the distribution of students across ability groups in the six public and one Catholic school in the study, Table 5.2 examines the achievement of the public and Catholic school students across ability groups. The data are based on the results of a statewide standardized test given in the ninth grade to public and Catholic school students. Table 5.2 presents the means and standard deviations of the test scores obtained by the ninth grade students in the year they par-

Table 5.2. Means and Standard Deviations of Student Test Scores by Ability Group, School Sector, and Subject

	English					Mathematics			
	Public (N=2581)		Catholic (N=233)			Public (N=2574)		Catholic (N=233)	
	9th					9th			
Very Basic						29.6	(18.2)		
Basic	24.0	(14.4)	44.4	(14.4)	Basic	50.5	(18.9)	56.2	(17.7)
Regular	51.7	(18.5)	71.0	(15.6)	Regular	67.6	(17.6)	73.3	(16.3)
Honors	76.4	(15.0)	92.9	(5.6)	Honors	85.9	(10.6)	91.2	(8.6)
Advanced	89.8	(7.8)			Advanced	92.2	(9.0)	96.7	(3.3)
Total	57.9	(23.9)	74.1	(18.6)	Total	61.3	(25.7)	74.6	(20.7)
	Public (N=2470)		Catholic (N=233)			Public (N=2157)		Catholic (N=233)	
	10th					10th			
Very Basic						31.4	(16.9)		
Basic	24.1	(13.8)	43.4	(12.7)	Basic	47.5	(17.5)	54.2	(15.4)
Regular	48.1	(18.4)	69.2	(16.0)	Regular	65.5	(17.6)	75.7	(15.7)
Honors	74.6	(15.0)	92.1	(6.8)	Honors	85.7	(12.3)	96.0	(3.8)
Advanced	89.4	(8.4)			Advanced	92.9	(7.0)		
Total	57.9	(23.7)	74.7	(18.2)	Total	63.2	(24.6)	77.1	(18.1)

ticipated in the study, and by the tenth grade students who took the test the previous year. Omitted from the analysis are those students who did not take the test or who had missing information on other variables. These missing data explain the smaller sample reported in Table 5.2 as compared to Table 5.1.

Table 5.2 shows that Catholic school students are academically stronger than their public school counterparts at every corresponding ability group level in ninth and tenth grades in English and Mathematics. For example, the mean test score for the Catholic school in ninth grade Basic English is 44.4, compared to 24.0 in the public schools. The mean test score for Catholic school students in ninth grade Advanced Mathematics is 96.7, compared to 92.2 in the public schools.

Differences of this magnitude between Catholic and public school students at the same ability group level may be explained in terms of the higher overall achievement of Catholic school students. However, in multivariate analyses controlling for selection factors, and prior achievement in particular, Catholic school students continue to perform more successfully than public school students. This result suggests that it is more than ability differences that explain the Catholic school advantage. School practices and policies, such as the way that ability grouping is implemented, and the nature of the curriculum and level of instruction offered in various ability group levels, may account for at least some of the achievement differential between the two school sectors. Although Table 5.1 shows that public schools offer students high ability classes, Table 5.2 suggests that the Catholic school curriculum is more rigorous since it challenges students at all levels. The findings also suggest that ability group designations in the public schools are inflated, since courses that present the same curriculum are given a higher ability group label in the public schools than in the Catholic school.

Another way that Catholic and public schools differ is in the rate at which their students take courses to satisfy graduation requirements. All of the students in the study were required to take four years of English and two years of Mathematics to graduate. The most straightforward way for students to meet the English requirement would be to take one English course during each semester of high school. Table 5.3 reveals the extent to which Catholic and public school students follow this pattern. The data show that over 99 percent of the Catholic school students took an English course at their own grade level every semester. In contrast, 3 percent to 7 percent of the public school students enrolled in no English course during the semester when the data were collected. Unless these students take two English classes in some semester, take an English class during summer school, or take longer than four years to graduate, they will fail to earn a high school diploma.

While students have more leeway in scheduling their required Mathematics courses, almost all Catholic school students complete two years of Mathematics during their first two years of high school. Nearly 7 percent of public school students fail to do so. In other words, Catholic students are making steadier progress toward graduation than public school students by systematically meeting the graduation requirements.

Table 5.3 also shows a difference in the number of Mathematics courses that public and Catholic school students take. Even though only two years of Mathematics is required, 98 percent of the eleventh grade students and 84 percent of the twelfth graders in the Catholic school are enrolled in a Mathematics course. In contrast, 70 percent of the eleventh graders and less than half of the twelfth graders in the public schools are enrolled in a Mathematics course. These results reveal a striking difference between the two sectors in the emphasis placed on Mathematics education.

The way that schools schedule students for classes makes it possible for them to take courses above or below their grade level. For example, a ninth grade student could take a tenth-grade English class or a twelfth grade student could take an eleventh-grade Mathematics class. Table 5.3 shows that several public school students take classes out of grade sequence. In a few of these cases, students are accelerating in English or Mathematics. However, the majority of public school students who take a class out of sequence do so because they are failing to make satisfactory

Table 5.3. Distribution of Students across Ability Group Categories by School Sector and Grade in English and Mathematics

	English				Mathematics			
	Public (N=4128)		Catholic (N=435)		Public (N=4128)		Catholic (N=435)	
	9th				9th			
No class	224	5.4%	3	0.7%	260	6.3%	3	0.7%
Grade level ability grouped class	3632	88.0%	432	99.3%	3700	89.6%	429	98.6%
Off-grade level grouped class	272	6.6%	0	0%	168	4.1%	3	0.7%
	Public (N=3309)		Catholic (N=424)		Public (N=3309)		Catholic (N=424)	
	10th				10th			
No class	140	4.2%	2	0.5%	228	6.9%	2	0.5%
Grade level ability grouped class	2928	88.5%	422	99.5%	2566	77.5%	378	89.2%
Off-grade level grouped class	241	7.3%	0	0%	515	15.6%	44	10.4%
	Public (N=2758)		Catholic (N=384)		Public (N=2758)		Catholic (N=384)	
	11th				11th			
No class	88	3.2%	2	0.5%	836	30.3%	6	1.6%
Grade level ability grouped class	2567	93.1%	382	99.5%	1360	49.3%	343	89.3%
Off-grade level grouped class	103	3.7%	0	0%	562	20.4%	35	9.1%
	Public (N=2303)		Catholic (N=389)		Public (N=2303)		Catholic (N=389)	
	12th				12th			
No class	151	6.6%	2	0.5%	1281	55.6%	61	15.7%
Grade level ability grouped class	2119	92.0%	385	99.0%	789	34.3%	264	67.9%
Off-grade level grouped class	33	1.4%	2	0.5%	233	10.1%	64	16.5%

progress. For example, a ninth grader may fail too many courses to advance to tenth grade but may have passed ninth grade English, and thus be allowed to enroll in a tenth-grade English class.

Catholic school students, however, seldom take courses out of sequence. Typically, they pass all their required courses and move ahead together to the next academic level. If a Catholic school student does take a course out of sequence, he or she is usually pursuing extra courses in a subject of interest. For example, some Catholic school students take an additional Mathematics course in eleventh or twelfth grade, such as Calculus or Probability and Statistics. When students advance through their required courses in a systematic manner, they have the advantage of being able to depend on a stable course schedule from year to year. They also benefit from the communal identity that they form as a member of a grade cohort.

This empirical study demonstrates three ways that the assignment of students to ability groups differs across school sector. First, Catholic school students are more likely to be assigned to the Regular English and Mathematics ability groups than public school students. Public schools accommodate the greater diversity of student ability in their classrooms relative to Catholic schools by creating a more differentiated curriculum and assigning more students to higher and lower ability groups. Second, Catholic school students are more likely to be assigned to a lower group than public school students with similar test scores. This suggests, for example, that the Regular group in a Catholic school is comparable in curriculum content, instructional level, and student ability to the Honors group in a public school. This difference between group labeling in public and Catholic schools is important for guidance counselors to know if they are preparing course schedules for students who are transferring from one sector to another. College admissions officers also need to take this information into account when evaluating student transcripts. Third, the study shows that Catholic school students advance through high school in a more structured manner than public school students. The latter are more likely to take courses off sequence. Public school students also take significantly fewer English and Mathematics courses during high school than Catholic school students. The typically higher achievement levels of Catholic school students are likely influenced by these organizational differences.

School organization also affects the assignment of students to ability groups. Constraints imposed by school level variables can affect placement independent of student characteristics. Hallinan (1991) shows that the number of ability groups in high school tends to remain constant from year to year. This stability limits the capacity of the school to respond to the needs of incoming cohorts of students (Garet & DeLany, 1988). For example, enrollments may close, forcing students to take a less demanding course, or students may be assigned to a more advanced class than appropriate, to ensure that a school meets class size requirements. These structural constraints reduce the academic benefits of ability grouping.

Since Catholic schools tend to be smaller than public schools, they typically have fewer ability groups. Moreover, Catholic schools have a narrower range of achievement than public schools. A smaller number of ability groups and a narrow distribution of achievement make it easier for Catholic schools to assign appropriate group levels. Moreover, assigning a student to an inappropriate ability group is likely to have a smaller effect on student learning in Catholic schools because the achievement differences across ability groups are not as great as in public schools.

Interestingly, attending a Catholic school prior to enrolling in a public high school has an effect on ability group placement for those students entering high school. Hallinan (1991) shows that students who attended a Catholic school for eighth grade have a slightly higher probability of being assigned to an Honors group in English and Mathematics in ninth grade than their peers who attended a public school for eighth grade.

Mobility across Ability Groups

Ability group assignments are not necessarily permanent. Schools that permit students to change ability group levels, based on academic considerations, can correct initial placements that are discovered to be inappropriate and make accommodations for different learning rates. Flexibility in assignments also improves ability group homogeneity, since students can be reassigned to classes that suit them better. Several models have been proposed to describe the pattern of movement across ability groups. These models were formulated when tracking was still practiced, and they depict mobility across general, vocational, and academic tracks. However, the models are useful depictions of movement across academic ability groups as well.

Turner (1960) claimed that track change could be depicted either as a sponsored mobility model or a contest mobility model. Sponsored mobility occurs when students are selected early in their schooling to belong to an elite group and receive special opportunities and resources. Selected students remain in the elite group throughout their school careers. Contest mobility is based on merit and ability. Students are allowed to move upward and downward across ability groups depending on their performance. Turner argued that streaming in British schools fits a sponsored mobility model while a contest mobility model represents tracking in schools in the United States. However, Rosenbaum (1978) proposed a different model of track mobility. He suggested a tournament model where students who do well can advance to a higher track; if they do poorly, they move to a lower track and lose the opportunity for future upward mobility. Rosenbaum found some empirical support for this model.

Hallinan and Sørensen (1983) described mobility across ability groups as a vacancy competition. They claimed that students can move to a higher ability group only when a position becomes open, that is, only when another student exits from the group. When a position becomes available, the student ranking highest according to some set of criteria is offered the slot. Similarly, a student can move to a lower ability group only when a position becomes available. School characteristics such as class size, space, and teacher resources determine the rate of mobility. Other mobility models include Garet, Agnew, and DeLany's (1987) matching model, in which school officials and students make course assignments jointly. Schools determine which courses are offered and at what levels, and students choose from among these options. Mobility occurs, but it is constrained by the master schedule.

Barr and Dreeben (1983) suggested that a technical model describes ability group mobility, at least in elementary schools. Characteristics of ability groups, including number, size, and student composition, are determined by school personnel, based on distributional characteristics of the student population. Teachers can change the size of these groups, depending on the needs of students. The technical model allows for mobility according to student learning need. With the possible exception of the matching model, all these models are based on the assumption that mobility is motivated solely by academic goals.

These models of track and ability group mobility are ideal types. Whether a particular model is a reasonable representation of group mobility in a particular school depends on the assignment policy in that school. The theoretical models assume that mobility is based primarily on academic considerations and give less attention to the roles of student background and school organizational characteristics in placement decisions. Regardless of how well any given model fits in a particular school, all the models have heuristic value. Each one can assist schools in making explicit the rationale that they use for mobility decisions.

In a study of six public high schools, Hallinan (1996) found considerable mobility in English and Mathematics among students at all grade levels. Most changes in ability group assignments occurred at the beginning of a school year, although some took place during the year as well. Upward mobility was more common than downward mobility. This was due primarily to the fact that many students dropped a course or took it in summer school rather than moving to a lower ability group. Moreover, many students dropped out of school after tenth or eleventh grade, reducing the number who would move to a lower group. The study showed that the considerable amount of ability group mobility in the schools resulted in more homogeneous ability groups. The fact that many students assigned to lower groups were able to move to higher ones suggests that they were given opportunities to improve their skills in order to meet the prerequisites for more advanced courses.

Lucas and Good (2001) examined ability group mobility in the sophomore cohort of the HSB survey. They found considerable mobility across ability groups in the study, with more than half the students changing group levels between sophomore and senior year in both English and Mathematics. Students were more likely to move downward than upward in both English and Mathematics for all race, ethnicity, and SES categories. In both analyses, dropouts were excluded. Since many students moved to a lower group and subsequently returned to a higher one, the researchers reject the tournament model as a valid portrayal of mobility in these schools.

Hallinan (1994) found that Catholic school students in the study experienced less mobility across ability groups than public school students. Since great care was taken in the initial assignment of Catholic school students to ability groups, fewer incorrect assignments seemed to occur. Moreover, the achievement distribution in Catholic schools was narrower than in public schools, allowing for greater homogeneity in ability groups. This provided the opportunity to ensure a good fit between student capabilities and ability group level. In addition, Catholic school students in the study had fewer scheduling conflicts than public school students. When conflicts did arise, the counselor typically made course decisions based on academic considerations.

Ability group mobility generally is viewed as a positive policy, at least when change is designed to improve learning opportunities. When students in public schools change ability groups based on academic considerations, they are expected to improve their course work. In Catholic schools, ability group mobility is infrequent, though not due to rigidity in the assignment process. Rather, initial assignments in Catholic schools are made with such care that not many changes are necessary. When changes do occur, they appear to be made by school personnel in keeping with the school's high academic standards. Thus, the mobility process in Catholic schools serves to maintain and possibly increase the homogeneity of ability groups. In public schools, the wider distribution of student achievement makes more course adjustments necessary to maintain group homogeneity. However, when change for nonacademic reasons is permitted, group heterogeneity increases and learning opportunity may be reduced.

CONCLUSION

Ability grouping is a common and controversial practice found in most contemporary middle and secondary schools in the United States. Proponents claim that ability grouping facilitates learning by enabling teachers to tailor instruction to the aptitude of the students. Critics argue that ability grouping discriminates against minority and low SES students, thus creating inequities in their learning opportunities. In an effort to better understand how ability grouping affects student achievement, this chapter compares ability grouping in Catholic and public schools. Sector differences in the structure of ability groups, determinants of placement, and flexibility in assignments should explain the higher academic achievement of Catholic school students.

One significant difference between this practice in Catholic and public schools is seen in the distribution of students across ability groups. In Catholic schools, the large majority of students are deemed Regular, while in the public schools, students are distributed more equally across ability groups. Moreover, Catholic school students are typically assigned to a lower group than their public school counterparts who have the same measured ability. A student who would be placed in an Honors class in a public school would likely be assigned to a Regular class in a Catholic school.

These structural characteristics imply that the public and Catholic schools differ in the content of their curriculum. Low-achieving public school students are more likely than Catholic school students to be assigned to low ability groups, suggesting that they are offered a less demanding curriculum and weaker instruction. Higher ability public school students are more likely to be assigned to higher groups than their Catholic school counterparts. However, these students attain achievement scores that are no higher than those obtained by Catholic school students in the Regular ability group. This implies that the curriculum for the Regular students in a Catholic school is as rigorous or more so than the curriculum in an Honors or Advanced group in a public school. Catholic school students who take Honors and Advanced courses have higher achievement scores than those at the same group level in the public schools, which suggests that the curriculum for the Catholic school students is more difficult in these courses than in the public schools. In general, the research provides consistent evidence that students in Catholic schools, regardless of ability, are expected to succeed when they are offered a rigorous and challenging curriculum. Low-ability public school students have more opportunities to take less demanding courses, while high-ability public school students are offered fewer academic challenges than in Catholic schools.

Another difference is seen in the way that students are assigned to ability groups in the two school sectors. Catholic school teachers and counselors invest considerable time in making assignments before the beginning of an academic year. They rely primarily on quantitative measures of achievement, such as grades and standardized test scores, as well as on their familiarity with the students. As a result, subsequent change in placement is seldom needed. Public school counselors have more difficulty in assigning students to ability groups, due to the larger number of students whom they must schedule and the wider range of student ability. Moreover, public schools try to take into account parental preference and student choice as well as quantitative and qualitative measures of achievement. These factors lead to less accuracy in placement decisions, resulting in the need for more class changes over the course of the school year. These differences in the assignment process also result in the creation of more homogeneous ability groups in Catholic schools. As a result, the ability groups in Catholic schools more closely reflect the overall goal of ability grouping, which is to facilitate learning by matching student aptitude to curriculum level.

Some researchers claim that the higher achievement of Catholic school students is attributable to selection factors. Most Catholic high schools have rigorous admission standards. This results in an academically stronger student population. Moreover, students who attend Catholic schools are likely to have highly motivated parents who are willing to invest in their children's education and take an active interest in their progress.

While selection factors may play a role in the Catholic school advantage, it is not an adequate explanation of the higher achievement of Catholic school students. Research shows that even when background factors and ability are controlled, these students perform better than their public school counterparts at all ability group levels. Moreover, Catholic schools have been remarkably successful in improving the test scores of students in inner-city schools despite their weak academic backgrounds and poor preparation. As the research reported in this paper indicates, within school factors, such as the way that ability grouping is practiced, account for much of the success of Catholic school students. Furthermore, another factor that influences teaching and learning is the Catholic mission of service. This commitment leads to an inclusive school environment that supports and encourages all students to succeed academically, especially those who have special learning needs.

The aim of ability grouping is to provide students with a curriculum and pedagogy that offer a challenge commensurate with their capabilities. A comparison of the way that ability grouping is practiced in Catholic and public schools demonstrates features that directly link to student achievement. These features are not all necessarily related to school sector. All schools can take great care in the assignment of students to ability groups, in the provision of a challenging curriculum at all ability group levels, in holding high expectations for student performance regardless of ability, and in fostering a school environment that promotes and supports learning. Research holds the promise that the result would be higher achievement for all students.

Note

The authors gratefully acknowledge support for this research from the Institute for Educational Initiatives at the University of Notre Dame and from the U.S. Department of

Education, Grant # ED R215K010011A. We are also grateful to Warren Kubitschek for his assistance with the analyses.

References

Alexander, K. L., & Cook, M. (1982). Curricula coursework: A surprise ending to a familiar story. *American Sociological Review, 47,* 626–640.

Alexander, K. L., Cook, M., & McGill, E. L. (1978). Curriculum tracking and educational stratification: Some further evidence. *American Sociological Review, 43,* 47–66.

Alexander, K. L., & McGill, E. L. (1976). Selection and allocation within schools: Some causes and consequences of curriculum placement. *American Sociological Review, 41,* 963–980.

Barr, R., & Dreeben, R. (1983). *How schools work.* Chicago: University of Chicago Press.

Betts, J. R., & Shkolnik, J. L. (2000). The effects of ability grouping on student achievement and resource allocation in secondary schools. *Economics of Education Review, 19,* 1–15.

Braddock, J. H. (1981). The issue is still equality of educational opportunity. *Harvard Educational Review, 54,* 490–496.

Bryk, A. S., Lee, V. E., & Holland, P. B. (1993). *Catholic schools and the common good.* Cambridge, MA: Harvard University Press.

Camarena, M. (1990). Following the right track: A comparison of tracking practices in public and Catholic schools. In R. Page & L. Valli (Eds.), *Curriculum differentiation: Interpretive studies in U.S. secondary schools* (pp. 159–182). Albany: State University of New York Press.

Coleman, J. S., Campbell, E. Q., Hobson, C. J., McPartland, J., Mood, A. M., Weinfield, F. D., & York, R. L. (1966). *Equality of educational opportunity.* Washington, DC: U.S. Government Printing Office.

Coleman, J. S., Hoffer, T., & Kilgore, S. (1982). Cognitive outcomes in public and private schools. *Sociology of Education, 55,* 65–76.

Eder, D. (1981). Ability grouping as a self-fulfilling prophecy: A microanalysis of teacher-student interaction. *Sociology of Education, 54,* 151–161.

Figlio, D. N., & Page, M. E. (2002). School choice and the distributional effects of ability tracking: Does separation increase inequality? *Journal of Urban Economics, 51,* 497–514.

Gamoran, A. (1987). The stratification of high school learning opportunities. *Sociology of Education, 60,* 135–155.

Gamoran, A. (1992). Access to excellence: Assignment to honors English classes in the transition from middle to high school. *Educational Evaluation and Policy Analysis, 14,* 185–204.

Gamoran, A., & Berends, M. (1987). The effects of stratification in secondary schools: Synthesis of survey and ethnographic research. *Review of Educational Research, 57,* 415–435.

Gamoran, A., & Mare, R. (1989). Secondary school tracking and educational inequality: Compensation, reinforcement, or neutrality? *American Journal of Sociology, 94,* 1146–1183.

Gardner, H. (1983). *Frames of mind: The theory of multiple intelligences.* New York: Basic Books.

Garet, M. S., Agnew, J., & DeLany, B. (1987). *Moving through the system: Curriculum decision making in high schools*. Unpublished manuscript.

Garet, M. S., & DeLany, B. (1988). Students, courses, and stratification. *Sociology of Education, 61*, 61–77.

Goldberg, M. L., Passow, A. H., & Justman, J. (1966). *The effects of ability grouping*. New York: Teachers College Press.

Goldberger, A. S., & Cain, G. G. (1982). The causal analysis of cognitive outcomes in the Coleman, Hoffer, and Kilgore report. *Sociology of Education, 55*, 103–122.

Greeley, A. M. (1982). *Catholic high schools and minority students*. New Brunswick, NJ: Transaction Books.

Hallinan, M. T. (1991). School differences in tracking structures and assignments. *Journal of Research on Adolescence, 1*, 251–275.

Hallinan, M. T. (1992). The organization of students for instruction in middle school. *Sociology of Education, 65*, 114–127.

Hallinan, M. T. (1994). School differences in tracking effects on achievement. *Social Forces, 72*, 799–820.

Hallinan, M. T. (1996). Track mobility in secondary school. *Social Forces, 74*, 983–1002.

Hallinan, M. T. (2002). Catholic education as a societal institution. *Catholic Education: A Journal of Inquiry and Practice, 6* (1), 5–26.

Hallinan, M. T. (2003). Ability grouping and student learning. In D. Ravitch (Ed.), *Brookings papers on education policy, 2003* (pp. 95–140*)*. Washington, DC: Brookings Institution Press.

Hallinan, M. T., & Kubitschek, W. N. (1999). Curriculum differentiation and high school achievement. *Social Psychology of Education, 3*, 41–62.

Hallinan, M. T., & Sørensen, A. B. (1983). The formation and stability of instructional groups. *American Sociological Review, 48*, 838–851.

Hoffer, T., Greeley, A. M., & Coleman, J. S. (1985). Achievement growth in public and Catholic schools. *Sociology of Education, 58*, 74–97.

Kerckhoff, A. C. (1986). Effects of ability grouping in British secondary schools. *American Sociological Review, 51*, 842–858.

Kubitschek, W. N., & Hallinan, M. T. (1996). Race, gender, and inequity in track assignments. In A. Pallas (Ed.), *Research in sociology of education and socialization* (Vol. 11, pp. 121–146). Greenwich, CT: JAI Press.

Lucas, S. R. (1999). *Tracking inequality: Stratification and mobility in American high schools*. New York: Teachers College Press.

Lucas, S. R., & Good, A. D. (2001). Race, class, and tournament track mobility. *Sociology of Education, 74*, 139–156.

Mondale, S., & Patton, S. B. (Eds.). (2001). *School: The story of American public education*. Boston: Beacon Press.

Oakes, J. (1985). *Keeping track: How schools structure inequality*. New Haven, CT: Yale University Press.

Pallas, A. M., Entwisle, D. R., Alexander, K. L., & Stluka, M. F. (1994). Ability group effects: Instructional, social, or institutional? *Sociology of Education, 67,* 27–46.

Powell, A. G., Farrar, E., & Cohen, D. K. (1985). *The shopping mall high school.* Boston: Houghton Mifflin.

Rees, D. I., Brewer, D. J., & Argys, L. M. (2000). How should we measure the effect of ability grouping on student performance? *Economics of Education Review, 19,* 17–20.

Rosenbaum, J. E. (1978). The structure of opportunity in school. *Social Forces, 57,* 236–256.

Scarr, S., & Weinberg, R. A. (1976). IQ test performance of black children adopted by white families. *American Psychologist, 31,* 726–739.

Slavin, R. E. (1990). Achievement effects of ability grouping in secondary schools: A best-evidence synthesis. *Review of Educational Research, 60,* 471–499.

Sørensen, A. B., & Hallinan, M. T. (1986). The effects of ability grouping on growth in academic achievement. *American Educational Research Journal, 23,* 519–542.

Stodolsky, S., & Lesser, G. (1967). Learning patterns in the disadvantaged. *Harvard Educational Review, 37,* 546–593.

Turner, R. H. (1960). Sponsored and contest mobility and the school system. *American Sociological Review, 25,* 855–867.

Useem, E. L. (1992). Getting on the fast track in mathematics: School organizational influences on math track assignment. *American Journal of Education, 100,* 325–353.

6 | Student Learning

Sector Differences in Achievement Gains across
School Years and during the Summer

William Carbonaro

Prior studies of student learning in public and private high schools provide important insights into how school organization affects academic outcomes (Bryk, Lee, & Holland, 1993; Coleman & Hoffer, 1987; Gamoran, 1996). However, major gaps remain in our knowledge of sector differences in student learning. While sector differences in high school achievement have been studied, nothing is known about sector differences in elementary school achievement. In addition, no studies have examined whether summer learning varies among private and public school students. These gaps regarding sector differences in learning are important because they highlight our limited understanding of how school sector affects student outcomes.

The lack of studies of sector differences in student learning in elementary school makes it impossible to answer a key question regarding school sector and achievement: Can sector differences in student learning be generalized across the span of students' K-12 academic careers? There are two reasons why this question is critically important. First, it addresses the issue of how large sector differences are in student learning. Small differences at each grade level might add up to large differences in achievement over the course of a student's K-12 career. Second, the question of whether sector differences in learning can be generalized across grade levels has implications for theories that purportedly explain why school sector is important. Popular explanations for these differences fail to address whether the factors that they identify apply to elementary and middle schools as well as to secondary schools. If consistent private school advantages are found across all grade levels, these theories gain support. If not, they clearly require rethinking.

The lack of information on sector differences in *summer learning* also limits our understanding of how school sector and student learning are related. Students learn both when school is in session (from fall to spring) and when it is not (during the summer). If private school students enjoy greater achievement gains in the summer when compared with public school students, it is possible that prior studies have overestimated how much public and private schools contribute to sector differences in learning. By separating *in-school* learning from *out-of-school* learning, our understanding of how sector differences in school organization affect student achievement will be enhanced.

In this chapter, the Early Childhood Longitudinal Study (ECLS) is used to address both of these limitations in prior research. The results indicate that (1) sector differences in learning vary across grade levels; (2) summer learning rates vary by school sector; and (3) estimates of sector differences in learning that exclude summer learning deviate from those that include it. Implications for understanding how school sector affects student outcomes and future research in this area will be discussed.

Student Learning and School Sector: Variable Effects across Grade Levels

Most quantitative studies of sector differences have analyzed two nationally representative data sets: High School and Beyond (HS&B) (Zahs, Pedlow, Morrissey, Marnell, & Nichols, 1995) and the National Education Longitudinal Study of 1988 (NELS:88) (Ingels, Scott, Lindmark, Frankel, & Myers, 1992). Unfortunately, these data sets provide a truncated record of students' academic careers that focuses exclusively on secondary school. For example, HS&B researchers studied sector differences in student learning gains from the spring of tenth grade through the spring of twelfth grade (Bryk et al., 1993; Hoffer, Greeley, & Coleman, 1985). Studies of the NELS:88 data have examined sector differences in learning gains from (1) the spring of eighth grade through the spring of twelfth grade (Hoffer, 1998); (2) the spring of tenth grade through the spring of twelfth grade (Morgan, 2001; Morgan & Sørensen, 1999); and (3) the spring of eighth grade through the spring of tenth grade (Gamoran, 1996). By focusing on only high school learning and estimating sector differences in learning across two or more grades at once, the true relationship between school sector and student learning may be distorted.

In studies using HS&B and NELS:88, sector differences in gains across grades were assumed to be continuous and linear. However, it is possible that observed sector effects on learning differed across academic years. Studies of the NELS:88 data suggest that sector effects vary depending upon how gains are measured. Hoffer (1998) found a Catholic school advantage in all four NELS:88 tests when examining eighth to twelfth grade gains, but Gamoran (1996) saw gains only in reading and math, both of which were statistically insignificant after controlling for differences in the composition of the student body. This inconsistency across studies suggests that sector differences in learning may be less important early in students' high school careers but increase in importance toward the end of high school.

Figure 6.1 provides a hypothetical illustration of the limitation inherent in measuring student gains across grade levels. In this example, gains in learning are estimated by using the spring tenth and twelfth grade tests. By estimating the sector differences in gains at these two time points, we see that the hypothetical results are consistent with the findings of prior research: Private school students enjoy greater academic gains between the first and second time points. The main limitation in this analysis is that student learning in the spring of eleventh grade is unobserved. Consequently, it is impossible to discern whether sector differences among

Figure 6.1. Hypothetical Sector Differences in Achievement Gains with Constant and Varying Effects of School Sector across Grade Levels

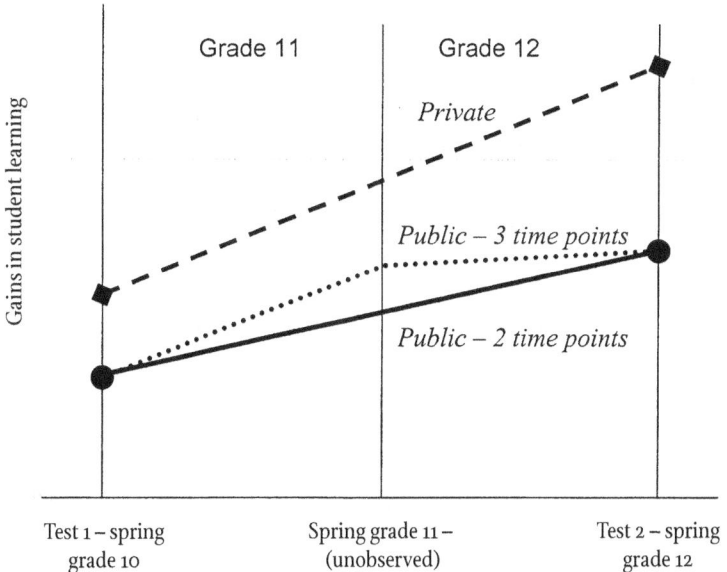

students are present in both grade levels, or whether they apply to only one academic year but not the other. For example, let us assume that the gains for private school students are equal in eleventh and twelfth grades. The dotted line in Figure 6.1 represents one possible pattern for public school gains. As the figure demonstrates, learning gains in the two sectors are equal in eleventh grade but diverge in twelfth grade, where public school students fall behind private school students. While this is a hypothetical example, it is not implausible to think that sector differences in gains might be isolated to twelfth grade. Since more students in private schools attend four-year colleges (when compared with public school students), it is possible that the twelfth grade curriculum is academically more rigorous in private high schools than in public high schools.

One key issue raised by the hypothetical example from Figure 6.1 echoes an important question raised by Jencks (1985) in his evaluation of the recent research on school sector: Are the differences in gains across sector in the last two years of high school also present throughout the full range of students' academic careers? If the differences in student gains across sectors are present throughout students' careers, the overall magnitude of the effects of school sector might be substantial.

In addition, and perhaps more important, consistent sector differences across students' academic careers might suggest that there are some fundamental sector differences in school organization that make private schools more effective than public schools. Numerous studies suggest that sector differences in high school learning are due to sector differences in learning opportunities (Bryk et al., 1993; Gamoran, 1992, 1993). Bryk et al. argue that Catholic high schools provide superior learning opportunities for students because they are *communally organized* and less bureaucratic than public schools, due to a pervasive ethic of caring. In a slightly different vein, Chubb and Moe (1990) believe that private schools are generally more effective in providing instruction for students because market forces require them to be accountable to consumers (i.e., parents).

Neither explanation for why private schools provide better learning opportunities specifically addresses the issue of whether sector effects are found equally in elementary, middle, and secondary schools. Regardless, if consistent sector differences in gains across grade levels are observed, both seem to be plausible preliminary explanations for such differences. However, if consistent sector differences in gains across grade levels are not observed, then questions regarding these explanations should be raised since there is no reason to suspect that private/Catholic elementary schools are less communally organized or more bureaucratic than private/Catholic high schools. Instead, sector differences in learning might reflect idiosyncratic differences in curriculum offerings, expectations for students, or other factors that do not reflect students' K-12 academic careers.

Summer Learning and Sector Effects

Prior research on student learning suggests that academic gains are not restricted to the time that students spend in school. Students continue learning during the summer months (albeit at a slower rate) when school is not in session (Entwisle, Alexander, & Olson, 1997; Heyns, 1978). One of the most interesting findings regarding summer learning pertains to socioeconomic and racial differences. During the school year, socioeconomic status (SES) does not predict student gains in achievement (Entwisle et al., 1997; Heyns, 1978). For example, Entwisle et al. found that high SES and low SES students gained the same amount in math and nearly the same in reading during elementary school. However, during the summer months, students with high SES continued to show impressive gains in both reading and math, while students with low SES failed to show gains in either subject. This pattern also applies to comparisons of black and white students, although the results are somewhat more pronounced when examining family background (Heyns, 2002).

Figure 6.2. Hypothetical Sector Differences in Achievement Gains with Constant and Varying Effects of School Sector across Summers

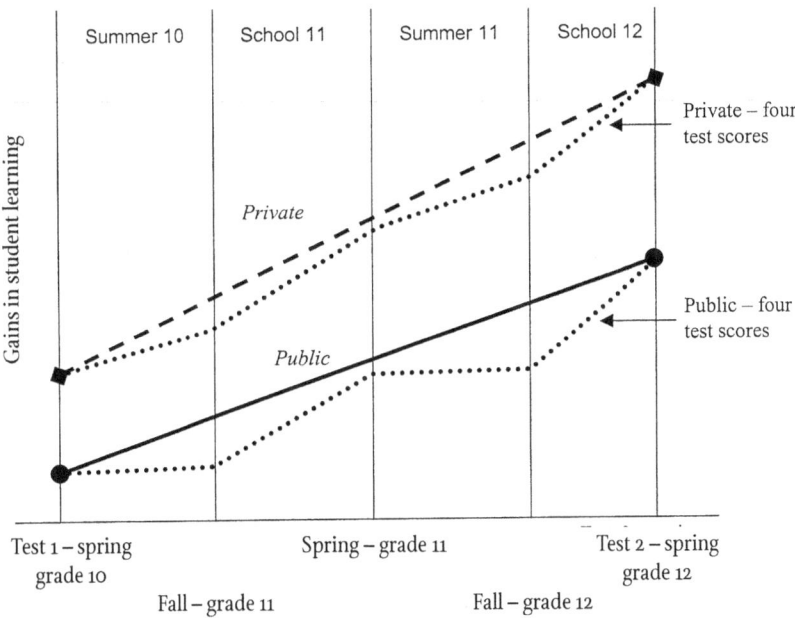

These findings regarding summer learning raise an important issue for studies of sector differences in student learning. One significant difference among private and public schools involves the SES of students attending these different schools: On average, students in private schools come from families with a higher SES and are more likely to be white than those attending public schools (Bryk et al., 1993; Coleman, Hoffer, & Kilgore, 1982). Since families with a higher SES are more likely to engage in practices that promote student gains during the summer (Lareau, 2000), students attending private schools might experience greater learning gains during the summer months when compared with public school students.

How might public-private differences in summer learning affect estimates of sector differences in student learning? Figure 6.2 displays another hypothetical example to illustrate the potential problem. As in Figure 6.1, the example in Figure 6.2 examines the last two years in high school. Unlike Figure 6.1, where the data are divided into academic years, Figure 6.2 further divides the data into both academic years and summers. Doing so emphasizes that two summers and two school years are nested between the spring of tenth and twelfth grade. The solid and dashed lines represent the divergence in gains by school sector that prior studies of sector effects have documented. The dotted lines below each of these represent a hypothetical series of gains if test scores were available at all four time points. In Figure 6.2, eleventh and twelfth grade gains during the school year are assumed equal across school sector; however, summer gains are allowed to differ across sectors, so that public school students have no net gain during the summer, but private school students have a positive net gain that is smaller than gains made during the school year.

The two sets of lines tell very different stories. The first set indicates that private school students outgain public school students in the time between the end of tenth and the end of twelfth grade. Scholars have interpreted these effects to be related to students' experiences within school. However, the second set of lines that accounts for summer learning reveals that students are learning at similar rates across sector when they are in school. The difference in the initial set of lines is due entirely to differences in rates of summer learning. The hypothetical example in Figure 6.2 assumes stark differences across sector that may or may not reflect reality in order to forcefully convey an important point: Prior studies showing sector differences in learning do not provide direct evidence that sector differences in student gains reflect different rates of learning while children are in school.

Given that prior studies of school sector control for student SES and race, it is possible that any sector differences in summer learning are purged from the estimates of sector differences in learning. However, since SES serves as a proxy for behaviors that families use to enhance summer learning, differences in such behaviors across sector may still remain when controlling for SES. Unlike the regression approach, which always risks this type of omitted variable bias, estimates of sector differences that isolate learning during the summer provide a superior way of examining this issue because they focus solely on learning that occurs during the school year.

Data

Data analyzed in this study came from the kindergarten and first grade samples of ECLS, a nationally representative sample of 21,000 students, and their parents, and teachers. In kindergarten, the students were assessed in both the fall and spring. In first grade, 25 percent of the students from the longitudinal cohort were randomly selected for assessment in the fall, while the full longitudinal cohort was tested in the spring. The ECLS sampling design is ideally suited for the questions raised in this study because (1) it allows data from early in students' school careers to be analyzed; (2) it enables gains in learning to be estimated separately by school years; and (3) it allows estimates of summer learning to be isolated from achievement gains during the school year.

Analytical Sample

Five samples, described in Figure 6.3, are used in the analyses that follow. Each sample corresponds to a specific set of learning gains: For example, the first sample (Model 1) includes students with test scores from the fall and spring of kindergarten. As described in the methods section of this chapter, each sample

Figure 6.3. Five Estimates of Student Learning Gains

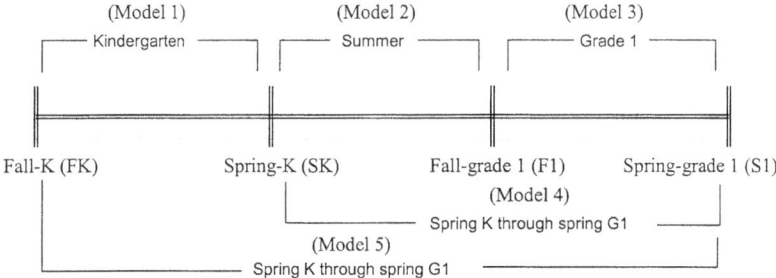

provides distinct estimates of sector effects in student learning. Since ECLS employs a longitudinal design, there is an overlap in students across samples.

The five samples are constructed by using listwise deletion based on the test scores that define each cohort. The sample sizes differ markedly because the first-grade fall sample is only one-quarter the size of the other three sample waves. Normally, attrition from a sample of this magnitude would be very problematic. However, since the fall first-grade test sample is a random subsample of the larger one, listwise deletion will not bias the results. Inspection of the data revealed that there was no difference in fall kindergarten (FK), spring kindergarten (SK), and spring first-grade (S1) test scores for students who were included in the fall first-grade (F1) cohort and those who were not. In addition, there were no differences in the basic demographic composition of the students who were included in the F1 sample and those who were not. Hence, in this case, listwise deletion provides unbiased estimates that maximize the statistical power of the analytical models for each sample.

Dependent Variables

In order to examine gains in student learning, gain scores for each subject (reading, math, and general knowledge) were created to serve as the dependent variables in the analyses. For example, when examining kindergarten gains in math, the FK score was subtracted from the SK score, and this difference served as the dependent variable in the analysis. Means and standard deviations for these gain scores are provided in Table 6.1.

Independent Variables

Standard controls for students' background characteristics, such as gender, race/ethnicity, and socioeconomic status, were used in the analyses. Additional controls for family background included whether students' families are intact (i.e., whether children live with both of their biological parents), their mother's age at first child's birth, the number of siblings, and whether English is their first language. For analyses that included a kindergarten assessment, a dummy variable indicating whether a student attended an all-day program was included as a predictor of learning gains. Students in full-day kindergarten learn more than those attending a half-day program, and, more important, full-day attendance varies across school sector (Carbonaro, 2002). In addition, the students' age at their initial assessment as well as the number of weeks between the assessments served as additional controls in the analyses. Students who had more time between their fall and

Table 6.1. Means and Standard Deviations for Selected Variables Used in the Multivariate Analyses

Dependent Variables	Mean
Reading gains	
FK-SK (kindergarten)	10.22
	(6.35)
SK-F1 (summer)	5.28
	(5.52)
F1-S1 (grade one)	17.24
	(8.16)
SK-S1	22.82
	(8.98)
FK-S1	33.07
	(10.34)
Math gains	
FK-SK (kindergarten)	8.08
	(5.00)
SK-F1 (summer)	4.98
	(5.06)
F1-S1 (grade one)	10.61
	(5.69)
SK-S1	15.55
	(6.11)
FK-S1	23.61
	(6.61)
General knowledge gains	
FK-SK (kindergarten)	5.10
	(4.04)
SK-F1 (summer)	2.96
	(3.86)
F1-S1 (grade one)	4.79
	(4.00)
SK-S1	7.51
	(4.39)
FK-S1	12.55
	(4.83)

Independent Variables	Mean
Reading scores	
Fall kindergarten (FK)	23.25
	(8.79)
Spring kindergarten (SK)	33.29
	(10.99)
Fall grade one (F1)	38.84
	(12.96)
Spring grade one (S1)	55.80
	(13.83)

Table 6.1. Means and Standard Deviations for Selected Variables Used in the Multivariate Analyses (*cont.*)

Independent Variables	Mean
Math scores	
Fall kindergarten (FK)	19.83
	(7.25)
Spring kindergarten (SK)	27.85
	(8.76)
Fall grade one (F1)	32.80
	(9.55)
Spring grade one (S1)	43.37
	(9.18)
General knowledge scores	
Fall kindergarten (FK)	22.52
	(7.51)
Spring kindergarten (SK)	27.27
	(7.85)
Fall grade one (F1)	30.22
	(7.94)
Spring grade one (S1)	34.40
	(7.68)
School sector	
Kindergarten	
Public (omitted)	.79
Catholic	.11
Private, secular	.06
Other religious	.04
Grade one	
Public (omitted)	.82
Catholic	.11
Private, secular	.05
Other religious	.02
Kindergarten and grade one	
Public (omitted)	.79
Catholic	.11
Private, secular	.05
Other religious	.02
Some other combination	.03

Note: Standard deviations are in parentheses.

spring assessments were undoubtedly exposed to more instruction than students with less time between assessments, and hence they were more likely to have greater achievement gains. Finally, students' initial test scores in reading, math, and general knowledge were included as predictors of learning gains. (Means and standard deviations for these variables are provided in Table 6.1.) For example, when looking at summer learning, the three test scores from the spring (not fall) of kindergarten were added as controls in the models. Together, this full array of controls should account for any student differences across sectors that might account for sector differences in learning gains over time.

Indicators of school sector divided students into four groups: public; Catholic; private, secular; and private, other religious (i.e., non-Catholic). (Percentage breakdowns for each cohort are provided in Table 6.1.) It is likely that private, secular and private, other religious schools are more heterogeneous categories than public or Catholic. However, there is sufficient homogeneity within the four categories to make each a coherent one that is distinct from the others. Information regarding school sector was collected during each of the four survey waves. The sector variables for the kindergarten and first grade samples were created from the spring reports, since the fall reports were available only for one-fourth of the first graders. Some students attended schools in different sectors for kindergarten and first grade. These changes were easily accommodated in the models that assessed kindergarten and first grade gains separately—separate measures in each year allowed the students' school sector to vary across kindergarten and first grade. However, difficulties emerged with the summer and cross-grade-level models. For the summer learning models, the first grade report of school sector was used because any summer learning effects in the cross-grade-level models should show up as a sector difference that is interpreted as a first grade gain. For the cross-grade-level analyses, separate dummies to denote students who switched and the nature of the switch (e.g., public-K to private-G1, private-K to public-G1, and mixed private sector) were created and added as controls in the analyses. (Since I have no strong theory regarding the effects of switching and the coefficients for these variables were significant in only a few cases, the coefficients for these variables were not included in the tables.)

Methods

The major goal of this study is to estimate sector differences in learning gains during kindergarten, first grade, and the summer between them. A summary description of the models used in the analyses is displayed in Figure 6.3. This figure describes five estimates of gains in student learning: (1) gains during kindergarten (FK-SK); (2) gains during the summer between kindergarten and first grade (SK-F1); (3) gains during first grade (F1-S1); (4) gains from the spring of kindergarten to the spring of first grade (SK-S1); and (5) gains from fall kindergarten to spring of first grade test scores (FK-S1). Models 1 and 3 provide estimates of sector effects by grade level, and Model 2 provides estimates of sector effects on summer learning. The results from Models 1 through 3 are then compared with the results from Models 4 and 5 to examine whether separate estimates of learning by grade level and summer learning suggest different estimates of sector effects than the conventional models, where gains were estimated across grade levels and summer recess.

These five models are applied to the three outcomes of interest: growth in student learning in reading, math, and general knowledge. Design effects from the ECLS sample will be corrected by using information about the sampling strata and primary sampling unit (PSU) in combination with the survey command in Stata (see StataCorp, 1999).

Results

Do Sector Differences in Student Gains Vary across Grade Levels?

The first set of analyses examined whether sector differences in learning gains vary by grade level. By examining fall to spring gains for kindergarten and first grade, it is possible to see whether both the magnitude and direction of any sector effects vary by grade level. Table 6.2 displays the unadjusted learning gains for kindergarten and first grade in reading, math, and general knowledge. These models use gain scores as the outcome, and dummy variables for school sector are the only controls. Thus, the models examine sector differences in achievement growth (not achievement levels). Differences in prior achievement among students across sectors were accounted for in the unadjusted models, but sector differences in other factors that are related to achievement gains were unaccounted for in the model. Table 6.3 shows the significant differences displayed in Table 6.2 as percentage differences from the average gain for a public school student. For example, a 10 percent advantage (+10%) for private, secular school students in reading indicates that, on average, these students gain 10 percent more than public school students in that subject for that academic year.

The intercepts in Table 6.2 are the public school gains. The nonpublic dummy variables indicate whether the gains in a given sector are significantly different from the average public school gain. Public school gains in both kindergarten and first grade are quite large. Public school students are learning one standard deviation or more in both kindergarten and first grade.

Table 6.2. Unadjusted Gains across School Sector

School Sector	Kindergarten (1)	Summer (2)	1st Grade (3)	SK-S1 (4)	FK-S1 (5)
			Reading skills		
Intercept (public)	10.117***	5.088***	17.397***	22.691***	32.802***
Catholic	.284	.547*	1.280**	.438*	.941**
Private, secular	1.003***	1.596***	2.238***	2.628***	3.624***
Other religious	.349	.715	-4.009***	-2.264***	-1.510**
			Math skills		
Intercept (public)	8.004***	4.989***	10.952***	15.759***	23.721***
Catholic	.292*	.361	-1.101***	-.839***	-.670***
Private, secular	.879***	-.327	-.196	-.706**	.388
Other religious	-.108	-.583	-3.312***	-2.870***	-2.750***
			General knowledge		
Intercept (public)	5.137***	2.971***	4.877***	7.618***	12.677***
Catholic	-.030	-.302	-.321	-.545***	-.601***
Private, secular	-.303*	.676**	-.073	-.224**	-.559**
Other religious	-.170	-.716*	-1.152**	-1.189***	-1.264***

*$p < .05$; **$p < .01$; ***$p < .001$

Table 6.3. Sector Differences in Unadjusted Gains as a Percentage of Public School Gains

School Sector	Kindergarten (1)	Summer (2)	1st Grade (3)	SK-S1 (4)	FK-S1 (5)
			Reading skills		
Catholic		+10.8%*	+7.4%**	+1.9%*	+2.9%**
Private, secular	+10.0%***	+31.4%***	+9.9%***	+11.6%***	+11.0%***
Other religious			-23.0%***	-10.0%***	-4.6%**
			Math skills		
Catholic	+3.7%*		-10.0%***	-5.3%***	-2.8%***
Private, secular	+11.0%***			-4.4%**	
Other religious			-30.2%***	-18.2%***	-11.6%***
			General knowledge		
Catholic				-7.1%***	-4.7%***
Private, secular	-5.8%*	+22.7%**		-2.9%**	-4.4%**
Other religious		-24.1%*	-23.6%**	-15.6%***	-10.0%***

Note: Blank cells in the table indicate that the coefficient was not statistically significant at the .05 level.
*$p < .05$; **$p < .01$; ***$p < .001$

The results indicate that there are significant sector effects in learning gains, but these gains vary both by grade level and by academic subject. When comparing Catholic and public school students, Catholic school students enjoy greater learning gains in first grade reading and kindergarten math; however, public school students have greater gains in first grade math. Gains are the same among Catholic and public school students in general knowledge for both academic years. Private, secular school students outperform public students by roughly 10 percent in reading for both kindergarten and first grade. However, the private school advantage in math gains is limited to kindergarten. In general knowledge, public school students outperform private school students in kindergarten but hold no advantage in first grade. Finally, for private, other religious school students, the pattern is consistent across all three academic subjects: In kindergarten, achievement gains are the same among public and other religious school students, but in first grade, achievement gains for other religious school students are anywhere from 23 percent to 30 percent less than those enjoyed by public school students.

While the unadjusted models provide some sense as to how gains vary across sector and across grade levels, it is possible that sector differences among students rather than sector differences in schooling account for the observed differences in gains across sector. To eliminate such differences, controls for differences in student background characteristics such as SES, race, gender, and initial academic achievement were included as predictors of learning gains. The results of these analyses are reported in Tables 6.4 and 6.5.

Overall, sector differences in adjusted gains were slightly different than the sector differences in unadjusted gains displayed in Tables 6.2 and 6.3. For Catholic school students, the positive effect in first grade reading remains, but there is now a significant negative effect in kindergarten reading. Also, the negative effect in first grade math gains is no longer significant in the adjusted models, but the positive math unadjusted gains in kindergarten become negative in the adjusted model. For private, secular schools, the positive effect in reading during kindergarten is no longer significant, but the other effects observed in the unadjusted models remain significant (although the magnitude of the effects differs). Finally, for private, other religious schools, negative effects now appear in reading and math in kindergarten. A substantial proportion of the other religious school gap in unadjusted gains is explained by background factors: For reading and math, the negative adjusted public-other religious differences in gains decrease by roughly 60 percent and 50 percent, respectively. Despite these differences between the adjusted and unadjusted models, there is enough agreement between the two sets to conclude that both the magnitude and direction of the relationships between school sector and learning gains differ from kindergarten through first grade.

Does Summer Learning Vary across School Sector?

While the results from Tables 6.2 through 6.5 indicate that some sector differences in learning gains are present during the school year, the question remains: Are sector differences in summer learning present as well? Tables 6.2 and 6.3 show differences in unadjusted summer gains across school sector (see column 2). Catholic school students gain roughly 11 percent more in reading during the summer than public school students. However, public and Catholic school summer gains do not differ in math and general knowledge. Private, secular school students have even more impressive summer gains: Compared with public school students, private, secular school students gain 31.4 percent and 22.7 percent more in reading and general knowledge, respectively. In contrast, private, other religious school students have the same gains as public school students in reading and math, but actually gain 24 percent less in general knowledge during the summer than public school students.

Table 6.4. Adjusted Gains across School Sector

School Sector	Kindergarten (1)	Summer (2)	1st Grade (3)	SK-S1 (4)	FK-S1 (5)
			Reading skills		
Intercept (public)	8.074***	-4.990***	18.592***	10.819***	20.947***
Catholic	-.565**	.017	1.144**	-.286	-.616**
Private, secular	.296	1.063**	2.816***	1.532***	1.826***
Other religious	-.670*	-.679	-1.706*	-3.247***	-3.740***
			Math skills		
Intercept (public)	3.627***	-2.608	11.360***	11.649***	17.501***
Catholic	-.286*	.290	-.231	-.681***	-.928***
Private, secular	.366*	-.486	.147	-.152	-.021
Other religious	-.841***	-1.034*	-1.644**	-2.688***	-3.181***
			General knowledge		
Intercept (public)	5.249***	3.573***	7.877***	10.206***	13.967***
Catholic	-.061	-.052	.239	-.078	-.165
Private, secular	-.327*	.301	.097	-.030	-.299
Other religious	-.260	-1.015**	-1.160**	-.918***	-.941***

Note: Controls for race, gender, SES, whether the student came from an intact family, whether English was the first language spoken in the home, the age at which the mother first gave birth, the number of siblings in the household, the child's age at the first time point for the gain score, and the elapsed time in weeks between the two time points used to create the gain score are included as predictors of learning gains in all of the models in the table.
*$p < .05$; **$p < .01$; ***$p < .001$

The adjusted scores are especially revealing when examining summer learning, because SES and the home environment play a larger role in affecting achievement gains when school is not in session (Heyns, 2002). In addition, if the summer sector effects disappear after controlling for student background characteristics, conventional models that measure student gains across summers may not bias estimates of sector effects. If the sector differences in summer gains remain significant in the adjusted models, the possibility remains that the conventional measures of sector effects might be biased.

The adjusted models (see column 2 in Tables 6.4 and 6.5) indicate that sector differences in summer learning are still present during the summer even after controlling for student background characteristics. The positive Catholic school effect in reading is no longer significant in the adjusted model. The private, secular effect on reading remains significant, but the magnitude of the relationship is reduced by roughly one-third. However, the positive private, secular school effect in general knowledge observed in the unadjusted model is no longer significant in the adjusted model. Finally, the gap in summer learning between public and other school students in general knowledge remains significant and grows larger in the ad-

Table 6.5. Sector Differences in Adjusted Gains as a Percentage of Public School Gains

School Sector	Kindergarten (1)	Summer (2)	1st Grade (3)	SK-S1 (4)	FK-S1 (5)
			Reading skills		
Catholic	-5.6%*		+6.5%**		+1.8%**
Private, secular		+20.8%***	+16.1%***	+6.8%***	+5.5%***
Other religious	-6.6%*		-9.8%***	-14.3%***	-11.4%***
			Math skills		
Catholic	-3.5%*			-4.3%***	-3.9%***
Private, secular	+4.6%*				
Other religious	-10.5%**	-20.7%*	-15.0%***	-17.1%***	-13.4%***
			General knowledge		
Catholic					
Private, secular	-6.3%*				
Other religious		-34.2%**	-23.7%*	-12.1%***	-7.4%***

Note: Controls for race, gender, SES, whether the student came from an intact family, whether English was the first language spoken in the home, the age at which the mother first gave birth, the number of siblings in the household, the child's age at the first time point for the gain score, and the elapsed time in weeks between the two time points used to create the gain score are included as predictors of learning gains in all of the models in the table.
*$p < .05$; **$p < .01$; ***$p < .001$

justed model. In addition, a statistically significant negative effect on summer learning emerges in math for private, other religious school students in the adjusted model.

When sector differences in summer learning are compared with sector differences during the school year, two conclusions can be drawn. First, sector differences in summer learning are less common than sector effects during the school year (see Table 6.5). Second, when sector effects are present during the summer, they are larger in magnitude than the sector differences in learning gains during the school year. The larger sector differences in the summer suggest that the out-of-school environments of students in different sectors are more unequal than the learning environments that they encounter during the school year.

Are Conventional Estimates of Sector Effects Biased?

The analyses previously discussed lead to two conclusions: (1) sector effects differ in significance and magnitude in kindergarten and first grade; and (2) summer learning varies significantly across school sector. One important question remains unanswered: Do conventional measures of sector effects (i.e., those that are estimated across grade levels and summers) lead to different conclusions about sector differences in student learning than the *revised* estimates account for in these differences by grade level and in summer learning? By comparing the conventional and revised estimates of sector effects, it is possible to identify whether the failure to account for sector differences in learning by grade level and during the summer distort our understanding of how student learning varies across school sector.

First, do estimates of sector differences in yearly gains differ from estimates of gains that combine academic years? To answer this question, kindergarten and first grade gains were compared with gains combining academic years. In Tables 6.2 and 6.3, unadjusted gain scores in columns 1 (kindergarten) and 3 (first grade) were compared with those in columns 4 (gains spanning the spring of kindergarten through the spring of first grade) and 5 (gains spanning the fall of kindergarten through the spring of first grade). The results indicate that the different sets of estimates lead to different conclusions about sector effects. For example, in reading, Catholic school students enjoy greater gains relative to public school students in first grade, but not in kindergarten. The conventional estimates of the Catholic school effect in reading are significant, but notably smaller in magnitude than the estimate of first-grade reading gains. For private, other religious schools, the conventional gains displayed in columns 4 and 5 are smaller than those of public school students, but the differences are much less pronounced when compared with the gains that are specific to kindergarten and first grade. The adjusted models tell a similar story (with some slight differences), and the overall conclusion is the same: Sector differences in gains computed across academic years overlook important differences in sector effects from year to year.

Table 6.6 summarizes the discrepancies in sector differences in gains by grade level. The coefficients in Tables 6.2 and 6.4 are removed in Table 6.6 and replaced

Table 6.6. Differences in Estimates of Sector Effects across Models

		Seasonal Gains			Combined Years		Consistency in Results?
				Unadjusted gains			
Sector	Subject	FK-SK	SK-F1	F1-S1	SK-S1	FK-S1	
Catholic	Reading	o	+	++	+	++	No
	Math	+	o	---	---	---	No
	G.K.	o	o	o	---	---	No
Private, secular	Reading	+++	+++	+++	+++	+++	Yes
	Math	+++	o	o	--	o	No
	G.K.	-	++	o	--	--	No
Other religious	Reading	o	o	---	---	--	No
	Math	o	o	---	---	---	No
	G.K.	o	-	--	---	---	No
				Adjusted gains			
Sector	Subject	FK-SK	SK-F1	F1-S1	SK-S1	FK-S1	
Catholic	Reading	-	o	++	o	++	No
	Math	-	o	o	---	---	No
	G.K.	o	o	o	o	o	Yes
Private, secular	Reading	o	+++	+++	+++	+++	No
	Math	+	o	o	o	o	No
	G.K.	-	o	o	o	o	No
Other religious	Reading	-	o	---	---	---	Yes
	Math	--	-	---	---	---	Yes
	G.K.	o	--	-	---	---	No

Note: The information in this table is derived entirely from the results displayed in Tables 6.2 and 6.4. A "+," "++," or "+++" sign indicates a statistically significant effect at the .05, .01, and .001 levels (respectively). A "-," "--," or "---" sign indicates a statistically significant effect at the .05, .01, and .001 levels (respectively). A "o" indicates that the sector effect is not statistically significant at the .05 level. "Yes" indicates that there is a statistically significant coefficient at the .05 level, with matching signs in the FK-SK, F1-S1, and either SK-S1 or FK-S1. "No" indicates that these conditions are not met. "G.K." refers to general knowledge.

with symbols that denote (1) whether there is a significant effect for a given sector in a given subject; (2) its direction; and finally, in the last column, (3) whether the indicators of gains by grade level (columns 1 and 3 in Tables 6.2 and 6.4) are consistent with the conventional cross-grade indicators (columns 4 and 5 in Tables 6.2 and 6.4). For the unadjusted gains, only one set of estimates shows consistency: Private, secular students hold a positive advantage in both the conventional and yearly estimates of gains in reading. However, none of the other comparisons indicates consistent results. The adjusted results show slightly more consistency: Three of the nine comparisons show consistent results between the yearly and conventional estimates. In particular, the estimates for private, other religious schools are consistent in reading and math but not in general knowledge. Only one of three estimates for Catholic schools (general knowledge) and none of the three estimates for private, secular schools are consistent. Hence, Table 6.6 suggests that conventional estimates are likely to overgeneralize sector effects across grade levels and hence distort our understanding of when sector differences are present in students' academic careers.

Next, do sector differences in summer learning distort estimates of sector differences of gains from schooling? Table 6.7 provides estimates of student gains with and without summer learning gains. In this case, the conventional estimate of student learning that includes summer learning is the gain score from the fall of kindergarten to the spring of first grade (shown in column 5 in Tables 6.3 and 6.5). In contrast, the revised estimate of student gains that excludes summer learning is simply the sum of the estimates of learning during kindergarten and first grade (columns 1 and 3 in Tables 6.2 and 6.4) divided by the sum of the unadjusted public school gains in kindergarten and first grade for each subject. If the two estimates are very similar, then the sector effects on student learning are not biased by sector differences in summer learning. If the two estimates are substantially different, then the sector differences in summer learning are likely biasing the conventional estimates of sector differences in learning gains.

Among the unadjusted gains, most of the differences in the two sets of estimates are fairly small, although some, such as reading gains in private, other religious schools, are fairly large. Interestingly, the bias in the conventional estimates is actually downward, rather than upward, as predicted. In two cases, there is a lack of agreement regarding statistical significance among the conventional and revised estimates.

Comparison of the adjusted conventional and revised estimates tends to show more substantial differences between the two. Accounting for sector differences in summer learning does little to change either estimates of Catholic school effects in reading and general knowledge or the private, other religious school effects for

Table 6.7. Differences from Public School Gains with and without Summer Learning

	Unadjusted Gains			Adjusted Gains		
	Conventional estimate (with summer included)	Revised estimate (excluding summer gains)	Difference between estimates	Conventional estimate (with summer included)	Revised estimate (excluding summer gains)	Difference between estimates
Sector	Reading skills					
Catholic	+2.9%	+4.7%	↓1.8%	+1.8%	+2.1%	↓0.3%
Private, secular	+11.0%	+11.7%	↓0.7%	+5.5%	+10.2%	↓4.7%
Other religious	-4.6%	-14.5%	↓9.9%	-11.4%	-8.6%	↑2.8%
	Math skills					
Catholic	-2.8%	-4.3%	↓1.5%	-3.9%	-1.5%	↑2.4%
Private, secular	N.S.	+4.6%	↓4.6%	N.S.	+1.9%	↓1.9%
Other religious	-11.6%	-17.5%	↓5.9%	-13.4%	-13.1%	↑0.3%
	General knowledge					
Catholic	-4.7%	N.S.	↑4.7%	N.S.	N.S.	0.0%
Private, secular	-4.4%	-3.0%	↑1.4%	N.S.	-3.2%	↓3.2%
Other religious	-10.0%	-11.5%	↓1.5%	-7.4%	-11.6%	↓4.2%

Note: The information in this table is derived entirely from the information displayed in Tables 6.2 and 6.4. For the FK-S1 estimates of sector effects, "N.S." indicates that the coefficient was not statistically significant at the .05 level. For the estimates of sector effects that exclude summer learning, "N.S." indicates that neither the kindergarten nor first grade coefficient was statistically significant at the .05 level. Shading indicates that the summer learning coefficients in tables 2 and/or 4 were statistically significant at the .05 level. A down arrow (↓) indicates that the conventional estimate of the sector effect is downwardly biased. An up arrow (↑) indicates that the conventional estimate of the sector effect is upwardly biased.

math. However, several estimates of sector effects differ substantially when comparing the conventional and revised coefficients. For example, the conventional estimate of the private, secular effect in reading is only about half that of the revised estimate. The private, other religious effect on general knowledge is also underestimated by the conventional measure of student gains: Using the conventional indicator of student learning reveals a negative effect on general knowledge that is 63 percent as large as the effect suggested using the revised estimator. In two cases, the conventional indicator of student gains overstated the size of the sector effects: The conventional estimate of the Catholic school effect on math gains is 2.5 times larger than the revised estimate, and the conventional estimate of the private, other religious school effect on general knowledge is roughly 1.3 times greater than the revised estimate. Finally, in two cases, there is lack of agreement in statistical significance between the conventional and revised estimates. For private, secular math and general knowledge, the conventional indicator is not statistically significant, unlike the revised estimate.

Are conventional indicators of sector effects likely to be biased when there are significant sector differences in summer learning? Table 6.7 indicates that this is generally true in two of the three cases where significant sector effects on summer learning were observed in Table 6.5. However, inaccuracy in the conventional estimates was not limited to cases where there were significant sector effects.

In sum, the analyses suggest two shortcomings in conventional estimates of sector effects. First, as expected, conventional estimates of sector effects tended to overgeneralize sector differences across grade levels. Second, the conventional estimators did not adequately describe sector differences in learning that occurred during the school year from learning that occurred during the summer. However, while it was hypothesized that the conventional estimates of sector effects would be upwardly biased, errors tended to run in both directions (i.e., estimates of sector effects on learning that were too high or too low). Hence, the conventional estimators may suffer from a reliability problem rather than a problem related to bias.

Discussion

Two questions regarding school sector and student achievement were examined in this study: (1) do sector effects observed in high school generalize to other grade levels; and (2) do sector effects apply to summer learning, and, if so, do these sector differences in summer learning affect conventional estimates of sector effects on learning? In general, the analyses reported here suggest that (1) sector effects vary across grade levels and generally do not correspond well with the findings of prior research on school sector differences in high school learning; and (2) summer learning varies by sector, and conventional estimates of sector differences in learning are somewhat distorted when such differences are not accounted for. The substantive and methodological implications of these findings will now be discussed in an attempt to further understand sector differences in academic achievement and to propose future studies in this area.

School Sector and Student Learning in Elementary School

The findings reported here provide a dramatic contrast with prior research on school sector that should prompt a rethinking of how and why student achievement varies across school sector. While prior research suggests that Catholic school students outperform public school students in high school by a modest amount (see Bryk et al., 1993; Coleman & Hoffer, 1987; Hoffer, 1998), Catholic school students do not appear to enjoy the same consistent advantages early in their academic careers. This important finding suggests that the Catholic school effect may be limited primarily to high school. In addition, the most consistent sector effect observed in the analyses was the negative effect of private, other religious schools on student learning. While other studies have suggested that private school effects are limited to Catholic schools (Coleman & Hoffer, 1987; Coleman et al., 1982; Gamoran, 1996), the results reported here indicate that other types of private-public comparisons are worthy of examination.

What explains these differences between research on school sector and student learning at the beginning and the end of students' academic careers? To answer this question, it is useful to recall Bidwell and Kasarda's (1980) distinction between *schools*, which they refer to as "an organization that conducts instruction," and *schooling*, by which they mean "the process through which instruction occurs" (p. 401). This distinction highlights the process of translating a school's resources into student learning. Hence, differences in school organization that are related to curriculum, instruction, teacher quality, professional development, and other factors in regard to student learning are all likely and viable explanations for sector differences in student outcomes.

However, while sector differences in the social organization of *schools* affect *schooling* in high school, this may not be the case in elementary schools. For example, much of the research on school sector explores how Catholic high schools are communally organized in contrast to the more bureaucratic structure found in public high schools (e.g., Bryk et al., 1993). Are these public-Catholic differences in school organization absent in elementary school? Perhaps public schools are just as likely as Catholic schools to be caring institutions that are communally organized. Or, perhaps such differences matter less in elementary schools because they play out in ways that do not strongly impact students' learning opportunities.

Another possible explanation worthy of examination is variation in curriculum and instruction across school sector at different points in students' academic careers. For example, it is possible that curricular demands may be relatively equal across sectors in elementary (and perhaps middle) school, but important sector differences may emerge when students enter high school. Thus, the timing of *when* students in different sectors are exposed to a given part of the curriculum might explain *why* sector differences in student learning vary across grade levels.

An examination of these and related questions would greatly enhance our understanding of how school sector affects students' learning over the course of their K-12 careers. Fortunately, the ECLS provides good data for exploring some of these issues in greater depth in future studies. However, as discussed next, new data sources to explore these possibilities are likely needed to broaden our understanding of sector differences in student learning.

Rethinking the Measurement of Sector Effects on Student Learning

Two concerns about analytical limitations due to data shortcomings were examined in this study. The first focused on whether conventional measures of learning gains distort our understanding of sector effects on learning by falsely assuming that sector differences are constant across grade levels. The analyses revealed that sector effects differed across grade levels, and, consequently, conventional measures of sector effects fail to pinpoint exactly when sector differences emerge in students' careers. The second focused on whether sector differences in summer learning might bias the conventional estimates of sector effects. There was some evidence that sector differences in summer learning distorted estimates of sector differences in learning during the school year. Both of these findings raise important issues for research on sector differences in student learning that must be addressed.

First, as Jencks (1985) argued, it is difficult to assess the size of sector differences in learning when gains are measured in the last two years of high school because such differences may not apply to students' prior ten-plus years of schooling. The results reported here largely validate the relevance of this concern: (1) sector differences in learning are not consistent across kindergarten and first grade; and furthermore, (2) sector differences in learning during kindergarten and first grade are not consistent in magnitude or direction with those found in high school. One way to satisfy this concern about measuring sector effects would be to (1) calculate learning gains by comparing test scores at the beginning of elementary and at the end of high school; and (2) examine the sector differences in gains among those who stayed in the same sector for elementary and secondary school. Since sector differences would be estimated over the entire course of students' elementary and secondary careers, the problem of varying sector differences in achievement gains across grade levels would no longer be a concern.

While this strategy is technically correct, it suffers from two limitations. First, even if significant sector differences in K-12 gains are observed, it remains unclear as to how or when these differences in student learning emerge. One possibility is that small, but similar, sector differences in student achievement gains are present at each grade level. Alternatively, students in different sectors may experience similar rates of growth until high school, at which time achievement gains across sectors begin to diverge. Each of these possibilities suggests a different substantive conclusion as to why sector effects emerge. The first possibility—constant, incremental change over time—would suggest that schools in different sectors have fundamental differences in organization and/or governance that translate into different levels of overall effectiveness in instructing students. In contrast, the results indicating the sudden emergence of sector differences at a given point in students' careers would suggest a more idiosyncratic explanation focusing on sector differences in course-taking patterns, curriculum, or instruction that is specific to a given level of schooling. While it would be valuable to know which explanation of K-12 sector differences is correct, it is impossible to do so by measuring K-12 gains without any estimates of yearly gains.

There is a second shortcoming in measuring K-12 gains without estimating annual gains in student learning. The following example illustrates the problem. If public school students gain a quarter of a standard deviation more than private school students in elementary school, but private school students outgain public school students by the same amount in high school, the K-12 estimate of public-private differences in learning would be zero. While in a technical sense the K-12 model would correctly describe the overall sector effect as zero, this finding obscures the critically important finding that sector effects vary across grade levels.

The second issue of concern in estimating sector differences in learning focuses on sector differences in summer learning. While measures that estimate yearly gains in achievement would be very helpful in studying the importance of school sector for student outcomes, they would have the added benefit of providing estimates of summer learning as well. The results presented here indicate that unaccounted-for sector differences in summer learning sometimes bias the estimates of sector effects. Since the K-12 estimates of learning gains would also include gains from many summer intervals, there is the distinct possibility that sector differences in summer learning would contaminate the estimates of K-12 learning.

In addition, there is reason to believe that examining more summer intervals at different points in students' careers might lead to increased bias and/or unreliability in estimates of sector effects. First, it is possible that sector differences in summer learning become more pronounced after first grade. As students begin receiving grades and are assessed on exams for possible placement in honors classes and/or gifted programs, parents with a higher SES may engage in structured and carefully targeted academic preparation during the summer. In addition, as students age and grow more independent, they become capable of spending time outside the home, and their learning opportunities in the summer may begin to diverge. Affluent students, who are more likely to attend private school, may enroll in summer programs and camps that encourage their academic knowledge and skills. In contrast, less affluent students, who are more likely to attend public schools, may spend more time with their peers, who will not provide the high-quality learning opportunities that more affluent students receive. Finally, as they get older and can read, write, and study on their own, students in different sectors may make different choices about how to spend their free time during the summer (e.g., watching television vs. reading books), which create greater sector differences in summer learning.

Future Directions for Research on School Sector

The results reported in this chapter suggest that the conventional wisdom on sector differences in student achievement needs substantial revision. By focusing on high school learning and ignoring possible sector differences in summer learning, prior research has provided an incomplete picture of how school sector affects student learning. This study begins to fill in the gaps in our understanding of how school sector is related to student achievement by examining sector differences in learning at the beginning of students' school careers as well as learning that occurs during the summer.

However, to advance our knowledge in this area, new studies with better data are still needed. In particular, the findings reported here suggest that fall-spring data across students' K-12 careers are most appropriate for examining sector effects on learning. One promising strategy would involve collecting fall and spring achievement data on a sample of public and private school students currently enrolled in kindergarten through twelfth grade. Two years of data collection would provide estimates of test score gains for one summer and two school years for each age cohort. By combining data from the various longitudinal samples from each age cohort, a dynamic snapshot of sector differences in summer and in-school learning from kindergarten through twelfth grade could be created. In addition, data on school attributes, such as school organization and curriculum, could easily be added to the analyses to explain sector differences in learning. The potential benefits of such a study would be enormous because it would provide a more complete and precise picture of how school sector is related to students' academic achievement than does the present body of research.

NOTE

Research for this paper was supported by the Institute for Educational Initiatives at the University of Notre Dame, with funds from the U.S. Department of Education (Grant

No. R215K010011-01) for the Comparative Analysis of Best Practices in Public and Private Elementary and Secondary Schools. The author would like to thank Maureen Hallinan, Barbara Schneider, and Sean Reardon for their helpful comments, and Yinghao Lu for his valuable research assistance on this paper.

REFERENCES

Bidwell, C. E., & Kasarda, J. D. (1980). Conceptualizing and measuring the effects of school and schooling. *American Journal of Education, 88*, 401–430.

Bryk, A. S., Lee, V. E., & Holland, P. B. (1993). *Catholic schools and the common good*. Cambridge, MA: Harvard University Press.

Carbonaro, W. (2002, April). *School sector differences in achievement among kindergarten students: Does instruction account for school effects?* Paper presented at the annual meeting of the American Educational Research Association, New Orleans, LA.

Chubb, J. E., & Moe, T. M. (1990). *Politics, markets, and American schools*. Washington, DC: Brookings Institution.

Coleman, J. S., & Hoffer, T. (1987). *Private and public high schools: The impact of communities*. New York: Basic Books.

Coleman, J. S., Hoffer, T., & Kilgore, S. (1982). *High school achievement: Public, Catholic, and private schools compared*. New York: Basic Books.

Entwisle, D., Alexander, K., & Olson, L. (1997). *Children, schools, and inequality*. Boulder, CO: Westview Press.

Gamoran, A. (1992). The variable effects of high school tracking. *American Sociological Review, 57*, 812–828.

Gamoran, A. (1993). Alternative uses of ability grouping in secondary schools: Can we bring high-quality instruction to low-ability classes? *American Journal of Education, 102*, 1–22.

Gamoran, A. (1996). Student achievement in public magnet, public comprehensive, and private city high schools. *Education Evaluation Policy Analysis, 18*, 1–18.

Heyns, B. (1978). *Summer learning and the effects of schooling*. New York: Academic Press.

Heyns, B. (2002). Summer learning. In D. Levinson, P. Cookson, Jr., & A. Sadovnik (Eds.), *Education and sociology: An encyclopedia* (pp. 115–120). New York: Routledge Falmer.

Hoffer, T. (1998). Social background and achievement in public and Catholic high schools. *Social Psychology of Education, 2*, 7–23.

Hoffer, T., Greeley, A. M., & Coleman, J. S. (1985). Achievement growth in public and Catholic schools. *Sociology of Education, 58*, 74–97.

Ingels, S., Scott, L., Lindmark, J., Frankel, M., & Myers, S. (1992). *National education longitudinal study of 1988: First follow-up: Student component data file user's manual*. Chicago: National Opinion Research Center.

Jencks, C. (1985). How much do high school students learn? *Sociology of Education, 58*, 128–135.

Lareau, A. (2000). *Home advantage: Social class and parental intervention in elementary education*. (2d ed.). Lanham, MD: Rowman & Littlefield.
Morgan, S. (2001). Counterfactuals, causal effect heterogeneity, and the Catholic school effect on learning. *Sociology of Education, 74*, 341–374.
Morgan, S., & Sørensen, A. B. (1999). Parental networks, social closure, and mathematics learning: A test of Coleman's social capital explanation of school effects. *American Sociological Review, 64*, 661–681.
StataCorp. (1999). *Stata statistical software: Release 6.0*. College Station, TX: StataCorp.
Zahs, D., Pedlow, S., Morrissey, M., Marnell, P., & Nichols, B. (1995). *High school and beyond: Fourth follow-up: Methodology report*. Chicago: National Opinion Research Center.

7 | Sector Differences in Opportunities for Parental Involvement in the School Context

Gail M. Mulligan

Studies of academic achievement generally show that private school students outperform their public school peers on common measures such as standardized test scores and graduation rates (Coleman, Hoffer, & Kilgore, 1982; Hallinan, 2002). Some researchers argue that these differences in achievement levels are at least partially a result of sector effects; that is, differences in the way that public and private schools educate their students result in differences in academic outcomes. Public and private schools do differ on a number of characteristics that can affect achievement, including the types of courses that schools require of all students (Lee & Bryk, 1988) and the manner in which schools in different sectors discipline students (Coleman & Hoffer, 1987).

One characteristic related to school achievement that has been studied in regard to public-private school differences is parental involvement. Research suggests that parents of students in private schools are more involved in their children's education than parents of public school children (Coleman & Hoffer, 1987; Muller, 1993). These higher levels of involvement may be partially accounted for by private school parents' higher average incomes and educational levels (U.S. Department of Education, 1995), characteristics that are related to greater involvement among all parents (Lareau, 1987; Nord, Brimhall, & West, 1997; Stevenson & Baker, 1987). They also may result from a greater interest in or concern for education on the part of private school parents: the very act of choosing a school and paying tuition may be a reflection of greater interest and thus is a form of parental involvement in and of itself (Coleman, Schiller, & Schneider, 1993).

Greater parental involvement also may result from the practices of private schools themselves. To a great extent, parental involvement in the school environment—for example, volunteering in a classroom or attending an open house—is controlled by school personnel. Teachers and administrators are responsible for determining if, when, and how often activities that allow for such involvement are offered. Parents can take part only when school personnel afford them this opportunity. Research shows that the policies and practices of schools do affect levels of parental involvement (see Epstein, 1990). There is evidence that private schools more effectively facilitate the involvement of parents than do public schools (Goldring & Bauch, 1993; Vaden-Kiernan, 1996). However, this evidence is limited. The majority of studies on parental involvement focus on differences in individual-level characteristics rather than on school policies and practices that can influence parents' participation. This study adds to the understanding of ways in which teachers and administrators can affect parental involvement in the school context by using nationally representative data to examine differences between public and private schools in the opportunities that they provide to parents.

Exchange Theory and Sector Differences in Opportunities for Involvement

This study situates the general discussion of parental involvement within a social exchange framework, which also can be used to hypothesize about possible differences in opportunities for involvement between public and private schools. Within this framework, the parent-school relationship is conceptualized as an interpersonal one that involves the exchange of valued goods or rewards. A basic proposition of exchange theory is that people enter into a relationship when they feel that there is something to be gained, that is, when they can benefit from it. There are benefits for school personnel and parents in their relationships with one another. They exchange many types of goods, including information, support, and respect for the role that each individual plays in the lives of the students. Parents also gain satisfaction from seeing their children's accomplishments firsthand. The need or desire for these rewards motivates parents and school staff to seek and maintain relationships with one another.

The reciprocal nature of the exchange relationship also results in costs for the individual. In order to have others provide rewards, the individual must also provide something in return (Blau, 1964). Costs are incurred by both schools and parents in the process of overcoming constraints to their relationship. Parents and school personnel spend time and energy on this relationship that could be devoted to other pursuits. For example, school personnel often have to find time outside of the regular workday to fulfill the commitments of their jobs, as is the case with back-to-school nights. They lose time with their families or time to prepare the next day's lesson as a result of spending evening hours at the school. Parents, on the other hand, may have to take time off from their jobs in order to meet with teachers. Their cost is a financial reward (income) forgone by choosing involvement at school over attendance at work.

According to exchange theory, if individuals perceive that the costs of a relationship far outweigh its benefits, they may avoid it or leave it altogether (Thibaut & Kelley, 1959). Extending this proposition to the general parent-school relationship, one may hypothesize that as the costs of providing opportunities for involvement to parents increase, the actual number of opportunities offered by school personnel decreases. Alternatively, as the costs of not offering opportunities for involvement increase, the number of opportunities provided by the schools increases.

In this study, particular characteristics of schools constitute the context in which school personnel and parents make decisions about their relationships with one another. These characteristics can affect opportunities by constraining or facilitating the ability of teachers and administrators to offer these opportunities to parents. Conceivably, organizational features of the school or the school climate surrounding parental involvement can make it difficult or undesirable for school personnel to seek relationships with parents. Any attempt to overcome these difficulties or constraints results in costs for those teachers and administrators who are trying to offer opportunities for involvement. As these costs increase, school personnel become less willing or able to form and maintain relationships with parents.

In analyzing the relationship between the organizational characteristic school sector and opportunities for involvement, consideration must be given to the nature of the parent-school relationship in private schools, which is different from that in public schools. There are two prevalent perspectives in the study of the relationship between parents and private schools; researchers identify the relationship as (1) adhering to market principles; or (2) existing within an environment focused on the development of communities. Using either perspective, it can be expected that private schools will offer more opportunities for parents to become involved than public schools.

In the market model of the parent-private school relationship, parents are considered to be consumers of the school's goods because they are paying for their children's education. Private schools are dependent upon their students' families for the income necessary to run the school. As a result, school personnel are pressured to meet the needs and desires of the parents on whom they are dependent for resources and, ultimately, employment. This is not true of public schools, which receive financial resources from public funds. As such, private schools have a greater need to satisfy any desires that their parents have for involvement. They also must assure the parents that their children are having quality educational experiences. Facilitating this might include inviting parents to school to see classes and activities firsthand and making them aware of school events through newsletters and personal communication.

While there is a component of consumerism that exists between parents and personnel in Catholic schools, research suggests that their relationship is not driven solely by financial reasons. Catholic schools place special emphasis on developing a sense of community among school personnel, students, and parents (Bryk, Lee, & Holland, 1993). An integral part of this communal orientation is the shared commitment of parents and school personnel to create community and an academically enriching environment for all students. Researchers assert that this vision of the school as community enables Catholic schools to produce higher achievement levels and lower dropout rates than those found in public schools (Coleman, 1988; Coleman et al., 1982). Thus, a method by which Catholic school personnel succeed as educators is by creating and maintaining relationships with parents. For this reason, they may be highly motivated to offer parents opportunities to be involved at the school. However, parents of Catholic school students may not want to concern themselves with the daily functioning of their children's schools, instead opting to attend only those events to which parents have traditionally been welcomed. Parents of Catholic high school students are more interested in school activities such as parents' nights and children's programs than they are in the governance of the school (Bryk et al., 1993). Without parents' desire for involvement in certain activities, Catholic school staff may see no need to offer such opportunities.

For all private schools, whether operating strictly according to market principles or with a communal orientation toward education, there are costs to not providing involvement opportunities. These can include loss of funding and students if parents become dissatisfied with their school experiences and decide to educate their children elsewhere. Without parental involvement, school personnel may also fail to develop a community atmosphere, which represents a failure to adhere to the basic mission of some schools. In all cases, school staff must weigh the monetary, time, and energy costs associated with providing opportunities for involvement against the costs associated with not providing them.

In recent decades, there has been a movement to improve public education by creating schools with private-like characteristics, including magnet and charter schools. Often these schools purport a school-as-community orientation commonly found in Catholic schools. Many also require increased parental involvement for their students to attend (Cookson, 1994). As a result of this orientation, these types of public schools also are expected to provide greater opportunities for parental involvement than are regular public schools.

The nature of the relationship between parents and school personnel is not the only source of possible differences between public and private schools in the involvement opportunities offered to parents. National data show that public and private schools differ on other characteristics that also may affect these opportunities (see Alt & Peter, 2002). In examining differences among school types, it is important to take into account these other factors that may explain any observed differences in opportunities.

In general, public schools are larger than private schools. In the private sector, Catholic schools typically educate more students than other types of private schools. School size itself may be related to the number of opportunities for involvement, because the number of students and parents whose interests and desires must be accommodated affect school offerings. On the one hand, size may exhibit a negative relationship with opportunities for involvement as a result of the expenditures required to provide these opportunities. As the numbers of students and parents increase, the time, energy, and monetary costs associated with providing opportunities for all of them increase.

On the other hand, smaller schools may not be able or have the need to offer as wide an array of opportunities as larger schools (Alt & Peter, 2002). With a larger student body, schools have to provide extracurricular activities that encompass a wide range of interests. The cost of not doing so may be discontent among the students. These extracurricular activities also allow parents to attend school functions in order to observe their children. Similarly, with a larger parent population, schools may find it easier to attract enough parents to support a parent-teacher organization or a fair. Regardless of the direction of the relationship between opportunities and school size, it is important to account for this factor when making observations about differences in opportunities by school sector.

School resources constitute another factor simultaneously related to school sector and opportunities. As previously stated, the provision of opportunities brings many kinds of costs. Schools with greater financial and human resources can more easily bear these costs. As a result, they are less constrained by cost factors. Therefore, as their resources increase, schools should be able to offer a greater number of opportunities. When the socioeconomic characteristics of student populations are used as indicators of school resources, private schools seem to have an advantage. They are less likely than public schools to enroll students who qualify for free or reduced-price lunch programs and less likely to have student populations that are 30 percent or more minority (Alt & Peter, 2002). In fact, they are less likely than public schools to educate minority students at all. However, private schools tend to be smaller than public schools, and small schools tend to have limited fiscal and human resources (Bryk, 1995). Evidence shows that while more extracurricular activities are offered in Catholic schools with greater fiscal resources, overall these activities tend to be limited because Catholic schools have limited budgets (Bryk et al., 1993). Recent data suggest that private schools have at least one advantage with respect to human resources; although their absolute numbers of personnel may be smaller than those in public schools, their student/teacher ratios tend to be lower than they are in public schools (Alt & Peter, 2002).

Another aspect in which public and private schools differ is the working climate for personnel. Teachers in private schools are more likely than their counterparts in public schools to report that they have control over school practices and policies, that there is cooperation among teachers and a sharing of beliefs regarding their school's central missions, and that their work is supported by both administrators and parents (Alt & Peter, 2002). It is possible that aspects of school climate related to parental involvement, such as institutional backing for involvement and the power afforded to parents to influence daily school activities, also differ among schools in different sectors.

These aspects of the school climate may be important determinants of whether or not schools offer parents opportunities to be involved. According to exchange theory, an actor's willingness to accept the costs of a relationship depends on the value that he or she places on the outcome or reward. The value placed on parental involvement essentially mediates the effect of structural constraints on the provision and facilitation of opportunities for involvement. When the school climate values and encourages parental involvement, personnel will see benefits from creating relationships with parents, including positive evaluations of their work. As a result, they will be more likely to offer parents opportunities to be involved and to incur the associated costs. They also may experience costs from not creating these relationships, because they will be defying institutional norms or pressure, which will result in negative evaluations of their job performance. In contrast, when little institutional support is given to the home-school relationship, personnel may see no benefit in making the effort to generate relationships with parents. If they consider parental involvement to be unimportant or even detrimental to their ability to educate, they will be less eager to encourage it.

Personnel in private schools may place greater importance on parental involvement than do public school personnel as a result of their dependence upon parents for tuition fees and their emphasis on the development of community. Research shows that the parent-school relationship is important to parents, personnel, and students in Catholic high schools (Bryk et al., 1993), which may result in a greater degree of willingness to accept the costs of providing opportunities. Also, norms encouraging parental involvement may be better communicated from administrators to teachers in private schools, since private school teachers are more likely than public school teachers to report that goals are communicated clearly and staff members are recognized for doing a good job (Alt & Peter, 2002).

Last, when hypothesizing about the differences between sectors in opportunities for involvement, the balance of power and dependence between school personnel and parents is also an important consideration. As the relationship is envisioned here, personnel have more power than parents within the school context, because they determine opportunities for involvement. For this reason, the desires of parents are less likely to supersede those of personnel in decisions regarding such opportunities. However, school personnel who feel that parental involvement is important have an interest in making parents their partners in the educational process. When parents are afforded more influence in the school environment, they become more powerful actors. If parents have power to influence their children's school experiences, they can pressure teachers and administrators to provide them with more opportunities when they are desired. Therefore, it is expected that as parental power increases, the opportunities for involvement offered by the school also will increase. Private school parents are expected to exert more power within their schools than public school parents, because they have the ability to withdraw both their children and their money, and because some private schools view their students' parents as an integral part of the school community.

DATA AND METHODS

Data for this study come from the fall and spring kindergarten waves of the Early Childhood Longitudinal Study, Kindergarten Class of 1998-1999 (ECLS-K). The ECLS-K employed multistage probability sampling, which produced a nationally representative sample of schools that educate kindergartners in the United States (U.S. Department of Education, 2001). The unweighted sample includes 866 schools from all sectors for which information was available from school administrators. When weighted appropriately to account for the complex sampling design, oversampling, and nonresponse, the data represent is 72,260 schools. Information used in this study comes from self-administered questionnaires completed by administrators.

Several statistical methods are used to examine sector differences in the opportunities provided for parents to be involved in the school context. Descriptive analyses are used to present an overall picture of the frequency and types of activities offered by schools in different sectors. Comparisons are made among different types of schools, and any observed differences are tested for statistical significance.

Linear regression techniques are used to estimate the relationship between school sector and opportunities for involvement provided by the school while controlling for other organizational characteristics. The complex nature of the ECLS-K sampling design required an adjustment of the standard errors of the estimates in order to obtain more accurate evaluations of the precision of these estimates and more reliable tests of significance (U.S. Department of Education, 2001). In this study, standard errors are computed using Taylor series approximation.

Measures

Dependent Variable: Opportunities for Parental Involvement at the School Level

In the spring wave of the kindergarten year, administrators were asked whether several activities that involve parents were provided by the school. These activities included PTA, PTO, or parent-student-teacher organization meetings; teacher-parent conferences; school performances to which parents were invited; classroom programs such as class plays, book nights, or family math nights; and fairs or social events planned to raise funds for the school. Original responses from administrators were recoded in the following manner in order to obtain a measure approximating the actual number of opportunities for involvement offered by the school: Never = 0, Once per year = 1, 2 to 3 times per year = 2.5, 4 to 6 times per year = 5, and 7 or more times per year = 7. The answers were then summed across all five groups of activities to produce an overall indicator of the number of opportunities for involvement. Possible scores range from 0 to 35. Schools with higher scores on this measure provided more opportunities for involvement than schools with lower scores on this measure.

School Sector

The main independent variable in this study is the sector to which schools belong. For some analyses, a dichotomous distinction is made between public and private schools. In other analyses, schools are identified as belonging to one of four categories: a regular public school, a magnet school or public school of choice, a religious private school, or a secular private school. A dummy variable was created for each of the four school types, where a "1" indicates that the school is of that particular type and "0" indicates that the school is not of that particular type.

Additional Measures of School Characteristics

As previously indicated, measures of school characteristics are included in these analyses to control for other differences among schools in different sectors. These include: school size, type, resources, and location; characteristics of the student and teacher populations; general parental power; and institutional support for the parent-school relationship.

School size. The size of the school is measured by the number of students enrolled at the time when administrators filled out their questionnaires. The data set contains a categorical measure of size, where 1 = 0-149 students, 2 = 150–299 students, 3 = 300-499 students, 4 = 500-749 students, and 5 = 750 students or more.

School type. Schools are identified as being public or private early childhood centers by a dummy variable coded "1" if the school is an early childhood center and "0" if it is not. These schools educate children in only a limited number of grades, which probably results in their offering parents fewer opportunities for involvement.

School resources. Controlling for school resources within this study proved problematic. Educational researchers commonly employ a measure of the percentage of students within each school who are eligible for free and reduced-price lunches lunches as an indicator of the average socioeconomic status of the student body, which in turn reflects school resources. Although the ECLS-K includes a composite measure of eligible students, as indicated by administrators, this information is missing for 26 percent of the sample schools. Using this measure in analyses would have resulted in a substantial loss of cases. Therefore, this research utilizes two best-alternative measures related to school resources. The first is a dummy measure indicating whether the *school operates a schoolwide Title 1 program* (coded 1 = yes, 0 = no). Schools in which more than 50 percent of the student population are low income qualify for schoolwide Title 1 programs. This measure essentially indicates that at least one-half of a school's student population comes from a low-income background.

A second measure of school resources indicates any *additional sources of funding*. Schools that receive funding in addition to basic funding from the state or from tuition payments conceivably have extra money available to spend on the provision of opportunities for involvement. Specifically, administrators indicated whether their schools receive funding from state compensatory funds, community fund-raising, PTO fund-raising, local and/or national businesses, special education programs or agencies, auxiliary services or affiliated enterprises, Medicaid, impact aid, bilingual aid, migrant aid, or other grants. A score of "1" was assigned for each type of assistance. These scores were then summed across all eleven types of additional funding, resulting in a score that ranges from 0 to 11. The total number of *full-time equivalent school personnel* also is used as a measure of human resources available to provide opportunities for involvement.

School location. The ECLS-K provides a composite measure of *urbanicity*, which indicates whether a school is located in one of three areas: a central city; urban fringe or large town; or small town or rural area. Dummy variables were created for each of these locations and labeled city, suburb, and rural, respectively ("1" indicates that the school is located in such an area, and "0" indicates that the school is not located in that area).

Size of schools' minority-student populations. The data set provides a categorical measure of the *percentage of minority students* within each school. It is coded in the following manner: 1 = less than 10 percent minority, 2 = 10 percent to less than 25 percent minority, 3 = 25 percent to less than 50 percent minority, 4 = 50 percent to less than 75 percent minority, 5 = 75 percent or more minority.

General parental power. General parental power within the school is indicated by a series of measures representing parents' influence in different areas. The first measure indicates whether *parents are represented on a school-based management committee*. It is coded "1" if yes, and "0" if no.

The second measure of parental power indicates *parental influence in administrators' job evaluations*. Specifically, administrators were asked how much parent and community support, as well as parental involvement in school activities, influences their job evaluations. The more these factors influence these evaluations, the more costly it becomes to not offer opportunities for parental involvement or to not make efforts to create positive relationships with parents. Failure to do so can result in the loss of a job. Therefore, the greater the influence or power that parents have in this area, the greater the number of opportunities for involvement. Administrators indicated whether parents have (0) no influence; (1) some influence; or (2) major influence. A scale measure was created by summing the responses to these two areas affecting job evaluation, resulting in a measure of influence ranging from 0 to 4. Higher scores reflect greater parental influence on the administrator's job evaluation.

Institutional support for teacher-parent contact. The *value placed by the institution on the parent-school relationship* is indicated by administrators' responses to the question of how much emphasis he or she places on kindergarten teachers communicating well with parents. Available responses included (1) no or minor emphasis; (2) moderate emphasis; and (3) major emphasis. Categories 1 and 2 were collapsed into one, because only one administrator reported that the school places no or minor emphasis on communicating well with parents. The resulting measure is a dummy variable where "1" indicates that the school places major emphasis on such communication, and "0" indicates that the school places less emphasis on it. Greater emphasis on good communication with parents reflects greater institutional support for the home-school relationship.

Administrators also can give institutional support to the home-school relationship by training teachers to develop effective interrelationships with parents. Researchers suggest that such training is essential but lacking in teacher-education programs (Bermúdez, 1993; Davies, 1993). Teachers do not have the necessary skills to encourage parental involvement, especially with those who are considered difficult to contact. Therefore, initiating these relationships represents real costs to teachers because they have to undertake the process with little formal training, and they may become frustrated by their inability to connect with some parents. The costs of creating positive home-school relationships are reduced for teachers when they are taught the necessary skills and when they are supported by the administration and other teachers. Administrators were asked how often their schools provide *workshops for teachers* that focus on parental involvement. This measure is coded such that 1 = Never, 2 = Once per year, 3 = 2 to 3 times per year, 4 = 4 to 6 times per year, and 5 = 7 or more times per year. Higher scores reflect greater training for generating parental involvement.

FINDINGS

Table 7.1 presents basic statistics for the full, weighted sample of schools included in this study. Public schools compose 65 percent of the weighted sample. Roughly 16 percent of these public schools are schools of choice or magnet schools. Of the 25,257 private schools, 41 percent are non-Catholic religious schools, 27 percent are Catholic, and 32 percent are secular. About 13 percent of the sample are composed of early childhood centers.

Table 7.1. Descriptive Statistics for Weighted Sample of Schools Educating Kindergartners by School Sector

School Characteristics	Total Sample Mean	s.e.	Public Schools Mean	s.e.	Private Schools Mean	s.e.
Opportunities for involvement	18.33	.32	20.17	.32	14.78	.52
School size	2.60	.05	3.07	.07	1.73	.06
Full-time-equivalent school personnel	35.53	1.02	44.54	1.51	18.43	1.26
Percent minority	2.41	.07	2.53	.09	2.17	.10
School is early childhood center	.13	.02	.08	.01	.23	.03
School is located in urban area	.37	.02	.32	.03	.46	.04
School is located in suburban area	.37	.03	.36	.03	.39	.04
School is located in rural area	.26	.02	.32	.03	.15	.03
School runs schoolwide Title 1 program	.42	.02	.56	.02	.16	.02
Sources of additional funding	3.37	.09	4.19	.11	1.87	.11
Parent impact on administrator's job evaluation	2.48	.05	2.57	.05	2.33	.09
Parental presence on school-based management committee	.48	.02	.64	.02	.17	.03
Emphasis on good communication with parents	.88	.01	.87	.02	.91	.02
School offers teacher workshops	2.13	.04	2.18	.05	2.04	.07

(standard errors indicated by "s.e.")
Source: U.S. Department of Education, National Center for Education Statistics, Early Childhood Longitudinal Study, Kindergarten Class of 1998–1999.

Statistical comparisons show that public and private schools are quite different with respect to the organizational characteristics included in these analyses. As a group, private schools have significantly smaller enrollments, smaller percentage of minority students, and fewer sources of additional funding than public schools. Also, compared to public schools, a significantly lower percentage of private schools operate schoolwide Title 1 programs or are located in rural areas, while a greater percentage of them are located in urban areas and are classified as early childhood centers. There are also significant differences on those measures related to parental power. Contrary to expectations, parents in private schools have less influence on administrators' job evaluations, and a smaller percentage of private schools have parents represented on a school-based management committee.

Private schools, on average, have fewer full-time equivalent staff than do public schools. However, this measure was excluded from regression analyses, because it was highly correlated with school size. An additional measure indicating the teacher/student ratio was also created, but it was found to be unrelated to opportunities. As a result, this measure was dropped from the analyses. Due to insignificant differences in the frequency with which schools in different sectors offer workshops on parental involvement and the emphasis that administrators place on good communication, these measures also were omitted from further analyses.

Differences in Opportunities for Involvement

For the full sample, as shown in Table 7.1, the average number of opportunities for involvement in the previous year is 18.33. Some substantial differences are found among schools in different sectors. Public schools offer an average of 20.17 opportunities per year while private schools offer an average of 14.78, a difference that is highly significant. Among public schools, the difference between regular public schools and public schools of choice is small and insignificant. As a result, no distinctions are made between these schools in further analyses. However, there are significant differences between some types of private schools. Catholic schools offer considerably more opportunities for involvement (17.28 per year) than other religious private schools (14.52) or secular private schools (12.75). The difference in the number of offered opportunities between non-Catholic religious and secular private schools is not significant.

Factors Predicting Opportunities for Involvement

Results from the regressions of opportunities for involvement on schools' characteristics are presented in Table 7.2. Model 1 includes only a dummy variable indicating that a school is private, where public schools constitute the reference category. The effect of the private measure on opportunities is highly significant, with the beta coefficient indicating the difference between the public and private school means. In Model 2, the global measure of private school is replaced by the three dummy variables indicating different types of schools within the private sector, again using public schools as the reference category. The relationship between each type of school and opportunities is highly significant. Contrary to the hypotheses, the relationship of private school to opportunities is negative, whether one uses a global measure for private school or distinguishes among types of schools within the private sector. Catholic schools, private schools pertaining to a non-Catholic religious denomination, and secular private schools all offer fewer opportunities for involvement than public schools. Secular private schools offer the fewest: seven less per year than public schools. Catholic schools, on average, offer approximately three fewer per year than public schools. School sector alone accounts for 18 percent of the variance in opportunities for involvement.

As discussed above, public and private schools differ on important characteristics that may also be related to the opportunities that schools provide for parental involvement. Model 3 includes these factors along with the measures of the three categories of private schools. When these other factors are included, the effects of the school sector measures are reduced but not eliminated. Even when controlling

Table 7.2. Opportunities for Involvement Regressed on School Characteristics

School Characteristics	Model 1	Model 2	Model 3
Constant	20.17***	20.17***	14.35***
	(.32)	(.32)	(1.12)
Private school	-5.39***	-----	-----
	(.58)		
Secular private		-7.41***	-3.34**
		(.95)	(1.18)
Catholic		-2.88***	-3.01**
		(.62)	(1.13)
Other religious private		-5.65***	-1.42*
		(.96)	(.72)
Urban			.26
			(.65)
Rural			-.86
			(.66)
School size			.62**
			(.23)
Percent minority			-.01
			(.20)
Early childhood center			-2.62**
			(.87)
Schoolwide Title 1			-.62
			(.47)
Additional funding			.58***
			(.15)
Parental presence on school management committee			1.02
			(.61)
Job evaluation			.59**
			(.21)
R-square	.16	.18	.27
N Unweighted	820	820	756
Weighted	68,216	68,216	62,733

*$p < .05$; **$p < .01$; ***$p < .00$
(standard errors in parentheses)
Source: U.S. Department of Education, National Center for Education Statistics, Early Childhood Longitudinal Study, Kindergarten Class of 1998–1999.

for other factors, Catholic, non-Catholic religious, and secular private schools all offer fewer opportunities for involvement than do public schools.

Differences in the Types of Opportunities Offered

Focusing on a global measure of opportunities may lead to the incorrect assumption that public schools always offer parents more opportunities to be involved in all types of activities. It may be the case that private schools offer more opportunities for meaningful contact with school personnel that can enhance learning, for example, through parent-teacher conferences, but they offer fewer opportunities for parents to attend other school functions such as sporting events. Comparisons among different school types were made to determine whether differences in offerings of individual activities existed.

The means for each activity that together compose the overall opportunity measure (parent-teacher organization meetings, teacher-parent conferences, school performances to which parents are invited, classroom programs, and fund-raising events), broken down by school type, are presented in Table 7.3. In general, t tests show that public schools offer each of these activities significantly more often than each type of nonpublic school, with one exception: fund-raising. Catholic schools plan fairs or social events to raise funds significantly more often than public schools, other religious schools, and secular private schools. Among nonpublic schools, Catholic institutions generally offer each type of activity more frequently than the other two types of schools. Contrary to predictions, secular private schools offer parents the fewest opportunities to be involved in school decision making, as indicated by the low average number of times that PTO meetings are held during the year.

DISCUSSION AND CONCLUSION

Results from this study show that there are sector differences in the opportunities provided for parents to be involved in the school context. Even when accounting for other factors, private schools offer fewer opportunities overall than public schools. Catholic schools offer more activities to parents than other types of private schools but fewer than the average public school. These findings contradict what was expected, given the nature of the relationship between personnel and parents in private schools. Existing research offers plausible explanations for these findings.

Parents of private school students may not feel that they need to be involved, because they may have a greater level of trust that teachers and administrators are giving their children a quality education than do parents of public school students. A study on Catholic high schools suggests that this is true of Catholic school parents. Trust in school personnel, who believe that they are morally obligated to act in the students' best interest, leads parents to be less involved in the day-to-day aspects of the school environment (Bryk et al., 1993). This same study suggests that some of this trust stems from the fact that Catholic schools educate a large number of disadvantaged children. These children's parents, with low levels of education

Table 7.3. Mean Frequency of Individual Opportunities for Involvement by School Sector

Involvement Activity	All Schools	Public	Catholic	Other Religious	Secular Private
PTA, PTO, or parent-student-teacher organization meetings	5.14 (.13)	5.78 (.12)	4.71 (.20)	4.13 (.33)	2.91 (.41)
Teacher-parent conferences	2.61 (.06)	2.75 (.07)	2.38 (.14)	2.34 (.15)	2.34 (.19)
School performances to which parents are invited	4.36 (.10)	4.80 (.11)	3.95 (.17)	3.71 (.27)	3.01 (.24)
Classroom programs such as class plays, book nights, or family math nights	3.40 (.11)	3.99 (.12)	2.72 (.18)	2.04 (.25)	2.27 (.29)
Fairs or social events planned to raise funds for the school	2.71 (.11)	2.84 (.13)	3.46 (.22)	2.42 (.23)	1.68 (.24)

(standard errors in parentheses)
Source: U.S. Department of Education, National Center for Education Statistics, Early Childhood Longitudinal Study, Kindergarten Class of 1998–1999.

and perhaps little knowledge of what their children need to succeed, leave education in the hands of the people whom they believe are better able to provide it. Also, current rhetoric surrounding the debate over school choice reveals a common belief that private school education is superior to public school education. This belief may lead parents of children in non-Catholic private schools to place similar levels of trust in their schools' staff.

Private school parents also are shown to be more satisfied with various aspects of their children's schools than parents of public school children (Hausman & Goldring, 2000; U.S. Department of Education, 1992), which may result in their seeing less of a need to concern themselves with the daily functioning of the school. Parents whose children are having problems or who are dissatisfied with the schools might have contact with teachers and administrators on a more regular basis (Muller & Kerbow, 1993; Vaden-Kiernan, 1996). In general, decreased parental presence in the daily activities and governance of private schools, accompanied by less pressure from parents for contact with school personnel, results in fewer opportunities for involvement overall.

While the full regression model presented above accounted for a substantial amount of the variation in opportunities for involvement (27 percent), there probably exist other characteristics of school organization and personnel that are simultaneously related to sector and opportunities, whose inclusion may further reduce the relationship between private school and opportunities. In particular, differences in resources may not be adequately controlled for in this study. Catholic schools in particular operate on very limited budgets, which may explain why they are simply unable to offer more formal opportunities for involvement. Had resources been better controlled for through inclusion of different measures, the effect of private school may have been reduced further or eliminated altogether.

Last, this study only examines relatively formal opportunities for involvement in the school context, that is, those activities that may require substantial planning and are offered schoolwide. Involvement in the school context also includes less formal communication between parents and personnel, for example, when parents and teachers set up times for individual conferences apart from regularly scheduled, schoolwide times.

Similarly, involvement at the classroom level is not captured within the measure of opportunities used for these analyses. It is at this level that parents probably have the closest contact with the school as they interact with teachers, the people who are most responsible for their children's education. Relationships between teachers and parents may differ considerably between private schools that foster a communal environment and public schools. Future analyses should examine whether the nature of the parent-school relationship in private schools does lead to greater opportunities for involvement at the classroom level and in less formal activities than those examined here.

Despite these limitations, results from this study clearly indicate that public schools offer more formal opportunities for parents to be involved than do private schools. These differences are partially explained by differences in the organizational characteristics of the school, most notably size and sources of additional funding. On average, public schools have larger student populations than private schools. They offer more extracurricular activities, such as school plays, to their students, which results in parents having more opportunities for involvement. With a larger parent population, public schools also seem better able to support organizations such as parent-teacher associations.

It was expected that private schools would have an advantage with respect to resources, yet these data show that they have fewer sources of additional funding than public schools. Many of the sources included in this study—for example, migrant aid—specifically address the needs of at-risk populations, whom private schools are less likely to educate. For this reason, they are less likely to qualify for such financial assistance. This lack of additional funding explains some of the difference between public and private schools in opportunities for involvement, because additional funding is highly and positively related to opportunities. The differences between public and private schools also are partially accounted for by the fact that, in this sample, a greater number of private schools are early childhood centers, which offer fewer opportunities for involvement than traditional schools. Contrary to expectations, differences in opportunities were not explained by differences in institutional support for parental involvement, as measured in this study. Public and private schools placed similar levels of emphasis on good communication with parents. They also offered their teachers roughly equal opportunities for training in regard to parental involvement, although the average in both types of schools was low, approximately once per year.

Findings from this study seem curious given that other research suggests private school parents are more involved in the school context than public school parents. It appears that private school parents are more involved despite the fact that they have fewer formal opportunities. While this study cannot provide insight into why this might be so, other literature supports several explanations. As previously discussed, private school parents' socioeconomic backgrounds may lead them to be more involved, no matter which school their children attend. At the same time, it might be the case that when parents choose their children's schools, they become more interested, and therefore involved in, their children's education. Last, private schools may be doing a better job than public schools of encouraging and facilitating involvement in extracurricular activities. Such an explanation supports the contention that private schools are more concerned about creating an atmosphere in which all members of the school community are welcomed and valued. No matter the explanation, opportunities for parental involvement represent another area in which the school experiences for both students and parents differ between public and private schools.

Note

I would like to thank Maureen Hallinan for her insights on the theoretical foundation of this study, Warren Kubitschek and Felicia LeClere for their analytical guidance, and Bill Carbonaro for his invitation to participate in the conference "Effects of School Sector on Educational Outcomes," University of Notre Dame, November 9–10, 2002, from which this paper emerged.

(The author is currently employed as an education statistician with the National Center for Education Statistics. This research was conducted while she was a graduate student at the University of Notre Dame, and the views expressed in her chapter do not necessarily reflect the position of the U.S. Department of Education.)

REFERENCES

Alt, M. N., & Peter, K. (2002). *Private schools: A brief portrait* (NCES Publication No. 2002-013). U.S. Department of Education, National Center for Education Statistics. Washington, DC: U.S. Government Printing Office.

Bermúdez, A. B. (1993). Teaming with parents to promote educational equality for language minority students. In N. F. Chavkin (Ed.), *Families and schools in a pluralistic society* (pp. 175–188). Albany: State University of New York.

Blau, P. M. (1964). *Exchange and power in social life.* New York: Wiley.

Bryk, A. S. (1995). Lessons from Catholic high schools on renewing our educational institutions. In M. T. Hallinan (Ed.), *Restructuring schools: Promising practices and policies* (pp. 81–98). New York: Plenum Press.

Bryk, A. S., Lee, V. E., & Holland, P. B. (1993). *Catholic schools and the common good.* Cambridge, MA: Harvard University Press.

Coleman, J. S. (1988). Social capital in the creation of human capital. *American Journal of Sociology, 94* (Suppl.), S95–S120.

Coleman, J. S., & Hoffer, T. (1987). *Public and private high schools: The impact of communities.* New York: Basic Books.

Coleman, J. S., Hoffer, T., & Kilgore, S. (1982). *High school achievement: Public, Catholic, and private schools compared.* New York: Basic Books.

Coleman, J. S., Schiller, K. S., & Schneider, B. (1993). Parent choice and inequality. In B. Schneider & J. S. Coleman (Eds.), *Parents, their children, and schools* (pp. 147–182). Boulder, CO: Westview Press.

Cookson, P. W. (1994). *School choice: The struggle for the soul of American education.* New Haven, CT: Yale University Press.

Davies, D. (1993). Benefits and barriers to parental involvement: From Portugal to Liverpool. In N. F. Chavkin (Ed.), *Families and schools in a pluralistic society* (pp. 205–216). Albany: State University of New York.

Epstein, J. L. (1990). School and family connections: Theory, research, and implications for integrating sociologies of education and family. In D. Unger & M. Sussman (Eds.), *Families in community settings: Interdisciplinary perspectives* (pp. 99–126). New York: Haworth.

Goldring, E. B., & Bauch, P. A. (1993, April). *Parent involvement and school responsiveness: Facilitating the home-school connection in schools of choice.* Paper presented at the annual meeting of the American Educational Research Association, Atlanta, GA (ERIC Document Reproduction Service No. ED358532).

Hallinan, M. T. (2002). Catholic education as a societal institution. *Catholic Education: A Journal of Inquiry and Practice, 6* (1), 5–26.

Hausman, C. S., & Goldring, E. B. (2000). Parent involvement, influence, and satisfaction in magnet schools: Do reasons for choice matter? *The Urban Review, 32* (2), 105–121.

Lareau, A. (1987, April). Social class differences in family-school relationships: The importance of cultural capital. *Sociology of Education, 60,* 73–85.

Lee, V. E., & Bryk, A. S. (1988). Curriculum tracking as mediating the social distribution of high school achievement. *Sociology of Education, 61*(2), 78–94.

Muller, C. (1993, April). *Parent involvement in education and school sector.* Paper presented at the annual meeting of the American Educational Research Association, Atlanta, GA (ERIC Document Reproduction Service No. ED361888).

Muller, C., & Kerbow, D. (1993). Parent involvement in the home, school, and community. In B. Schneider & J. S. Coleman (Eds.), *Parents, their children, and schools* (pp. 13–42). Boulder, CO: Westview Press.

Nord, C. W., Brimhall, D., & West, J. (1997). *Fathers' involvement in their children's schools* (NCES Publication No. 98-091). U.S. Department of Education. Washington, DC: National Center for Education Statistics.

Stevenson, D. L., & Baker, D. P. (1987). The family-school relation and the child's school performance. *Child Development, 58,* 1348–1357.

Thibaut, J. W., & Kelley, H. H. (1959). *The social psychology of groups.* New York: Wiley.

U.S. Department of Education. (1992). *Education research report: Parent satisfaction with schools and the need for standards.* Washington, DC: Office of Educational Research and Improvement (ERIC Document Reproduction Service No. ED352206).

U.S. Department of Education. (1995). *Use of school choice* (NCES Publication No. 95-742R). Washington, DC: National Center for Education Statistics.

U.S. Department of Education. (2001). *Early childhood longitudinal study, kindergarten class of 1998–1999: User's manual for the ECLS-K base year public-use data files and electronic codebook* (NCES Publication No. 2001-029). Washington, DC: National Center for Education Statistics.

Vaden-Kiernan, N. (1996). *Parents' reports of school practices to involve families* (NCES Publication No. 97-327). U.S. Department of Education, National Center for Education Statistics. Washington, DC: U.S. Government Printing Office.

8 | Children's Cultural Capital and Teachers' Assessments of Effort and Ability

The Influence of School Sector

Susan A. Dumais

The French sociologist Pierre Bourdieu is well known in American sociology of education for his theory of cultural capital, which states that upper-middle-class children are privileged in the educational system because their families possess cultural knowledge and language skills that are valued by teachers. For the past twenty years, sociologists have operationalized cultural capital in a number of ways and assessed its effects on educational outcomes with a variety of methods. Some researchers have used large data sets with samples of high school students, while others have conducted qualitative research, studying smaller groups of young children in more detail.

Despite the wealth of existing research on the subject, the current understanding of cultural capital has three limitations. First, the existing research on cultural capital and education has focused on students in public schools, ignoring the different ways that cultural capital may function in the private school sector. Past educational research has discovered differences in the academic climate of public schools and Catholic schools (for example, Coleman & Hoffer, 1987), but has not examined differences in the possession of or the effects of cultural capital. Bourdieu (1973) noted the importance of the school setting in his research, but few American educational studies have taken school sector into consideration. Second, differences between children at the very early stages of their educational career—the kindergarten year—have not been studied with regard to public-Catholic school differences in general, or with regard to cultural capital differences by school sector in particular. Third, few studies have considered cultural capital as part of Bourdieu's broader theoretical framework, which includes the concepts of one's orientation to the world (what Bourdieu referred to as habitus) and the setting in which people enact their cultural capital (what Bourdieu referred to as field).

In this chapter, Bourdieu's theoretical framework is employed to study the differences between kindergarten students who attend public schools and kindergartners who attend Catholic schools. In particular, the cultural resources possessed by the students are compared across the two school sectors, as are the orientations toward schooling possessed by the kindergartners' parents. The teachers' academic evaluations of the students based on their and their parents' possession of these resources are also compared by school sector. The findings from this study contribute to two areas of educational research that have not been linked in previous studies: school sector effects research, and cultural capital research. The findings also contribute to the understanding of the educational experiences of young children.

In the next section, the differences between public school and Catholic school environments are discussed. Bourdieu's theory of social reproduction and the concepts of cultural capital, orientation, and setting are presented, and past research on cultural capital and schooling is reviewed. A nationally representative sample of kindergarten students and their parents is analyzed to address how cultural capital and parents' orientation toward school affect teachers' perceptions of students' effort and ability, and how the effects of cultural capital and parents' orientation vary by school sector.

The Cultural Climate of Public and Catholic Schools

Compared to public schools, Catholic schools have lower per-pupil expenditures but higher average achievement test scores, higher rates of graduation, and higher rates of graduates going on to postsecondary education (Coleman & Hoffer, 1987; Bryk, Lee, & Holland, 1993; Sander, 1996). To explain this relationship, Coleman relied on a theory of social capital (Coleman & Hoffer, 1987; also see Schneider, 2000, for a detailed discussion of Coleman's theories). Social capital refers to the network of relationships within a family, or within a community, such as a school. This network generates trust and a set of norms. In particular, when parents of students in the same class know each other, social closure is achieved, which allows for the creation and maintenance of norms regarding learning and effort. Coleman and Hoffer (1987) described this type of environment as a functional community. These shared norms lead to higher student achievement levels than would be found in a school lacking such social closure. The Catholic school environment is more likely than the public school environment to generate social capital, in part because the students' parents are often involved with the church community affiliated with the school.

The different environments in public and Catholic schools may influence the relationship between students' background characteristics and their achievement outcomes. Within Catholic schools, teachers may have expectations for both students and parents that are different from the expectations at public schools. For example, if Coleman's theory of social capital is correct, teachers in Catholic schools may expect more parental involvement and student motivation, and the consequences for lacking these resources may be more severe in a Catholic school than in a public school. Furthermore, the value of a student's cultural knowledge may vary by school sector, with one type of school expecting students to be well versed in a variety of cultural skills and another being more forgiving of those students who do not have these skills at their disposal. These characteristics—parental interaction with the school, student motivation toward getting an education, and students' cultural resources—all relate to Bourdieu's theory of cultural capital and educational inequality.

Bourdieu's Theoretical Framework

Bourdieu argued that cultural capital, one's orientation toward the social structure and social institutions, and social setting all work together to generate social action, or what Bourdieu (1984) referred to as practice. All forms of social action, from decisions in the political realm to processes in the classroom, are based on the combination of these three factors.

The element of Bourdieu's theory that has received the most attention in sociological research is cultural capital. Along with economic, social, and symbolic capital, cultural capital serves as a way for groups to remain dominant or to gain status (see Bourdieu, 1997, for a discussion of the different types of capital). Cultural capital comes in three forms: (1) objectified cultural capital, which refers to objects, such as works of art, that require special cultural abilities to use and appreciate; (2) embodied cultural capital, which is the disposition toward appreciating and understanding objectified cultural capital; and (3) institutionalized cultural capital, which refers to educational credentials and the credentialing system. Objectified cultural capital refers to what is considered high art and tends to be found in museums, concert halls, and the homes of the upper classes. It is the second form of cultural capital—embodied—that most researchers try to operationalize in their studies, by showing students' interest in music or lessons in art or dance. The third form of cultural capital—institutionalized—develops as a result of one's having embodied cultural capital and successfully converting it via the educational system.

Bourdieu argues that cultural capital, particularly in its embodied form, serves as a resource that people can employ to gain or maintain power and privilege. While embodied cultural capital is a resource, one's orientation toward using that resource is critical in determining the type of social action that occurs. Bourdieu describes the concept of orientation as a "structuring structure, which organizes practices and the perception of practices" (1984, p. 170). It is generated by one's place in the social structure. By internalizing the social structure and one's place in it, an individual comes to determine what is possible for his or her life and develops aspirations and practices accordingly. This orientation reflects both a general worldview and one's relationship to different social institutions. A person's place in the class structure affects his or her orientation toward schooling, toward religion, and so forth.

The internalization of the social structure takes place during early childhood and is a primarily unconscious process, but the consequences go beyond individual actors. Bourdieu (1984) argues that the reproduction of the social structure results from people's orientations toward it. Based on their class position, people develop ideas about their individual potential. For example, working-class persons tend to believe that they will remain in the working class. These beliefs are then externalized into actions that lead to the reproduction of the class structure.

Finally, the actions that result from one's orientation and capital take place within specific settings. Bourdieu and Wacquant (1992) describe the social setting as a configuration of relations between social positions. Settings are spaces where dominant and subordinate groups struggle for control over resources. Each setting is based upon one or more types of capital (an intellectual setting would be organized around cultural capital, for example). Indeed, Bourdieu argues that capital does not exist or function except in relation to a setting.

Applying these three concepts—cultural capital, orientation, and setting—to education, Bourdieu (1973) argues that schools reproduce social inequality. He describes the school system as a particular setting within which the most valuable form of capital is cultural capital. Rather than individual talent, then, it is the possession of cultural capital that leads to academic success (Swartz, 1997).

Cultural capital is concentrated in the upper classes. Bourdieu (1984) finds that middle-class teachers also have high levels of cultural capital and tend to reward those students who possess it. Children who have more cultural capital (having been exposed to it in their upper-class families) will feel more comfortable in the school setting, will communicate easily with teachers, and therefore will be more likely to do well in school. Lower-class students, on the other hand, find the school environment different from their home environment and lack the capital necessary to fit in as well as the upper-class students. Even those lower-class students who do manage to accumulate cultural capital in school and advance successfully through the school system will be easy to distinguish from their upper-class peers, because their cultural capital will be more scholastic and conservative than those who were exposed to cultural capital in their homes (Bourdieu, 1984).

It is not cultural capital alone, however, that leads students to succeed in the school system. One's orientation toward the social structure also plays a role. Students' decisions to invest in their education, study hard, and go to college depend on their place in the class system and their understanding of whether people from that class tend to be successful academically (Swartz, 1997). For younger students, parents' orientation affects the early school years. Working-class parents do not feel comfortable in the school environment and have a harder time interacting with teachers than middle-class parents. Children witness their parents' interactions and attitudes and internalize them, creating larger differences in the working-class and middle-class orientations each year that the children spend in school. Bourdieu (1973) argues that one's orientation develops in relation to how much cultural capital he or she has; a person from the lower class is aware that people from that class tend to have very little cultural capital and that, without it, they are unlikely to succeed educationally. Therefore, students from the lower classes will tend to, on average, have lower expectations about succeeding in school and may be less likely to use what little cultural capital they have, because they do not see much chance to succeed academically.

The importance of cultural capital and parents' orientation toward schooling certainly may vary by setting. What is considered irrelevant in a public school, for example, may be considered vital in a Catholic school. Although these two research areas—school sector differences and cultural capital—have not been linked in the past, Coleman's views on norms and schooling can be linked to Bourdieu's concept of orientation. Both one's orientation toward schooling, and norms generated by social capital, are indications of one's disposition and commitment to particular values. One would expect that parents who enroll their children in a Catholic school have specific reasons for doing so, which may have to do with curriculum, discipline, or religious beliefs. An implication of this school choice, then, is that these parents have a different orientation toward the world and what they expect for their children than parents who send their children to public school. We should therefore expect to see a stronger parental academic orientation among Catholic school parents than public school parents, and this academic orientation should have an effect on students' educational outcomes. Indeed, a positive parental orientation may lead to the generation of social capital. As parents attend school events and open houses, they should become acquainted with other parents and begin to build the networks and shared norms that, Coleman argued, are important for student achievement.

Bourdieu's conceptual framework has not been without criticism. Swartz (1997) notes that in large, differentiated societies such as the United States, where there is not as strong a dominant culture as there is in France, cultural capital may not be as useful a concept. Additionally, a number of researchers have found that in American schools, cultural capital benefits not only students from privileged backgrounds but also all students who have it. This phenomenon has been referred to as the "cultural mobility" model (DiMaggio, 1982), in contrast to Bourdieu's cultural reproduction model. Nevertheless, the concept of cultural capital remains a major focus in the sociology of education and has been analyzed in a number of quantitative and qualitative studies.

Past Research: Quantitative Analyses

Research on cultural capital in America has operationalized a number of different variables as "cultural capital" and "educational success"; indeed, Kingston (2001) criticizes researchers' use of conceptually distinct variables under the "big umbrella of cultural capital." Nevertheless, the majority of studies in this area have found that cultural capital has a positive effect on whatever educational outcome is being studied. Some of the earliest studies of the effects of cultural capital in the United States were done by DiMaggio and Mohr (DiMaggio, 1982; DiMaggio & Mohr, 1985). Using a large data set of high school students from 1960, DiMaggio (1982) found that cultural capital had a significant effect on students' grades, even after controlling for ability and fathers' education. Using the same data set, DiMaggio and Mohr (1985) found that cultural capital had significant effects on several educational outcomes (educational attainment, college attendance, and college completion).

Kalmijn and Kraaykamp (1996) used data from the Surveys of Public Participation in the Arts, finding that parental cultural capital (attending arts events, encouraging their children to read) was associated with higher levels of schooling for children. Aschaffenburg and Maas (1997) relied on the same data set to show that cultural participation, particularly taking lessons in the arts, positively affected educational transitions (going to high school, completing high school, moving from high school to college, and completing college).

Roscigno and Ainsworth-Darnell (1999) used data from the National Education Longitudinal Study (NELS) to examine how cultural trips, cultural classes, and household educational resources (such as a dictionary and an encyclopedia) affected grades and achievement test scores. They found that all three forms of cultural capital positively affected both outcomes, and that the returns for cultural trips and educational resources were less for African American and low socioeconomic status (SES) students. Teachman (1987) focused exclusively on household educational resources, and, using data from the National Longitudinal Study of the High School Class of 1972 (NLS-72), found that, controlling for family background, educational resources had a positive effect on educational attainment.

In the United States, then, a number of different data sets have been used to show that participation in cultural activities and possession of educational resources in the home result in higher grades, higher achievement scores, and higher levels of educational attainment. Several studies have considered cultural capital in other countries, but the findings have not been as consistent as those in the United States. With data from the Netherlands, De Graaf, De Graaf, and Kraaykamp (2000) found that parental reading behavior had a positive effect on children's educational attainment, especially for children whose parents had low levels of education; parental participation in beaux arts, however, was not found to have any effect on attainment. Katsillis and Rubinson (1990) found that cultural capital (operationalized as participation in high culture) did not affect the grade point averages of high school seniors in Greece. Robinson and Garnier (1985) used fathers' education as a measure of embodied cultural capital in studying class reproduction in France, and they found that education played only a small role in reproducing ownership over the means of production.

None of these studies in the United States or in Europe considered the role of orientation toward the social structure in general, or toward schooling in particular. McClelland (1990) conducted the earliest quantitative study of orientation toward the social structure in American educational research, using the NLS-72 data to operationalize orientation as students' occupational aspirations, particularly whether or not they aspired to white-collar jobs. McClelland did not include cultural capital in her study, which examined how students either reach their educational and occupational goals or change them over time. More recently, Dumais (2002) used data from NELS to examine gender differences in the effects of cultural capital and orientation among eighth grade students; cultural capital was operationalized as students' participation in arts activities and orientation toward the social structure were operationalized as students' white-collar occupational aspirations. Dumais did find that orientation had an effect on students' grades, while cultural capital affected only the grades of girls.

Research including measures of orientation toward the social structure is only now beginning to be conducted. One important issue to consider in this research is how early in a student's life his or her orientation becomes salient. Quantitative studies have primarily come from surveys of students who are junior high school age or older, but several qualitative analyses have focused on younger children.

Past Research: Qualitative Analyses

Qualitative work from the late 1980s through the present has provided a rich description of the experiences that young students and their parents have with the school system and has considered the role of cultural capital. Overall, qualitative research has shown that there are class differences in the ways that children and parents interact with the school system, but it has not examined the consequences that these differences have for student achievement. The most thorough research to date on cultural capital in American elementary schools has been conducted by Lareau and her colleagues (Lareau, 1987; Lareau, 1989; Lareau & McNamara Horvat 1999; Lareau, 2000; Lareau, 2002). Lareau (1989) studied the relationships between parents of first-graders and school personnel in a predominantly working-class and a predominantly upper-middle-class school. At both schools, teachers and officials were middle class. Lareau argued that working-class parents lacked the resources (education, occupational status, and so forth) to feel comfortable in confronting teachers; she referred to these resources as cultural capital. She did not explicitly study the effect that parental involvement had on teachers' perceptions of students, although she did find that upper-middle-class parents tended to be most involved when their children were doing poorly, and working-class parents were most involved when their children were doing very well.

In another study, Lareau (2000) found that class differences were larger than racial differences when following the daily lives of white and African American working-class and middle-class boys in third and fourth grades. She found that the middle-class boys had very structured lives outside of school, filled with a variety of activities, while the working-class boys had much less structure and spent their free time playing and watching television (similar findings were described in Lareau, 2002). Lareau hypothesized that these differences would result in advantages for the middle-class boys: With a wide variety of experiences through their activities, they had different repertoires on which to draw, while the working-class boys did not have the same opportunities to gain experience and expertise. The differences in experiences might be interpreted as the difference between a working-class and a middle-class orientation, although Lareau did not explicitly state this.

Reay (1995) studied two primary school classrooms in England, one working class, and one middle class, and examined the differences in orientation between the two groups of students. While the middle-class students did not want to tidy up at the end of class (because they saw it as "someone else's job"), the working-class students were eager to help the teacher. Reay also observed a group of middle-class girls playing a computer game, and they assumed that they held the role of the mistress, while the working-class girls assumed that they held the role of the servant. This research provided a description of the different forms of orientation that students may possess, but it did not examine the effects of orientation on educational outcomes.

None of these studies of cultural capital and schooling addresses the differences that might occur by school sector. School type has been included as a control variable in some cultural capital studies (for example, Roscigno & Ainsworth-Darnell, 1999), but it has not been a major focus in this area of research. Furthermore, research in the area of public school-Catholic school differences has not addressed the concepts of cultural capital and orientation. Additionally, although more students are enrolled in Catholic elementary schools than in Catholic high schools, the majority of educational research on Catholic schools has focused on the secondary level. (An exception is Jepsen, 2003.)

A true test of Bourdieu's theory would take into account both cultural capital and orientation toward social structure or specific social institutions while also taking into consideration the setting, or the site of social action. Because past research has shown that the public school environment differs from the Catholic school environment in several key ways, it is reasonable to expect that the influences of cultural capital and orientation may also differ by school sector. The recent availability of a data set that follows children from the onset of their education and that includes children from both public and Catholic school sectors provides a unique opportunity to examine the early effects of cultural capital and orientation on students' educational experiences and outcomes.

The analyses in this chapter address three major questions: (1) Do public-Catholic school differences exist in the possession of cultural capital by kindergarten children and in their parents' orientation toward schooling? (2) How do children's cultural capital and parents' orientation toward schooling affect teachers' perceptions of kindergarten students' effort and ability? And (3) Do the effects of children's cultural capital and parents' orientation vary by school sector?

Analysis

Data and Sample

Data are from the public-use files of the Early Childhood Longitudinal Study, Kindergarten Class of 1998–1999 (ECLS-K). The ECLS-K follows a nationally representative sample of approximately 22,000 children from kindergarten through fifth grade; currently, data are available from the kindergarten and first grade waves of the study. The children's teachers, parents, and schools all provide information.

Data in these analyses are from the Spring 1999 Questionnaires for Parents and Teachers and from the direct child assessments (U.S. Department of Education, National Center for Education Statistics, 2001). Whites, African Americans, and Hispanics are all included in the sample. For these analyses, the sample is restricted to kindergartners in public and Catholic schools.

The two dependent variables come from the teacher's questionnaire. The first is the teacher's response to the question, "How often does the student work to the best of his or her ability?" The teacher can respond: never, seldom, usually, or always (a scale of 1 to 4). For public schools, this variable had a mean of 3.2 and a standard deviation of .7, while in Catholic schools, the mean was 3.3 and the standard deviation was .6. The second dependent variable asks the teacher to compare the student's language and literacy skills to other students in the same grade level; teachers may respond: far below average, below average, average, above average, or far above average (a scale of 1 to 5). For public schools, the mean of this variable was 3.1 and the standard deviation was 1.0, while for Catholic schools, the variable had a mean of 3.3 and a standard deviation of .9.

The independent variables include a dummy variable for gender (1 = female), a dummy variable for minority status (1 = African American or Hispanic), and a composite SES variable, generated from information on the parents' education, occupational status, and income. A direct assessment of the kindergartners' reading skills in the fall of 1998 is used as a control variable for ability; the IRT scale score for this assessment is used.

Parents in the ECLS-K report on two different types of cultural activities in which their children are involved outside of school: one-time cultural excursions, such as visiting a museum or going to a concert; and sustained lessons, such as classes in art, dance, drama, music, performance art, foreign language, or crafts. For all activities, the survey responses were "yes" (has participated) or "no" (has not participated).

Because the children in the ECLS are quite young, there are no survey questions asked of them directly in the kindergarten wave. Therefore, in order to examine orientation toward schooling, it is necessary to turn to the information that the parents provide about their own experiences with their children's schooling. The parents' experiences fall into two main categories—actions and attitudes—and each category can be seen as a reflection of the parents' orientation toward schooling. Among the actions that a parent could take are volunteering at the school, attending school events (such as play performances), attending open houses, and going to parent-teacher conferences. There are two questions that reflect parents' negative attitudes about schooling. The first asks whether the parent has found it more difficult to be involved with the child's schooling because he or she does not feel welcomed by the school. The second inquires whether the parent has found it more difficult to be involved with the child's schooling because there is nothing that interests him or her (the parent).

Cultural Participation, Parents' Orientation toward Schooling, and School Sector

In Table 8.1 the parents' reports of children's participation in cultural activities are given by school sector. In every activity except performance art, the Catholic school students have a higher participation rate than the public school children. The differences between the two groups are statistically significant for every activity except performance art lessons and foreign language lessons.

The most popular activities for all students—both public and Catholic—are the one-time cultural events. More than one-third of public school students have been to a concert, and 28 percent have been to a museum. Among Catholic school students, 43 percent have been to a concert, and 35% have been to a museum. The least popular are repeated lessons in areas such as drama, foreign language, music, and art. In the public school sector, 6 percent or fewer children participate in each of these lessons; in the Catholic school sector, fewer than 10 percent participate. Dance is the most popular type of lesson in both public and Catholic schools, with 14 percent of public school students, and more than one-quarter of Catholic school students, participating.

Overall, about 38 percent of public school students, and 25 percent of Catholic school students, take part in no cultural activities at all. Among the public school students, 15 percent participate in three or more cultural activities, compared to 21 percent of the Catholic school students. The average number of cultural activities is 1.2 for the public school students and 1.6 for the Catholic school students.

Table 8.1. Percentage of Children Participating in Selected Cultural Activities by School Sector

	Public	Catholic
One-time events		
Concerts	36.0%	42.7%***
Museums	28.4%	35.4%***
Lessons		
Dance	14.2%	26.1%***
Music	6.0%	7.1%*
Drama	1.2%	2.1%**
Art	6.2%	8.6%***
Performance art	14.0%	12.5%
Crafts	9.8%	13.2%***
Foreign language	4.6%	5.3%

Notes: Appropriate sample and design weights were used. The sample size varied by question and ranged from 12,958 to 12,967 for public school students and from 2,020 to 2,021 for Catholic school students.
*$p < .05$; **$p < .01$; ***$p < .001$
Source: Early Childhood Longitudinal Study, Kindergarten Class of 1998–1999

Catholic kindergarten students, then, are more likely to take part in a greater number and in a wider variety of cultural activities than public school children. In part, this may be due to SES differences between the student populations. The Catholic school students have a higher average SES level than the public school students; and in both schools, higher SES groups are more likely to participate in cultural activities. Nevertheless, the SES differences between school sectors do not account for all of the difference. For example, in the lowest SES quintile of students, the average number of cultural activities was .65 in public schools, but 1.3 in Catholic schools. On the other hand, within the top SES quintile, public school students took part in an average of 2.0 cultural activities, compared to 1.9 in Catholic schools. SES appears to have a greater influence on cultural participation in public schools than in Catholic schools. Indeed, a student's total number of cultural activities (all of the one-time events and lessons added together) had a correlation with SES of .33 in public schools and only .19 in Catholic schools.

In addition to differences in levels of cultural capital, Bourdieu argued that people have different orientations toward social structure and social institutions. Those who are from privileged backgrounds will feel more comfortable in academic settings and will be more likely to conduct intellectual conversations (Lareau, 1989). These differences in perspective may affect the ways in which the parents of kindergartners engage with the school system, teachers, and other parents.

Table 8.2. Percentage of Parents Who Agree with School Orientation-Related Statements by School Sector

	Public	Catholic
Actions		
Attended open house	71.5%	84.9%***
Attended parent-teacher conference	83.4%	91.2%***
Attended a school event	62.7%	82.7%***
Volunteered at school	43.7%	70.5%***
Attitudes		
Does not find school activities interesting	13.6%	7.6%***
Does not feel welcome at school	6.0%	3.6%***

Notes: Appropriate sample and design weights were used. The sample size varied by question and ranged from 12,944 to 12,975 for public school students and from 2,020 to 2,021 for Catholic school students.
*$p < .05$; **$p < .01$; ***$p < .001$
Source: Early Childhood Longitudinal Study, Kindergarten Class of 1998–1999

Table 8.2 presents several indicators of parental school orientation and the percentage of parents in each school sector who have them. For all four of the actions that parents could take, public school parents have a lower rate of participation than Catholic school parents; all of the school sector differences in parents' participation are statistically significant. The activity with the greatest gap between public school and Catholic school participation is volunteering at school: while 71 percent of Catholic school parents volunteer, only 44 percent of public school parents do so. The majority of parents in both schools engage in the other three activities.

Overall, the average number of activities in which the parents participate is 2.6 for public schools and 3.3 for Catholic schools. When one takes SES into consideration, the average number of activities for public school parents ranges from 1.9 in the lowest SES quintile to 3.3 in the highest SES quintile; for Catholic school parents, the average number of activities ranges from 2.9 in the lowest to 3.5 in the highest.

The other component of parental orientation—attitudes—consists of two questions about factors that lead the parents to be less involved in their children's schooling. The first question asks the parents whether they have been less involved in their children's schooling because they do not find school activities interesting. Fourteen percent of parents in public schools answer "yes" to this question, compared to 8 percent in Catholic schools. The second question asks parents whether they have limited involvement with the school because they don't feel welcome;

6 percent of public school parents, and 4 percent of Catholic school parents, respond "yes." Like the measures of cultural capital and the actions measures for parental orientation, SES plays a role here. Higher SES parents are less likely to agree with these two negative statements. Again, the SES differences are greater within the public school sector than within the Catholic school sector. The correlation between SES and parents' orientation is higher in public schools (SES and actions: .41; SES and attitudes: -.11) than in Catholic schools (SES and actions: .23; SES and attitudes: -.07).

Like the measures of cultural capital, the measures of parents' orientation are clearly associated with school sector. Catholic school parents have higher levels of involvement in their children's schooling than public school parents. Although the majority of parents from both school sectors disagree that they feel unwelcome at their child's school or are uninterested in school activities, public school parents are more likely to agree with these statements.

School Sector Differences in the Effects of Cultural Capital and Parents' Orientation toward School

Table 8.3 presents the pooled within-school regression estimates for two sets of models, with separate analyses for public and Catholic school students. The pooled within-school models, also called fixed effects models, control for school level variables, such as the urbanicity of an area, which might affect the availability of cultural resources. The final models are presented here. Earlier models, such as analyses with the cultural capital variables alone, with the orientation variables alone, with a sum total of cultural capital activities rather than separate variables for each activity, and so forth, had very similar results. Additionally, these analyses were conducted using ordered logistic regression and produced nearly identical results.

The dependent variable in the first set of models is how often the teacher believes that the student works to his or her best ability. A higher value of the dependent variable represents a more favorable evaluation by the teacher. In the model for public school students, the reading test score, being female, and SES all have significant positive effects on teachers' evaluations of students. However, the cultural capital variables—both attendance at arts events and taking arts lessons—do not have an effect on teachers' evaluations. This result is quite different from past studies that have examined the effects of cultural capital on middle school and high school students, where positive effects have consistently been found.

All four of the "actions" components of parents' orientation toward schooling have significant effects on teachers' evaluations of public school students' working

Table 8.3. Effects of Cultural Capital and Parental Orientation on Teachers' Perceptions of Students' Effort and Ability in Public and Catholic Schools

	Ability		Language Skills	
	Public	Catholic	Public	Catholic
Reading test score	.02***	.02***	.06***	.07***
	(.00)	(.00)	(.00)	(.00)
Female	.21***	.15**	.16***	.08
	(.02)	(.05)	(.02)	(.05)
Minority	-.04	-.06	-.12***	-.04
	(.02)	(.04)	(.03)	(.08)
SES	.05***	.07*	.13***	.10**
	(.01)	(.03)	(.01)	(.03)
One-time events				
Museums	-.01	-.02	.00	.00
	(.02)	(.04)	(.02)	(.05)
Concerts	.00	.03	.03	-.02
	(.01)	(.03)	(.02)	(.04)
Lessons				
Dance	.02	-.01	.04	-.03
	(.02)	(.04)	(.03)	(.06)
Music	.00	-.06	.03	-.07
	(.03)	(.06)	(.04)	(.07)
Drama	-.05	-.18	.02	-.05
	(.06)	(.10)	(.07)	(.13)
Art	-.01	.04	-.02	.15
	(.03)	(.05)	(.04)	(.09)
Performing	-.01	.07	.02	.05
	(.02)	(.05)	(.03)	(.05)
Crafts	-.02	.06	.04	-.05
	(.02)	(.04)	(.03)	(.08)
Languages	-.06	-.02	-.07	-.06
	(.03)	(.07)	(.03)	(.10)
Actions				
Open house	.06***	.02	.08**	.03
	(.02)	(.04)	(.02)	(.06)
Conference	-.07**	-.11*	-.10**	-.06
	(.02)	(.05)	(.03)	(.09)
School event	.05**	.12**	.02	.15*
	(.01)	(.05)	(.02)	(.06)
Volunteering	.06***	-.01	.07**	-.09
	(.01)	(.04)	(.02)	(.07)
Attitudes				
Not interested	-.02	-.01	-.01	-.03
	(.02)	(.05)	(.03)	(.09)
Not welcome	-.06*	-.11	-.14**	.04
	(.03)	(.06)	(.04)	(.14)
Constant	2.72***	2.71***	1.87***	1.61***
	(.03)	(.09)	(.05)	(.13)
Adj. R-squared	.19	.23	.38	.43
N	11033	1586	11073	1597

Notes: Standard errors are in parentheses. Appropriate sample and design weights were used.
*p < .05; **p < .01; ***p < .001
Source: Early Childhood Longitudinal Study, Kindergarten Class of 1998–1999

to ability. However, one of the variables—attending parent-teacher conferences—has a negative effect. In other words, teachers have less favorable evaluations of students whose parents have attended a parent-teacher conference, even after controlling for the students' ability levels. The ECLS data do not provide information about why the parent-teacher conferences take place, but perhaps conferences are more likely to occur if the student is having problems at school. The other three variables—attending open houses, attending school events, and volunteering at school—all have positive effects. Only one of the two attitudes variables—not feeling welcome at school—has an effect on teachers' perceptions.

The next model uses the same dependent variable—the teacher's perception of how often the student works to ability—but focuses on students in Catholic schools. A higher reading score, being female, and higher SES all correspond with more favorable teacher evaluations, as they did in the public school model. Neither the one-time events nor the cultural lessons have any effect on the teachers' evaluations. For both public school and Catholic school students, then, the possession of cultural capital is not associated with higher teacher evaluations of student effort. The variables indicating parents' orientation do not affect Catholic school teachers' evaluations in the same way that they affect public school teachers' evaluations. Attending school events results in a more positive evaluation, while going to parent-teacher conferences results in a more negative one. Attending open houses and volunteering at school do not have effects on Catholic school teachers' evaluations. Additionally, neither of the two attitudes variables has an effect in this model.

For both public school and Catholic school students, then, teachers are more likely to say that students work to their best ability if they are female, have higher test scores, or come from a higher socioeconomic background. Whether or not students take cultural lessons or attend cultural events has no effect on teachers' perceptions in the public or the Catholic schools. More of the parents' orientation variables have an effect in the public school model than in the Catholic school model. In public schools, all of the actions that parents could take affect teachers' perceptions, while only conferences and attending school events have an effect in the Catholic schools. Among the attitudes variables, only not feeling welcome has an effect in public schools, and neither variable has an effect in the Catholic schools.

The first set of models examined the effects of cultural capital and parents' orientation on teachers' assessments of students' working to ability. In the next set of models, the dependent variable is teachers' assessments of students' academic skills—in particular, how a student's language skills compare to other students at the same grade level.

In the public school model, the student's score on the reading test has a positive effect, as would be expected. Being female results in a more favorable teacher assessment, while minority status has a negative effect. Socioeconomic status has a positive effect on teachers' evaluations. The two components of cultural capital—one-time cultural activities and long-term lessons—do not have a significant influence on teachers' perceptions. This finding is similar to that of the previous set of models. The cultural activities that have been found to have an effect on adolescent students in past research do not have an effect on kindergartners.

Three of the actions variables of parents' orientation toward schooling have effects on teachers' perceptions, and the effects are in the same direction as they were in the previous set of models. Attendance at open houses and volunteering at school result in more favorable teacher evaluations, while going to parent-teacher conferences results in less favorable ones. Attending school events, which affected teachers' evaluations of working to ability, does not have an effect on their evaluations of students' skills in language arts. Of the two attitudes variables, only not feeling welcome has an effect on teachers' evaluations; not feeling welcome results in a lower teacher evaluation of students' skills. For public school students, then, teachers' assessments of effort and skill are affected similarly by parents' orientation, with the exception of attendance at school events, and not at all by cultural capital.

The estimates in the Catholic school model differ both from the public school models and from the previous Catholic school model focusing on effort. While higher reading test scores and higher SES levels result in more favorable evaluations of students' language arts skills, gender and minority status have no effect. As in all of the previous models, none of the cultural capital variables has any effect on teachers' perceptions. Only one of the parents' orientation variables—attendance at school events—has an effect on teachers' evaluations; the rest of the actions and attitudes variables have no effect. Interestingly, attendance at school events was the one action in the public school model that did not have an effect on teachers' evaluations.

Discussion

The answer to the first research question—whether cultural capital and parents' orientation to schooling differ by school sector—is clear: Catholic school students are more likely to participate in cultural activities, and Catholic school parents are more likely to be involved in and have positive feelings toward their children's schooling. Moreover, these school sector differences cannot be accounted for by the different socioeconomic makeup of the student bodies.

The second and third questions—how cultural capital and parents' orientation toward schooling affect teachers' perceptions of students, and whether these effects vary by school sector—have answers that contradict previous theories and research. Cultural capital, as it has traditionally been operationalized in educational research, does not significantly affect teachers' evaluations of students' effort or ability. This is true for students in both public and Catholic schools. Past research on American middle and high schools has consistently found a cultural capital effect on various educational outcomes, and the lack of an effect for kindergarten students is puzzling. One possible explanation is that kindergarten teachers, on average, have lower levels of cultural capital themselves and do not value it as much as teachers in the higher grades. Another possibility is that the effects of cultural capital build slowly over time, so that by second or third grade, the effects of cultural capital become evident in students' educational outcomes. Both of these possibilities should be explored in future research. The second possibility—that the effects of cultural capital accumulate over time—can be answered as the third grade and fifth grade waves of the ECLS are released.

A positive interpretation of this finding is that for kindergarten students, lack of access to cultural resources does not appear to have a negative effect. Students from less privileged backgrounds are not necessarily at an educational disadvantage (from a cultural capital perspective) if they do not take arts lessons or go to museums. The lack of a cultural capital effect may be because of the age of these children; it is possible that kindergartners are too young to display the embodied cultural capital that has been found in adolescent students. Conversely, the lack of a cultural capital effect may be due to the dependent variables used in the analyses. The measurement of teachers' perceptions of the students' effort and ability may be weak. Studies of older students have often used grades as the dependent variable. Unfortunately, the ECLS data do not contain any information on grades.

Parents' orientation toward schooling does affect teachers' evaluations, and these effects vary by school sector. In public schools, attending open houses, volunteering, and going to parent-teacher conferences all affect teachers' evaluations of both student effort and ability: The first two variables have positive effects, while the third has a negative one. Attending school events has a positive effect only for teachers' evaluations of students' effort. Additionally, in public schools, teachers' evaluations of effort and ability are both negatively affected when parents agree that they do not feel welcome at their children's schools.

In Catholic schools, however, another contradiction arises. Looking at past research on social capital and parental norms, one would expect parents' orientation in Catholic schools to have a strong effect for both dependent variables. The Catholic community should reward parents' involvement and efforts to generate social closure and see their children in a more favorable light. In fact, neither of the two attitudes variables has an effect on teachers' evaluations of effort and ability. Of the four actions variables, only attendance at school events has positive effects for both types of teacher evaluations, while parent-teacher conferences have a negative effect on teachers' evaluations of effort. Since this is one of the first studies of cultural capital and parental orientation in Catholic schools, it remains to be seen if these findings are replicated. Perhaps, like cultural capital, the effects of orientation toward schooling during the high school years are stronger than they are in kindergarten.

Teachers' perceptions can have serious repercussions—teachers decide into which ability groups to place the students, whether to hold a student back, and how much time to spend with each one—which in turn may exacerbate pre-existing educational inequalities. The findings in this study indicate that public school parents, in particular, need to be made aware of the importance of their involvement in their children's schooling and to be encouraged to attend open houses or volunteer at school.

While race and gender are included as control variables in the models, they are not the main focus of this study. Being female results in more favorable teacher evaluations of both effort and ability in public schools and of effort in Catholic schools, even after controlling for ability level. Minority status has an effect in only one model—public school teachers' evaluations of language skills—but this effect is negative, again after controlling for ability level. Future research should consider these issues of gender and race.

Past research has shown that school sector differences exist in the types of social relationships that parents have with other parents, with Catholic schools generating more of this social capital. In turn, social capital has been found to have a positive influence on the educational outcomes of students in the Catholic school sector. In this study, the distribution and effects of another important form of capital—cultural capital—were examined. Higher levels of cultural capital are found in the Catholic school sector, but cultural capital does not have any impact on kindergartners' academic outcomes in either sector. These findings indicate that Bourdieu's theory of cultural capital may not apply to the American educational system in the same way that he believed it applied to the French system. Cultural capital may not become relevant in generating educational inequalities in the United States until students reach secondary school.

Additionally, the findings of this study indicate that there are school sector differences in parents' activity levels and comfort levels with school involvement.

Catholic school parents are more involved and more comfortable in their children's schools, but, ultimately, it is only parents' attendance at school events that results in educational advantages for Catholic school students. This specific indicator of parents' orientation toward schooling is, in fact, the one most closely related to Coleman's notion of social capital. Attendance at school events is a way for parents to meet with other parents, generating the social closure that leads to shared norms.

To gain a complete understanding of the influence of school sector on the effects of cultural capital and parents' orientation toward schooling, researchers will need to study sector differences over time. Bourdieu argued that the generation of both cultural capital and orientation toward the social structure are lifetime processes, and, therefore, differences between school sectors that appear minor or even nonexistent during the first year of schooling may grow gradually over subsequent years. Continued longitudinal research in this area will be necessary to fully understand school sector differences in the accumulation of and benefits from cultural capital and orientation toward schooling.

Note

This research was supported by Louisiana State University's Council on Research Summer Stipend Program. I am grateful for the comments of Stanley Lieberson, Stephen L. Morgan, and the participants in the Center for Research on Educational Opportunity's seminar series at the University of Notre Dame.

References

Aschaffenburg, K., & Maas, I. (1997). Cultural and educational careers. *American Sociological Review, 62,* 573–587.

Bourdieu, P. (1973). Cultural reproduction and social reproduction. In R. Brown (Ed.), *Knowledge, education, and cultural change: Papers in the sociology of education* (pp. 71–112). London: Tavistock.

Bourdieu, P. (1984). *Distinction: A social critique of the judgment of taste.* Cambridge, MA: Harvard University Press.

Bourdieu, P. (1997). The forms of capital. In A. H. Halsey, H. Lauder, P. Brown, & A. S. Wells (Eds.), *Education: Culture, economy, and society* (pp. 46–58). Oxford, Eng.: Oxford University Press.

Bourdieu, P., & Wacquant, L. J. D. (1992). *An invitation to reflexive sociology.* Chicago: University of Chicago Press.

Bryk, A. S., Lee, V. E., & Holland, P. B. (1993). *Catholic schools and the common good.* Cambridge, MA: Harvard University Press.

Coleman, J. S., & Hoffer, T. (1987). *Public and private high schools: The impact of communities.* New York: Basic Books.

De Graaf, N. D., De Graaf, P. M., & Kraaykamp, G. (2000). Parental cultural capital and educational attainment in the Netherlands: A refinement in the cultural capital perspective. *Sociology of Education, 73,* 92–111.

DiMaggio, P. (1982). Cultural capital and school success: The impact of status culture participation on the grades of U.S. high school students. *American Sociological Review, 47,* 189–201.

DiMaggio, P., & Mohr, J. (1985). Cultural capital, educational attainment, and marital selection. *American Journal of Sociology, 90,* 1231–1261.

Dumais, S. A. (2002). Cultural capital, gender, and school success: The role of habitus. *Sociology of Education, 75,* 44–68.

Jepsen, C. (2003). The effectiveness of Catholic primary schooling. *Journal of Human Resources, 38,* 928–941.

Kalmijn, M., & Kraaykamp, G. (1996). Race, cultural capital, and schooling: An analysis of trends in the United States. *Sociology of Education, 69,* 22–34.

Katsillis, J., & Rubinson, R. (1990). Cultural capital, student achievement, and educational reproduction: The case of Greece. *American Sociological Review, 55,* 270–279.

Kingston, P. W. (2001). The unfulfilled promise of cultural capital theory. *Sociology of Education, Extra Issue,* 88–99.

Lareau, A. (1987). Social class differences in family-school relationships: The importance of cultural capital. *Sociology of Education, 60,* 73–85.

Lareau, A. (1989). *Home advantage: Social class and parental intervention in elementary education.* London: Falmer Press.

Lareau, A. (2000). Social class and the daily lives of children: A study from the United States. *Childhood, 7,* 155–171.

Lareau, A. (2002). Invisible inequality: Social class and childrearing in black families and white families. *American Sociological Review, 67,* 747–776.

Lareau, A., & McNamara Horvat, E. M. (1999). Moments of social inclusion and exclusion: Race, class, and cultural capital in family-school relationships. *Sociology of Education, 72,* 37–53.

McClelland, K. (1990). Cumulative disadvantage among the highly ambitious. *Sociology of Education, 63,* 102–121.

Reay, D. (1995). 'They employ cleaners to do that': Habitus in the primary classroom. *British Journal of Sociology of Education, 16,* 353–371.

Robinson, R. V., & Garnier, M. A. (1985). Class reproduction among men and women in France: Reproduction theory on its home ground. *American Journal of Sociology, 91,* 250–280.

Roscigno, V. J., & Ainsworth-Darnell, J. W. (1999). Race, cultural capital, and educational resources: Persistent inequalities and achievement returns. *Sociology of Education, 72,* 158–178.

Sander, W. (1996). Catholic grade schools and academic achievement. *Journal of Human Resources, 31,* 540–548.

Schneider, B. (2000). Social systems and norms: A Coleman approach. In M. T. Hallinan (Ed.), *Handbook of the Sociology of Education* (pp. 365–385). New York: Kluwer Academic/Plenum Publishers.

Swartz, D. (1997). *Culture and power: The sociology of Pierre Bourdieu.* Chicago: University of Chicago Press.

Teachman, J. D. (1987). Family background, educational resources, and educational attainment. *American Sociological Review, 52,* 548–557.

U.S. Department of Education. (2001). *Early childhood longitudinal study, kindergarten class of 1998–1999: User's manual for the ECLS-K base year public-use data files and electronic codebook* (NCES Publication No. 2001-029). Washington, DC: National Center for Education Statistics.

Contributors

Charles E. Bidwell is the William Claude Reavis Professor Emeritus in the Department of Sociology, University of Chicago.

Matthew Boxer is a graduate student in the Department of Sociology, University of Wisconsin-Madison.

William Carbonaro is an assistant professor in the Department of Sociology and a member of the Center for Research on Educational Opportunity, Institute for Educational Initiatives, University of Notre Dame.

Fengbin Chang is a research analyst in the Department of Sociology and the National Opinion Research Center, University of Chicago.

Scott Davies is an associate professor in the Department of Sociology, McMaster University, Hamilton, Ontario, Canada.

Robert Dreeben is professor emeritus in the Department of Education, University of Chicago.

Susan A. Dumais is an assistant professor in the Department of Sociology, Louisiana State University.

Brandy J. Ellison is a graduate student in the Department of Sociology and a member of the Center for Research on Educational Opportunity, Institute for Educational Initiatives, University of Notre Dame.

Adam Gamoran is professor of sociology and educational policy studies and director of the Wisconsin Center for Education Research, University of Wisconsin-Madison.

Maureen T. Hallinan is the William P. and Hazel B. White Professor of Sociology and director of the Center for Research on Educational Opportunity, Institute for Educational Initiatives, University of Notre Dame.

Lisa Hoogstra is director of Research Services in the Alfred P. Sloan Center on Parents, Children, and Work, University of Chicago.

Gail M. Mulligan is an education statistician with the National Center for Education Statistics, U.S. Department of Education.

Linda Quirke is an assistant professor of sociology at Wilfrid Laurier University, Brantford, Ontario, Canada.

Barbara Schneider is professor of sociology, co-director of the Alfred P. Sloan Center on Parents, Children, and Work, and a senior social scientist with the National Opinion Research Center, University of Chicago.

Holly Rice Sexton is a research associate in the Center for the Analysis of the Pathways from Childhood to Adulthood, Research Center for Group Dynamics, Institute for Social Research, University of Michigan.

General Index

ability grouping, 125–152, 219
    high school, 129, 133, 144
    student achievement, 126–128, 131–136
academic achievement, 73, 76–77, 82, 93
    sector differences, 4, 126–128, 147, 153, 173, 177
    summer learning, 153–177
ACT, 20
adolescent(s)
    altruistic behavior, 76–92
    Jewish identify, 101–103, 106–110
    peer influences, 73–74, 76–77, 79, 82–96, 135, 145, 177
    religiosity, 73–99
    well-being, 3, 73, 76–77, 79–83, 85–91, 102
altruistic
    activities, 74, 76, 83
    behavior, 76–92
    participation, 76–81, 84–93

behavioral outcomes, 73, 78–79, 86, 93

Catholic
    community, 127–128, 143, 156, 174, 184
    high school, 33, 77, 93, 127, 131, 144, 149, 156, 174, 186, 195, 209
    vs. public schools, 78, 86, 88–89, 92–93
    school advantage, 77–78, 127–128, 133–145, 147–149, 155
    school effect, 78, 168–169, 171–172, 174

school students, 126–149, 166–167, 169, 173–174, 211–220
charter/magnet schools, 27, 30–33, 39–41, 44, 62, 184
community/communal, 74–79, 103, 105–106
    Catholic, 127–128, 143, 156, 174, 184
    service, 81–84, 88–89, 92–93
cultural capital, 101–118, 201–220
    education, 102, 105–108, 118–19, 201–208, 218–219
    effects of, 201–202, 206–207, 209, 214–216, 218–220
    family, 101–102, 105–106, 109
    high school, 214, 218–219
    Jewish, 101–120
    Jewish religious identity, 101–103, 106–110
    kindergarten, 201–202, 209–220
    school sector, 101–121, 201–220
    sector differences, 214–217
    teacher perceptions/assessments, 201–220
curriculum
    high school, 43, 129
    Jewish schools, 101, 107–108, 111

Early Childhood Longitudinal Study, 4, 154, 159–160, 164, 174, 210
Early Childhood Longitudinal Study (ECLS-K), 187–190, 210–211, 216, 218–219
Edison Project, 21

225

education
    and cultural capital, 102, 105–108,
        118–119, 201–208, 218–219
    sociology of, 10, 62, 201, 206
educational
    management organization (EMO), 49
    market(s), 21–27, 39–69, 156,
        183–184
Educational Testing Service, 20
exchange theory, 182–186
extracurricular activities, 51–53, 76, 79,
    185–186, 197–198

family
    adolescent psychological well-being, 3,
        73, 76–77, 79–83, 85–91, 102
    challenge, 82–83, 87, 89, 91, 95–96
    cultural capital, 101–102, 105–106, 109
    Jewish, 101–102, 104–119, 121
    religiosity, 74–76
    ritual practices, 103, 108–117, 119, 121
    socioeconomic status (SES), 83, 125, 127,
        137, 146–147, 157, 168, 176, 198, 207,
        210, 212–217
for-profit schools, 41, 49–51, 61, 64–66

high school, 17–18, 23, 25, 32, 46, 49, 52–53,
        59, 158, 173–177, 201, 206
    ability grouping, 129, 133, 144
    Catholic, 33, 77, 93, 127, 131, 144, 149, 156,
        174, 186, 195, 209
    cultural capital, 214, 218–219
    curriculum, 43, 129
    graduation rates, 77–78
    sector differences, 155–156
    sector effects, 173
High School and Beyond (HSB), 126–127,
    137–138, 146, 154
Hughes, Bishop John Joseph, 16

identity
    Catholic, 128–130, 143
    Jewish, 102–103, 110–112, 118
    religious, 74–76, 101
innovation in educational markets, 21,
    39–69
institutional/new institutional theory,
    40–44, 62

Jewish
    affiliation, 101–106, 108–110, 112–117
    cultural capital, 101–120
    family, 101–102, 104–119, 121
    identity, 102–103, 106–110
    ritual practice, 103, 108–117, 119, 121
    schools, 101–121
    —curriculum, 101, 107–108, 111
    —sector differences, 101–121

kindergarten, 159–172, 175, 177, 187–188,
        191–192
    cultural capital, 201–202, 209–220

learning
    organizational, 23–24, 28, 30, 33
    in school vs. out of school, 154, 177
    sector differences in, 125–177
    student, 153–177
    summer, 153–154, 157–159, 163–164,
        167–169, 171–173, 175–177

market(s),
    educational, 21–27, 39–69, 183–184
    niches and hierarchies, 23, 25–28
    and schools, 21–22, 39–69, 156,
        183–184
    theory, 44, 47, 61–63

National Catholic Educational Association, 127
National Education Longitudinal Study of 1988 (NELS:88), 80–81, 83–85, 154–155, 207
National Longitudinal Study of the High School Class of 1972 (NLS-72), 207
new institutional/institutional theory, 40–44

Ontario College of Teachers (OCT), 54–56
opportunity to learn, 114, 117, 125, 136
organizational
    dimensions, 2, 9, 32–34
    form(s) of, 9–11, 18–21, 23–26, 30
    learning, 11, 23–24, 28, 30, 33
    structure, 39–69, 192

parental
    involvement, 181–200, 203, 208, 213–220
    orientation, 206, 213–215, 219
parent-principal relationships, 55, 60–61
parent-teacher relationships, 55–56, 59
pedagogy, 9, 24–25, 28–33, 40–41, 49–52, 55–61, 64–66, 125–126, 149
physical plant, 45, 51–52
psychological
    outcomes, 77–78, 93
    well-being, 3, 73, 76–77, 79–83, 85–91, 102
public vs.
    Catholic schools, 78, 86, 88–89, 92–93
    private schools, 79, 88–89
    religious schools, 78, 84, 86

religiosity, 73–99
religious
    identity, 74–75
    involvement, 75–76, 78–80, 82–92
    vs. public schools, 78, 84, 86

school(s)
    advantage, Catholic, 77–78, 127–128, 133–145, 147–149, 155
    budgets, 42, 53, 56–57
    charter/magnet, 27, 30–33, 39–41, 44, 62, 184
    choice, 1, 40–44, 188, 191–193, 196
    effect, Catholic, 78, 168–169, 171–172, 174
    effects, 90–92, 105–106, 118
    extracurricular activities, 51–53, 76, 79, 185–186, 197–198
    funding, 40, 42–43, 52, 183
    Jewish, 101–121
    market(s), 21–27, 39–69, 156, 183–184
    niche, 45–47, 53, 58, 61
    physical plant, 44–45, 51–53, 61, 87–89
    sector, 9, 11, 18–19, 23, 30, 32–34, 79, 83–84, 86, 88–90, 101–121, 173–177, 201–220
    students, Catholic, 126–149, 166–167, 169, 173–174, 211–220
    summer learning, 153–154, 157–159, 163–164, 167–169, 171–173, 175–177
    third sector, 39–63
sector differences
    ability grouping, 4, 126–128, 147, 153, 173, 177
    academic achievement, 4, 126–128, 147, 153, 173, 177
    cultural capital, 214–217
    high school, 155–156
    Jewish schools, 101–121
    organizational structure, 192
    parental involvement, 181–200, 213, 219–220
    third sector schools, 39–63
sector effect(s), 125, 152, 155–158, 160, 164, 166, 168–177, 175–177, 202
self-efficacy, 74, 78–82, 84–92
self-esteem, 74, 78–82, 84–92

social
    capital, 202–203, 218–220
    class, 201, 204–205, 207–209
    closure, 202–203, 219–220
    structure, 204–205, 207–209
socialization, 52, 53
socioeconomic status (SES), 83, 125, 127, 137, 146–147, 157–158, 166–167, 176, 189, 198, 212–217
sociology of education, 10, 62, 201, 206
standardized testing, 40, 41, 43, 44
    achievement, 126–128, 131–134, 136
    outcomes, 1, 154, 174, 176
summer learning, 153–154, 157–59, 163–164, 167–169, 171–173, 175–177

Surveys of Public Participation in the Arts, 206

teacher
    credentials, 41, 51, 53–56, 87–89
    perceptions/assessments, 202–203, 208–209, 214–220
    qualifications/certification, 40–41, 43–45, 53–56, 61, 191
testing culture, 57–58, 62–63
theory
    exchange, 182–186
    institutional/new institutional, 40–44, 62
    market, 44, 47, 61–63
third sector schools, 39–63

Author Index

Agnew, J., 145
Ainsworth-Darnell, J. W., 207
Alexander, K. L., 133, 135
Argys, L. M., 132
Aschaffenburg, K., 206

Bailyn, B., 14
Baker, D. P., 78
Barr, R., 146
Betts, J. R., 132
Bourdieu, P., 101, 104–106, 182–186 201–206, 209, 212, 219–220
Brewer, D. J., 132
Byrk, A. S., 1, 77, 127–128, 138, 156

Chubb, J. E., 156
Coleman, J. S., 1, 9–10, 118, 126–127, 131, 202–203, 205–206, 220
Cook, M., 133
Cremin, L. A., 12–13

Darbel, A., 105–106
DeGraaf, N. D., 207
DeGraaf, P. M., 207
DeLany, B., 145
Demos, J., 13
DiMaggio, P., 206
Dreeben, R., 146
Dumais, S. A., 207

Eder, D., 134
Ellison, C. G., 82
Entwisle, D. R., 135

Gamoran, A., 133, 137–138, 155
Ganzeboom, H. B. G., 105–106, 117–118
Garet, M. S., 145
Garnier, M. A., 207
Good, A. D., 146
Greeley, A. M., 127

Hallinan, M. T., 133–134, 137, 139, 144–147
Heckman, J., 80
Hirsch, E. E., 46
Hoffer, T., 1, 126–127, 134, 155
Holland, P. B., 1
Holtz, B., 106
Horowitz, B., 103–104, 110

Jencks, C., 156

Kaestle, C. F., 15–16
Kalmijn, M., 206
Katsillis, J., 207
Kilgore, S., 1, 126–127
Kingston, P. W., 206
Kraaykamp, G., 206–207
Kubitschek, 137

Lareau, A., 53, 208
Lee, V. E., 1
Leslie, W. J., 15–16
Lucas, S. R., 146

Mare, R., 137
Mass, I., 206
McClelland, K., 207
Meyer, J. W., 11, 19–20, 23, 40–41
Meyer, M. A., 118
Moe, T. M., 156
Mohr, J., 206
Muller, C., 82

Nagel, I., 19, 105–106, 117–118

Pallas, A. M., 135

Rathunde, K., 83
Reay, D., 209
Reese, D. I., 132
Reese, W. J., 15–16
Riordan, C., 78
Robinson, R. V., 207

Roscigno, V., 207
Rosenbaum, J. E., 145
Rossi, Alice S., 10
Rossi, Peter H., 10
Rowan, B., 20, 44, 62
Rubinson, R., 207

Schmidt, J., 76
Schneider, B., 77
Scott, W. R., 11
Selznick, P., 10–11
Shkolnik, J. L., 132
Sklare, M., 102
Sørensen, A. B., 145, 154
Stevenson, D., 77
Stluka, M. F., 135

Teachman, J. D., 207
Tolley, K., 15, 18
Turner, R. H., 137

Useem, E. L., 137

Weber, M., 21

www.ingramcontent.com/pod-product-compliance
Lightning Source LLC
Chambersburg PA
CBHW071017240426
43661CB00073B/2472